Praise for *On the Chocolate Trail: A Delicious Adventure Connecting Jews, Religions, History, Travel, Rituals and Recipes to the Magic of Cacao*

"This engaging journey into the extraordinary past of a much-loved product is packed with fascinating stories and thrilling bits of information."

—**Claudia Roden**, food writer and author of almost twenty classic works on Middle Eastern and Mediterranean cookery; most recently, the award-winning *The Book of Jewish Food*

"Bravo! ... Takes us on a roller coaster roll through the history of chocolate, from the beginning when it was only used as a drink to the present day.... A great read."

—**Joan Nathan**, award-winning cookbook author, *Jewish Cooking in America; Quiches, Kugels, and Couscous: My Search for Jewish Cooking in France*; and other books

"Meticulously researched and whimsically presented. Fascinating facts, amusing anecdotes and mouth-watering recipes.... An instant classic for chocolate devotees of all faiths!"

—**Francine Segan**, food historian, chocolate expert and James Beard nominated cookbook author of *Dolci: Italy's Sweets*

"A joy for history and chocolate buffs.... Traces the exciting and curious aspects of the evolution of chocolate. The reader is rewarded with fascinating nuggets of chocolate lore, as well as several yummy chocolate recipes."

—**Carole Bloom**, CCP, author, *Intensely Chocolate* and *Truffles, Candies and Confections*

"A treat! Part history, part travelogue, part cookbook, [it] ... will tantalize all readers and delight chocoholic ones."

—**Jonathan D. Sarna**, Joseph H. & Belle R. Braun Professor of American Jewish History, Brandeis University

"A knowledgeable, surprising and, of course, delicious book. Chocolate lovers (and that includes just about everyone) and Jewish historians alike will be delighted."
—**Leah Koenig**, author, *The Hadassah Everyday Cookbook*

"Fascinating and entertaining ... if you're interested in Jews or chocolate, you're gonna like this book. If you're interested in both, you're gonna love it :-). Like chocolate itself—wonderful as a gift, or you could just get one for you yourself."
—**Nigel Savage**, founder,
Hazon: Jewish Inspiration, Sustainable Communities

"Yes, separate milk from meat. And wool from linen. But do not separate Jews from chocolate. They shall be yoked together for all time. And now we have the definitive book on the topic, an eloquent and astutely researched history."
—**A.J. Jacobs**, editor-at-large, *Esquire* magazine; author of the *New York Times* bestseller, *The Year of Living Biblically: One Man's Humble Quest to Follow the Bible as Literally as Possible*, and other books

"A fascinating ramble through the history of chocolate and the roles—sometimes central, sometimes peripheral—that Jews have played in bringing it from the forests of Africa and Spanish America to your table. The recipes are a tasty bonus."
—**David M. Gitlitz and Linda Kay Davidson**, authors, *A Drizzle of Honey: The Lives and Recipes of Spain's Secret Jews*

"Calling all chocoholics.... I devoured this book. Readers beware! Stash fine chocolate in your pack before setting off on this delicious journey across time and space."
—**Pamela S. Nadell**, Patrick Clendenen Chair in Women's and Gender History, American University; author, *Women Who Would be Rabbis: A History of Women's Ordination, 1889–1985*

"A delightful, fascinating read full of history, religion, ethics, anecdotes and recipes that will make you hungry."
—**Paula Shoyer**, author, *The Kosher Baker: 160 Dairy-Free Desserts from Traditional to Trendy*

ON THE
Chocolate
TRAIL

A Delicious Adventure Connecting Jews, Religions, History, Travel, Rituals and Recipes to the Magic of Cacao

RABBI DEBORAH R. PRINZ

On the Chocolate Trail:
A Delicious Adventure Connecting Jews, Religions, History, Travel, Rituals and Recipes to the Magic of Cacao

2013 Quality Paperback Edition, First Printing
© 2013 by Deborah Prinz

For information regarding permission to reprint material from this book, please mail or fax your request in writing to Jewish Lights Publishing, Permissions Department, at the address / fax number listed below, or e-mail your request to permissions@jewishlights.com.

Library of Congress Cataloging-in-Publication Data

Prinz, Deborah.
 On the chocolate trail : a delicious adventure connecting Jews, religions, history, travel, rituals and recipes to the magic of cacao / by Deborah Prinz. — Quality paperback ed.
     volume ; cm
 Includes bibliographical references and index.
 ISBN 978-1-58023-487-0 (pbk.)
 1. Chocolate—History. 2. Cocoa—History. 3. Cacao—Religious aspects. 4. Cacao—Religious aspects—Judaism. 5. Cooking (Chocolate)
 I. Title.
 TX817.C4P75 2013
 641.6'374—dc23

                                        2012031818

10 9 8 7 6 5 4 3 2 1

Manufactured in the United States of America

Cover Design: Barbara Leff and Heather Pelham
Interior Design: Heather Pelham
Cover images: © FreeSoulProduction/shutterstock; © Aaron Amat/fotolia; © photo25th/iStockphoto; © Richard Vandenberg/iStockphoto

For People of All Faiths, All Backgrounds
Published by Jewish Lights Publishing
A Division of LongHill Partners, Inc.
Sunset Farm Offices, Route 4, P.O. Box 237
Woodstock, VT 05091
Tel: (802) 457-4000   Fax: (802) 457-4004
www.jewishlights.com

For my sweet-toothed mother and father,
Helen (*z"l*) and Ray Prinz,
my partner in adventure and chocolate, Mark,
our food-savvy children, Avigail, Rachel, and Noam,
and for Amiel, as he learns the delights of eating.

Contents

Part Two
Other Religious Chocolate Revelations

PREFACE

Choco-dar

"CONNECTIONS BETWEEN JEWS AND CHOCOLATE? That would be like looking for a needle in a haystack!" said a cultural historian and journalist when I mentioned this project, just hoping for some insights, for a few tips, or for some modest encouragement. I slumped back in my chair, realizing that she could be correct. There may be nothing to it. What had I been thinking? After all, I had not heard of this theme of chocolate and Jews in all of my years of Jewish studies from religious school through rabbinical seminary or since. It had been easy enough to design an *On the Chocolate Trail* business card and to create a website for the project; now it seemed as though that would be the end of it. To concoct a lecture or an article about my intrigue for chocolate and religion, much less an entire book, began to seem completely daunting.

At the same time, I could feel my inner Nancy Drew transforming me. I just knew in my gut that there had to be a story. My choco-dar—my internal, serendipitous radar for chocolate discoveries and experiences—would somehow feed this research to uncover the stories of Jews, religions, and chocolate. After all, choco-dar alerts had entered my life at fun and surprising moments, particularly when traveling. One such fortuitous experience occurred as my rabbi-husband, Mark, and I traveled in our VW van from south of Paris on a small road to Carpentras in southern France. Mark drove while my head sunk deep into my reading and my laptop. I randomly looked up just in time to notice a billboard boasting a bright orange checkmark against a black backdrop that I quickly recognized as the logo for Valrhona chocolate, which I happened to have seen for sale at a local San Diego market. I grabbed Mark's arm to urge him to pull over and park. Checking the map, we realized that we had chanced upon Tain-L'Hermitage, the small-town home of the international headquarters for Valrhona, reputed to be one of the best chocolate makers in the world. We traipsed into the company store where, to our delight and admittedly our gluttony, every item for purchase was also available for tasting, from curry-flavored chocolate, to chocolate-covered nuts, to bonbons, to hot chocolate. We sampled it all—or tried to. Then, as we paid for our selections, the cashier tossed in even more treats.

My choco-dar kicked in again later when we altered our route at the last minute to investigate Turin's chocolate by crossing the Alps from Sospel, France, into northern Italy. Mark calmly managed the van through the truly scary switchbacks in very mild weather on the French side. At the border tunnel's entrance, a red light stopped us—a very long red light, a light that remained red though there was no traffic. The light was equipped with a timer so we knew that, conscientious rabbi-travelers that we are, the wait would be a full twenty minutes. Finally, with the permission of the green light, we passed through to snow on the Italian side. As we marveled at the contrasting temperatures and the snow-whitened chalet rooftops sprinkling the mountainside, we caught sight of "*Venchi: Spaccio del Cioccolato.*" This roadside *Venchi* chocolate factory, in business since 1878, offered a well-stocked bar as well

The sign at the Venchi chocolate factory welcomed us warmly just after crossing the Alps.

as specialty chocolate balls made with Cuban rum. Without hesitation, we celebrated our arrival in Italy along this dramatic drive through the Alps into the winter chill with chocolate!

Admittedly, chocolate was the reason for our stop in Turin, where I hoped to sample the local specialty chocolate drink known as *bicerin*. We found what we were looking for, and much more, as my choco-dar revved up once again. They say that the intimate, low-ceilinged, candlelit setting of Caffè al Bicerin, founded in 1763, boasts the best *bicerin* in Turin. Always run by women, the Caffè's location near the Santuario della Consolata meant that women often broke their Lenten and Communion fasts there. The name of the drink and the Caffè recall the handle-less glass in which the *bicerin* is customarily served. As Mark and I savored the much anticipated *bicerin* with its layers of hot chocolate, coffee, and cream, we unabashedly stared across the small room where a couple of men scooped a thick, chocolaty substance out of a large bowl. Checking with the waitress, we learned that they were downing warm chocolate soup poured over hazelnut cake. We could not resist that *torta di nocciole con cioccolata calda*. What a rich two-course chocolate lunch that turned out to be!

After a bit of shopping in the Al Bicerin retail store next door—and, yes, amazingly more tasting—our intention to leave Turin was undone by my irrepressible choco-dar. Looking for a map for the next leg of our trip, we luckily learned about the Turin Chocolate Festival taking place at that very moment just a square away. Without discussion, we delayed our departure from Turin to enjoy our first, but not our last, chocolate festival, this one featuring chocolate makers from all over Europe. While we could not stay for the entire multiday, annual festival, with its chocolate-related entertainment, tastings, and classes, we did wander around the booths, gobbled up treats, and stocked up on delicacies such as chocolate pasta and a most delicious chocolate liquor. We reluctantly left Turin. A few days later our daughter, a religious studies major, asked if we had seen the Shroud of Turin. We rabbis licked the chocolate off our fingers and confessed, with some embarrassment, that we had completely forgotten about the Shroud.

In Spain my choco-dar activated again. We had read a text panel at the Barcelona Chocolate Museum explaining that Spain had hosted a Cistercian chocolate tradition with special ecclesiastical chocolate rooms. The next day, as planned, we headed to Belchite in the northeast of Spain to pay homage to the ruins of the 1937 Spanish Civil War where Mark's (middle) namesake, Sam Levinger, was fatally injured. I barely caught a glimpse of the sign off to the side of the road to the monastery. The sign led us to a last-minute stop at the Royal Abbey of Santa Maria de Poblet, a Cistercian monastery founded in 1151 at the base of the Prades Mountains, and its medieval monks' chocolate room.

My choco-dar also works pretty well Stateside. Years ago a couple of my lovely congregants, knowing of my interest in chocolate, wanted to introduce me to their family friend, chocolate expert Carole Bloom, author of several chocolate and dessert books. Carole was on a book tour at that time so we could not connect, even though we then both lived in San Diego County. However, a few years after our move to the East Coast, Mark and I took some yoga classes in Carlsbad, California, while on vacation and overheard the names of other people in the class. After our fourth class, I saw Carole enter a car with the license plate "DESSERT." When Mark and I stopped a few moments later at the nearby Chuao Chocolate store, we saw one of Bloom's books displayed. Her photograph confirmed my suspicion. Finally, after all those years, at the next yoga class I met her, thanks to my trusty choco-dar.

When we moved into our cozy New York City studio apartment, where this book was written, the corner super-market was in the midst of major renovations. It reopened six months later, with an entire room larger than the size of our apartment devoted only to chocolate. It now supplies our daily basic chocolate dosages.

Choco-dar also led me to *On the Chocolate Trail*. By happenstance I heard a story on National Public Radio about chocolate stores in Paris by chocolatier, foodie, and pastry chef David Lebovitz. Following up on his leads during a sabbatical trip to Europe, Mark and I came upon our first clues about chocolate and Jews. Thus began *On the Chocolate Trail*. Two rabbis—my adventuresome husband and I—on our chocolate exploration, tasting and unpacking connections of religions to chocolate production and commerce which furthered cacao's travels through the Western World. The fifteenth-century dispersion of Jews from Spain created a trail of Jewish business interests in chocolate that continues today. Choco-dar sometimes simply led me to chocolate eating; more significantly, it revealed heretofore unexplained links between religion and chocolate.

Acknowledgments

My choco-dar instincts and sleuthing were also triggered in libraries and archives, where this research was generously supported by a Starkoff Fellowship and a Director's Fellowship from the American Jewish Archives, Cincinnati, Ohio, as well as a Gilder Lehrman Fellowship from the John D. Rockefeller Jr. Library, Williamsburg, Virginia. Deepest gratitude is extended to the many people who assisted me, including the staff of the American Jewish Archives, the American Jewish Historical Society, the Hebrew Union College–Jewish Institute of Religion, the New York Society Library, and the John D. Rockefeller Jr. Library, as well as Josh Beraha, Rabbi Jillian Cameron, Rabbi Lisa Delson, Benjamin Fox-Rosen, Emily Geminder, Chana Kupetz, and Hilary Ramp. My husband, Mark Hurvitz, provided unfailing technical, navigational, photographic, tasting, and loving support.

I am very grateful to the rabbinic leadership of the Central Conference of American Rabbis, particularly appreciative chocolate eaters Rabbi Steven A. Fox, Rabbi Alan Henkin, Rabbi Dan Medwin, Rabbi Hara Person, and Rabbi Lennard Thal, as well as our wonderful staff. Amazing graphic artist, Barbara Leff, enthusiastically helped create the book cover. The staff of Jewish Lights hankered for this book's release. Publisher Stuart M. Matlins took a chance on a book outside the usual scope of his company and publishing program. Editorial and production vice president Emily Wichland kindly guided me through the stages of publication and skillfully helped shape the final manuscript. Thanks go as well to Justine Earnest, assistant editor; Jennifer Rataj, publicity manager; and the staff at Jewish Lights. Copyeditor Debra Corman deserves special acknowledgment for making this book happen. The following scholars generously responded to my queries, shared feedback, and in some cases read chapters or sections: Dr. Robert Ferry, Dr. Leo Hershkowitz, Dr. Stanley Hordes, Dr. Sara Malino, Dr. Marcy Norton, Kevin Profitt, Dr. Marc Raphael, Dr. Jonathan

Sarna, Dr. Michael Signer (z"l), Dr. Brigitte Sion, Dr. Susan Terrio, and Dr. Gary Zola.

Several others generously read chapters or the entire book, including Sally Goodis, Noam Gross-Prinz, Rabbi Alan Henkin, Agnes Herman, Avigail Hurvitz-Prinz, Chana Kupetz, Libbe Madsen, Dr. Jessica Prinz, Edwina Riblet, and Rabbi Sara Rich. Chocolate maven Dr. Judy Logback offered helpful suggestions. Pastry chef Hannah Gross read, interpreted, and implemented recipes and served as a fun food consultant. There were many chocolate tasters as well. I remain responsible for any errors but not for any resulting weight gain.

Chocolate discoveries occurred in our travels within the United States and to several countries, including Belgium, Egypt, England, France, Israel, Italy, Mexico, Spain, and Switzerland. I am grateful to the kind people who gave us tips, clues, and directions along the trail.

I hope that this first-ever book about Jews, religions, and chocolate will assist you in maximizing your choco-dar; I intend to continue to pay close attention to mine. As I bring this inquiry to a close, I am sated by the requisite chocolate snacking—whether traveling or at my computer, at food shows or in my neighborhood. There is now only one thing left to do: clean the chocolate smudges from my keyboard.

Introduction

PICK UP A PIECE OF CHOCOLATE AND PARTAKE IN AN
expedition into Jewish and religious history. *On the Chocolate
Trail* melds an enjoyment of chocolate with an exploration
of chocolate's religious narratives and rituals, unwrapping
tantalizing new themes in the first book on this topic. It
highlights unique Jewish connections to chocolate against a
historical backdrop of several other religions' engagement with
chocolate. Delight your mind and your taste buds as this book
unscrambles the mysteries of Jews, religions, and chocolate
along a trail of economic development spanning several
cultures, countries, centuries, continents, and convictions. This
chocolate journey layers curiosity, gratitude, pleasure, opportunity, and success onto an underside of disdain, critique,
abuse, and persecution. It embraces marginalized groups such
as Quakers and Jews and also notes individuals who came to
be known as "chocolate uncles." As chocolate is malleable,
so this story reflects the resourcefulness and resilience of the
chocolate lovers featured in this book.

   This chocolate path parallels the highway of Jewish history,
particularly that of Sephardi (Jews of Iberian descent) and
other Jewish migrations (as in the case of chocolatiers Eliyahu
Fromenchenko of Elite Chocolate from Eastern Europe to Israel,

Karina Chaplinsky from Argentina to Israel, Stephen Klein of Bartons from Vienna to New York, and Oded Brenner of Max Brenner from Tel Aviv to New York). It builds on deep pre-Columbian traditions and intersects with twists and turns of Catholic and Quaker chocolate encounters. Jews jump on that chocolate trail early in some places (New Spain, Oxford, Brabant); in significant Jewish centers (Amsterdam, New York, Newport); as great chocolate entrepreneurs (Chillon and others in New Spain, the Gomez family and Aaron Lopez in North America); and as experts (Amsterdam, Martinique, Bayonne). This New World product of chocolate blazed a new world of commerce, appetite, and opportunity for Jews as well as for others.

Jews and Christians meet on this chocolate trail. Faith traditions share chocolate consumption, ritual, and business interests. Today's commercial chocolate endeavors track back to a continuum of life-cycle and holiday use baked in pre-Columbian spiritual understandings. Jews and Christians displayed a fascination with the cacao trade, arriving at it from different perspectives and beliefs. Struggles around propriety, constraints, and enjoyment could be seen in both Judaism and Christianity. While there have been—and still are—abuses related to chocolate—from the Spanish Inquisition to the Holocaust, from Bayonne to West Africa—this path also nurtured and sustained. When we consider the visionary, ambitious, and versatile entrepreneurs who made a life of chocolate—the British Quaker companies and Milton Hershey, Camille Bloch and the Holocaust controversies in Switzerland, the unique business approach of Bartons—we also see that they contributed to the lives of others.

From chocolate use in religious settings, we learn food wisdoms about chocolate eating as a potentially sacred endeavor. Religious life has been enhanced by chocolate. Chocolate has been enhanced by religion. A challenge remains to develop a chocolate culture of ideals, expressing commitments grounded in Jewish and other faith values.

What Are Cacao, Cocoa, and Chocolate?

Let's start by understanding some of the basics of chocolate growing and manufacturing. The chocolate we love begins with trees. The cacao tree is native to the Amazon rainforests of South America. It is shaded by taller trees until it matures. Cultivated since approximately 1500 BCE, it has been transported to many other parts of the world such as Hawaii, Vietnam, Indonesia, and Mexico. The bulk of the growing currently happens in West Africa, particularly the Ivory Coast and Ghana. The tree needs the climate of twenty degrees north and south of the equator. The plant's scientific name is *Theobroma cacao*.

Cocoa pods grow off the side of the tree trunk, with a thick rind, filled with white pulp that encases thirty to fifty beans. The pods ripen throughout the year. Inside the pod are cocoa beans. There are primarily three types of beans: Criollo, Forastero, and Trinitario. Forastero is most widely available; Criollo is the highest quality; Trinitario is a hybrid of these two and is more disease resistant.

The beans are extracted from the pods while still in the country of origin. Once the pod is removed from the tree and its rind is discarded, the seeds and pulp are gathered for fermenting. This makes the sugars

The natural beauty of the cocoa tree and its pods.

acidic and alters the color of the beans from white to brown. At this point, they look like almonds.

The beans are spread over large surfaces for drying in the sun or through artificial heat. This enables shipping in bulk in jute bags usually via container boats. With a few exceptions, cacao is not processed into chocolate in the locale where it is grown. The sophisticated equipment is too expensive, as is temperature control in the Amazon heat.

Once at the chocolate factory, the beans are processed depending on the form of chocolate they are intended for.

1. Beans are sorted, cleaned, and roasted.

2. Beans are then cracked and de-shelled in a winnower, resulting in cocoa nibs, the broken pieces of cacao without the shell. The shells are blown away from the nibs.

3. Crushing the nibs creates a paste of the chocolate. This may be done by hand on a stone, as in the colonial period / age of discovery in Spain, North America, Bayonne, and Amsterdam; in a *tiendas de chocolate* electric mill, as in Mexico and other Central American countries today; or in machines of industrial companies in Europe and North America. The resulting "cocoa liquor" has no alcohol and is not yet sweetened. Sometimes this is called cocoa mass. A longer period of grinding yields a smoother-textured chocolate.

Shelling roasted cocoa beans by hand.

4. Through the grinding stage, the liquor/mass is separated from the cocoa fat/butter. They are recombined in varying quantities depending on the intended use of the chocolate—for baking, eating, or drinking.

5. The chocolate mixture is then conched—or massaged— to mix together the ingredients. Longer conching means higher-quality chocolate.

6. Finally the chocolate is tempered. This is the heating and cooling process that gives the chocolate a glossy look and hardness.

7. The taste of chocolate depends on many factors, including the type of bean, length of fermentation, form of processing, ratio of cocoa liquor to cocoa butter, quality of the additional ingredients in the product, and more.

Jews in Navigational Sciences Help Discover Cacao

The trailhead for this chocolate passion lies at the crossroads of the age of exploration and the discovery of the New World at the end of the fifteenth century. Jews of the time inherited

Ten Facts about Religion and Chocolate

1. Some people think that Jews brought chocolate to France.
2. The 1602 victory of the citizens of Geneva over the Duke of Savoy's attempt to destroy the Reformation is commemorated each December with soup pots made from chocolate.
3. The bishop of Chiapas, Mexico, was poisoned because he prohibited local women from drinking chocolate during Mass.
4. North American Jewish colonial traders were involved in the chocolate trade.
5. Junipero Serra depended on chocolate for his work in building missions in California in the eighteenth century.
6. Cistercian monks in Poblet, Spain, designated a special chocolate room.
7. At age sixteen, Austrian-Jewish confectioner Franz Sacher created the now famous Sachertorte.
8. Chocolate was first introduced to the Spanish court of King Ferdinand and Queen Isabella by Dominicans.
9. Inquisition jails in New Spain allowed the drinking of chocolate by prisoners.
10. Since Europeans first encountered chocolate, Jews and clerics have been on the chocolate trail.

the then radical concept of a round world from the fourth-century text "The earth is made as a ball" (Jerusalem Talmud, *Avodah Zarah* 42c). Medieval Jewish scientists advanced many innovations related to navigation that furthered New World discoveries. Explorers Christopher Columbus and Vasco da Gama consulted with Abraham Ben Samuel Zacuto regarding westward travel to the Near East. Zacuto plotted Columbus's route. Just as Columbus's voyage began, Zacuto faced charges from the Spanish Inquisition, the crusade against heretics by the Roman Catholic Church, and fled to Portugal, where he devised an improved metal astrolabe. This device, used to fix location in relation to the sun, stars, and moon, became the standard in subsequent exploits by colonialist adventurers. These and other advances by Iberian Jews set the backstory for the discovery of the New World's chocolate resources.[1]

Jews and Catholics First to Sight Cacao

Jews may have been among the first Europeans to see cacao in the New World, especially if Columbus was Jewish, as some believe.[2] Members of his crew were born Jews or descended from Jews. Conversos—a term usually used for Jews converted to Christianity and/or descendants of converted Jews—such as Alfonso de la Calle, a sailor; Rodrigo Sánchez of Segovia, a comptroller; and others crewed the first voyage of 1492. Luis de Torres was baptized just in time to act as Columbus's interpreter. Their journey was supported by the vastly wealthy converso Luis de Santangel, chancellor of King's household, comptroller-general of Aragon, who argued in favor of the proposed voyage to Ferdinand and Isabella. Santangel also used his own funds to help underwrite this and other expeditions.

All of these contributed to the discovery of a cacao bean–laden canoe during Columbus's fourth voyage, in 1502, in the Bay of Honduras, as reported by Columbus's son, Ferdinand:

Many of the almonds [cacao beans] which the Indians of New Spain use as currency; and these the Indians in the canoe valued greatly, for I noticed that when they were brought aboard with the other goods, and some fell to the floor, all the Indians stooped to pick them up as if they had lost something of great value.[3]

Follow the Chocolate Trail through the Chapters

The awareness of chocolate in the European world depended, in no small measure, on people of faith.

The first part of this book, "Forging the Jewish Chocolate Trail," reveals how Mark and I chanced on clues to a very long Jewish and religious chocolate trail through our travels to France, Spain, Belgium, and Israel.

Chocolate migrated to France, specifically to Bayonne in southwestern France, which generally spouts the claim that Jews introduced chocolate making to France. Chapter 1 explores other chocolate locales with Jewish specialists and how Jews were perceived to possess chocolate-making expertise. Today's elegant and plentiful French chocolate culture may very well be indebted to Jews.

Chapter 2 unpacks the seepage of pre-Columbian chocolate customs into New Spain's Jewish ritual practices. Seventeenth-century Inquisition records from New Spain document some of the earliest and abundant Jewish business involvement with chocolate. In this context, xenophobia injected suspicion and cruelty right into the chocolate and onto the Jews who drank it, sold it, and traded it. In some cases, chocolate outed Jews and in general divided Christians.

In colonial North America, the chocolate interests of Sephardi refugees could be uncovered in the holds of their ships, in their shops, and in their homes. Chapter 3 traces how Jewish merchants such as Aaron Lopez, Daniel Gomez, and others dipped deeply into cacao trading and the processing of chocolate. Rebecca Gomez was the only woman of her time to manufacture chocolate.

Despite distinct messages and rituals, Christmas and Chanukah connect through chocolate coin customs. Chapter 4 investigates how Chanukah and Christmas chocolate melt into gelt by unraveling some celebratory themes of these December holidays.

The fifth chapter looks into chocolate during and after World War II. It examines chocolate's use by the military, its role at the liberation of concentration camps, its succor and support for immigrants and refugees, and its contribution to survival and renewal. This contrasts sharply with the unbelievable deprivations of that time, making for an unusual period of chocolate experiences.

One could say that Israelis are *meshuga* (crazy) for chocolate. Chocolate permeates Israel, as observed in chapter 6. A chunk of Israel's growth as a state may be seen through its chocolate industry, which reflects both immigrant stories and the entrepreneurship of Israel.

The second part of this book, "Other Religious Chocolate Revelations," tracks the mysteries of chocolate's trek back and forth between the New World and the Old. Religious peoples—pre-Columbians, Catholics, Quakers, and others—stuck their fingers into the business of chocolate worldwide.

European Chocolate Processing

European countries pride themselves on distinct approaches to chocolate processing, measuring the microns to distinguish the chocolate in terms of texture:

- Belgian chocolate tends to be around twelve microns.
- British chocolate tends to be around twenty-four microns.
- French chocolate tends to be in the range of twelve to twenty microns.
- Swiss chocolate tends to be in the range of fifteen to twenty microns.

They struggled, as did Jews, with permeability and boundaries for their chocolate.

When Jews encountered chocolate, they did so in an environment full of Mesoamerican wonderment and awe, an earlier tradition that saw cacao as the divine food of the gods. Chapter 7 unveils the backdrop for the Jewish story as it details how the earliest chocolate drinkers in South and Central America, living before Columbus, idolized chocolate and saturated their cultic life with it.

Jews and Christians built upon this pre-Columbian chocolate dependency. Europeans' first contact with chocolate in the sixteenth century both excited and confused Catholics. Chapter 8 divulges how the Catholic faith diffused chocolate into Europe, into South America, and along the El Camino Real (or the Royal Road) in California even though Catholics were also beset with quandaries and conflicts about chocolate.

Quakers mixed chocolate into their dreams for a better society and into very lucrative businesses in Britain. Chapter 9 shows how their utopian visions spread from the chocolate factory outward to the community and how they influenced other chocolate companies, including Hershey's and Israel's Elite. At the same time, this chapter exposes how some of these companies compromised their ideals.

Many complexities surface when measuring our food values against our chocolate consumption and purchases. Chapter 10, "Shopping for the Best Chocolate: Values and Ethics," examines these issues through a discussion of fair labor and sustainability practices.

Your Chocolate Chronicle

If reading the stories within these chapters jogs your memory of a story of chocolate and religions, I invite you to hop onto the chocolate trail by posting your recollections at my blog. Please share them at Chocolate Chronicles at www.jews-onthechocolatetrail.org.

Recipes

If you are hankering to indulge in some chocolate as you meander along this chocolate trail, I invite you to try the recipes included with each chapter and also at the end of the book. A few of these recipes connect to yummy goodies we discovered in our travels. I also found some in historical materials as I researched. Others were introduced to us by friends. Mark created the citrus salad with cocoa nibs. We have devoured the results of each recipe.

Supplementary Material at the *Jews on the Chocolate Trail* Website

You will find a lot of helpful resources and educational material on the *Jews on the Chocolate Trail* website including *A Haggadah for a Chocolate Seder*, lesson plans for teaching about Jews and chocolate, traditional Jewish texts related to chocolate, additional photos, and data related to colonial chocolate use in North America. See www.jews-onthechocolatetrail.org.

Additional Resources

Several additional resources are included at the back of the book to enhance your exploration of Jews, religion, and chocolate, and possible travel experiences, including more recipes, a "Timeline of Chocolate and Religion," "A Consumer's Guide to Buying Ethically Produced Chocolate," and "Chocolate Museums and Tours around the World."

I hope that you enjoy the journey as this book guides you into these stirrings of age-old passions for chocolate and religion.

PART ONE

Forging the Jewish Chocolate Trail

Basque Chocolate Cake

This unique combination of chocolate and cherries directs our taste buds to the flavors of the Basque area of Bayonne, France, where Jews are said to have initiated local chocolate making.

Ingredients:

¾ cup unsalted butter
5½ ounces bittersweet chocolate
3 large eggs
¾ cup sugar
⅓ cup all-purpose flour
¾ cup black cherry preserves, for serving
Crème fraîche, for serving

Instructions:

Preheat the oven to 375°F. Lightly butter and flour a 9-inch round cake pan. In a large heatproof bowl set over a pan of simmering water, combine the butter and chocolate. Melt over moderate heat, stirring frequently, until smooth, about 4 minutes. Remove from the heat and let cool slightly. In a medium bowl, using an electric mixer, beat the eggs with the sugar at high speed until thick and pale, about 3 minutes. Add the flour and beat at low speed just until combined. Fold in one-third of the melted chocolate, then gently fold in the remaining chocolate; do not overmix.

Pour the batter into the prepared pan and bake for 20–30 minutes, or until a toothpick inserted into the center comes out clean. Invert the cake onto a rack and let cool.

In a saucepan, warm the cherry preserves over moderate heat. Cut the cake into wedges and serve with the cherry preserves and crème fraîche.

Quantity: 6–8 servings

Chapter One

Did Jews Introduce Chocolate to France?

"JEWS BROUGHT CHOCOLATE MAKING TO FRANCE," I read in the brochure I happened to pick up in a chocolate store in the Montparnasse neighborhood of Paris. Jews were the first to bring chocolate to France? How could this be? I wondered, channeling the professor who had doubted the efficacy of this project. This amazing morsel of history had been omitted in my serious Jewish education and had not surfaced in over thirty years of study about Judaism as a rabbi. I knew plenty of Jews devoted to eating chocolate. But I had no clue until then of any history tying Jews and chocolate together, much less about Jews introducing chocolate to France. Not until Paris.

Only a month earlier, during my morning workout on Valentine's Day, I had chanced upon a National Public Radio interview with a well known Paris food writer reporting on chocolate shops in Paris. Perfect. What a great way to see Paris, I thought. My husband, Mark, and I were in the midst of planning a late-winter sabbatical journey through several European countries in a VW van. He had thought that we should skip Paris and push on to the warmer south. I had never been to Paris and wanted to stop there. When I mentioned the chocolate in Paris, Mark immediately rerouted the trip.

I took my map of Paris and plotted chocolate store locations so that chocolate visits would accompany our touring: chocolate shop / the Louvre, chocolate shop / Eiffel Tower, chocolate shop / Paris Opera. We savored as many *chocolateries* on the list as possible, plus those that we discovered as we wandered the *arrondissements* (districts). Often when we inquired about the attendant's favorite, we were rewarded with samples, which became so numerous they lasted for months. While browsing and tasting in L'Atelier du Chocolat de Bayonne, a chocolate boutique on the Left Bank, itself a find as it was not on our original list, I read this astonishing passage in the company's literature:

> *À Bayonne l'origine de la fabrication et de la consomma-*
> *tion du chocolat semble remonter au début du VXIIème*
> *siècle, lorsque les Juifs pourchassés par l'Inquisition*
> *s'installèrent dans le bourg de Saint Esprit.*

Then I reread this sentence, wondering if my high school French had accurately captured its meaning. The booklet indeed claimed:

> At Bayonne the origins of the manufacturing and the consumption of chocolate happened at the beginning of the seventeenth century, when the Jews exiled from the Inquisition settled in the suburb of Saint Esprit.

It took a few moments for me to absorb this link between chocolate and the Jewish people. The sophisticated and elegant chocolate of France connects with Jews in Bayonne. This factoid might have sweetened our Jewish educations. How could we have missed out on this scrumptious detail?

Admittedly, as I noticed in that pamphlet, several theories exist about chocolate's arrival in France. Some credit royal marriages with bringing chocolate to France, either through the marriage of Anne of Austria (the Infanta of Spain) to Louis XIII in 1615 or through the marriage of Maria Teresa of Spain to Louis XIV in 1659. Others claim that chocolate arrived in France with clerics and monastic orders, gifts from those in Spain to their French counterparts. And others suggest that chocolate entered France as a medicine.[1]

Jews Specialize in Chocolate

As I considered this connection between chocolate and Jews in France, however, I realized that it made sense. Jews exiled from Spain in 1492 and then from Portugal in 1496 engaged in international trade as they continued their linkages to each other through birth, business, or family bonds. Over the years since its discovery by Europeans in 1502 in the New World and its import to Spain in approximately 1520, chocolate developed into a colonial extract industry. Jews still living in Spain or with family contacts in Spain would have easily learned about chocolate, even as the Spanish throne sought to maintain a monopoly over it.

With more detective work it became clear that in their relocations from Spain and Portugal, these Jews played a critical, if not unique part in the cocoa business. In addition to Catholic clerics, Jews who converted to Christianity or were descendants of converted Jews (conversos) diffused Spanish methods of chocolate making across Europe with specialty workshops in Bayonne, Amsterdam, and other European cities. For instance, the first coffeehouse in England, The Angle, which served hot chocolate, as later coffeehouses did, was opened by a converso Jew named Jacob in Oxford in 1650 at the time of the readmission of Jews

Jacob the Jew established the first coffeehouse in Oxford at this site. Along with coffee, the Angle served hot chocolate.

to England. Some sources refer to him as "Cirques Jobson, a Jew."[2] The Grand Café memorializes that site today.

In addition, chocolate making became a Dutch Jewish specialty, especially after the rise of the cocoa trade with Curaçao in the 1650s. Jews were considered excellent chocolate makers in what was called another typical Amsterdam Jewish industry. When appointed the Spanish ambassador to the Hague in 1655, Don Esteban Gammarra fretted that he would not be able to access his customary daily chocolate in this strange environment. To assuage his fear, his staff informed him that "the best chocolatiers—including a man named Pacheco, who flavored his chocolate with vanilla—were the Jews of Amsterdam."[3] Not only that, but in Belgium in 1663, Emanuel Soares de Rinero, a converso, received the first permit to fabricate chocolate in the Belgian province of Brabant.[4]

In the French Caribbean island of Martinique, Benjamin d'Acosta de Andrade, a Jew formerly of Bayonne, cultivated the first cacao trees. Owner of the two largest sugar plantations, he also established the first cacao-processing plant in French territory. As a result, chocolate eventually became the most important export from Martinique. D'Acosta de Andrade may have been the first to experiment with shaping cacao into pellet form.[5] Sadly, the growth of the profits from the Caribbean colonies prompted Jean-Baptiste Colbert, the chief minister of Louis XIV, to shift ownership of properties in the Caribbean settlements directly into the control of the French crown. When all Jews lost their property in 1664, D'Acosta de Andrade did, too. A 1681 petition circulated by Jesuit fathers accusing Jews of blaspheming Jesus and of killing babies born to their Christian slaves prompted the king's order expelling Jews from the French colonies in 1685, thus ending the Jewish chocolate business in Martinique of that period.[6]

Rabbi Jonathan Eybeshutz of Metz berated his congregation for their resistance to the spiritual reform of Judaism, this even though they were early adopters of chocolate.[7] In the eighteenth century in Denmark, when guild restrictions prevented Jewish involvement, Jews instead pursued trade in tea, coffee, and chocolate. These became known as "Jew trades," a phrase abolished when Jews became citizens in 1814.[8] It was a Jew, Franz Sacher, who created the Sachertorte,

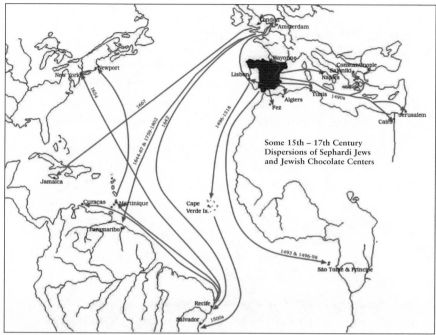

Some 15th – 17th Century
Dispersions of Sephardi Jews
and Jewish Chocolate Centers

The dispersion of Jews after the Expulsion from Spain corresponds to the early diffusion of chocolate from the New World.

a dense, dark chocolate cake made with apricot jam, at the age of sixteen in 1832. As a trainee at the home of the chancellor of Vienna, Prince Klemens Wenzel von Metternich, it fell to Sacher to create dessert for special guests when the head chef fell ill. Sacher's impromptu cake pleased the crowd. His son Eduard parlayed this into a great business, first at the Demel Bakery in Vienna and then at the Hotel Sacher. Today, Austrians debate the quality of the Demel and the Sacher versions of the pastry.[9]

Surprisingly, according to some chocolate mavens, it may have been Jews in France who first developed chocolate Easter eggs. These were passed around during church services to provide morsels of sustenance.[10]

Having learned about these striking early Jewish connections to chocolate in London, Amsterdam, Brabant, Martinique, and others, Mark and I hoped to tease out the Jewish chocolate

Complexities of Jewish Identity:
The Sephardi Diaspora

The events leading up to the establishment of the Inquisition and the Expulsion from Spain combined to create intricate descriptions of the Sephardi community, externally and internally defined.

Inquisition: The Roman Catholic Church campaign against suspected heretics that began before the twelfth century; the Inquisition in Spain was formally established in 1480, in Portugal in 1536, and in New Spain in 1571. New Spain, a viceroyalty of the Spanish empire, included much of North America, present-day Mexico, Central America, the East and West Indies, Puerto Rico, Jamaica, Cayman Islands, Trinidad, and the Bay Islands.

Expulsion: From Spain in 1492 and from Portugal in 1496.

The complexity of the Sephardi experience when expelled from Spain in 1492 led some scholars to speak of "diasporas within diasporas." This developed into a uniquely commercial diaspora that connected to the then "seaborne empires" of seventeenth-century Spain, Portugal, Britain, France, the Dutch Republic, and Denmark. These Sephardi Jews did not have monolithic experiences, though success sometimes came from the uncertainties they experienced. Some moved a great deal, while others were more settled. They lived in and moved among varied settings: Catholic or Protestant; Western Hemisphere or on the European continent; agricultural, mercantile, or urban.

Several terms refer to the nuanced Jewish identity of Jews in this period:

Anusim: Hebrew term for Jews and their descendants who were forcibly converted, many of whom continued to observe Judaism in secret.

Converso: Jew converted to Christianity and/or descendant of converted Jews.

Crypto-Jew (*Judios*): Hidden Jew secretly practicing Judaism and outwardly observing Christianity, forced to convert to Catholicism to escape the Inquisition. Some of these Jews traveled between Spain and Portugal and may have escaped both countries.

Hebreos Christianos Nuevos Judaizantes: Inquisition documents in Mexico called these "Judaizing Hebrew New Christians."

Marrano: The Portuguese derogatory term, meaning "pig" or "swine," for a Jew converted to Christianity.

Meshumadim: Hebrew word for voluntary converts without a desire to return to Judaism or to practice it secretly, sincere in their conversion to Catholicism.

Nation: In the late sixteenth century, after Spain annexed Portugal, Portuguese conversos migrated to Spanish cities such as Madrid and Seville. Spaniards called these Portuguese immigrants *Portugueses de la naçion Hebrea*, or "Portuguese of the Hebrew Nation," because they were thought to be less sincere in their conversions. With time, they took the name upon themselves out of a sense of pride, calling themselves *homens da nação*, or "Men of the Nation."

New Christian / *Christãos Novos*: Jews and descendants of Jews who converted to Christianity and descendants of converted Jews, a term that developed in Portugal.

Portuguese: Sometimes refers to Jews from Portugal who fled the Inquisition.

Sephardi (plural, Sephardim): Jew descended from Iberian ancestry; to be distinguished from Ashkenazi, or Jew descended from Western Europe.[a]

In Spain the conversos were pretty rapidly integrated into society. After 1530, Portugal still had conversos who were crypto-Jews, making up 3 percent of the population. Because of Portuguese hatred of Jews and therefore conversos, the category of *Christãos Novos*, or New Christian, developed, making it difficult to assimilate even when they returned to Spain after 1580.

A great advantage for Sephardi Jews in the development of the Atlantic trade of this period stemmed from the financial credit that could be extended based upon trust within the Jewish community. Whether Jews, conversos, or crypto-Jews, they collaborated to further their business interests. Kinship and mercantile ties remained strong, connecting these refugees in all areas of the world despite the thousands of miles separating them.[b] Travel and trade bound them along the shipping lanes as some of these Jews became active in the cacao trade.

story of Bayonne when we visited the southwestern region of France. Along with nearby St. Jean de Luz, the port of Bayonne offered both an accessible refuge and an easy transit point for Jews escaping the Inquisition on their way to freer destinations such as the Netherlands. Jews collecting or administering family estates in Spain or Portugal also found Bayonne convenient for such business.[11] As far as the Inquisition was concerned, any trip of an Iberian to Bayonne was certain indication of the "crime of Judaism."[12]

Jews Launch the French Chocolate Business

By the 1630s there were approximately sixty Jewish (probably converso) families living in Bayonne, France, which had formally admitted small numbers of conversos. Outwardly they lived as Christians. However, since the Inquisition was not strong in France, they slowly became more public about their Judaism. In 1654 the Jewish community sought assistance from the parish priest of the suburb of St. Esprit to purchase a cemetery plot, which was granted. He also allowed Jewish mortuary and funeral rituals there. Until 1668 Jewish deaths were recorded in the registers of the Christian burials. By the end of the century, the Jewish population of Bayonne had grown to eight hundred, with thirteen synagogues in St. Esprit.[13]

Bayonne Jews such as Emil Péreire, Isaac Péreire, Alvaro Luiz, Jacome Luiz, and Aaron Colace were crucial leaders in the contraband trade with Spain, including the business of exporting, re-exporting, and smuggling cacao.[14] Spain was the primary European market for chocolate at the beginning of the seventeenth century. Bayonne's extremely valuable port enabled traders to bypass the Spanish embargoes of 1621, creating lucrative economic traffic between Spain's Castile region and other Jewish communities, particularly Amsterdam. Aaron Colace opened a Bayonne office to monitor the market between Spain, Amsterdam, and Caracas, primarily shipping Caracas cacao between Amsterdam and Spain.[15] In just a six-month period from 1621 to 1622, at least thirty Dutch vessels unloaded goods in Bayonne's port for secret transport to Madrid by mule train through the mountain passes. Given this tremendously profitable trade through Bayonne, in which Jews played a key role, merchants of Amsterdam petitioned to open a Dutch consul office in Bayonne in 1624. These ties between the Bayonne Jewish merchants and the Amsterdam Jewish community furthered the commerce of cacao.

Because of this chocolate trade and because of the local Jewish chocolate makers, Bayonne became known as a chocolate center.[16] In September 1725 it was reported that Bayonne chocolate was sold in marble-sized balls prepared on a stone (*à la Pierre*), or as known in the New World, a metate. With time, the reputation of Bayonne chocolate was so well established that dealers in Carcassonne, a fortified town in the southwest region of France—a significant distance in those days—preferred chocolate primarily from the Bayonne area. Bayonne chocolate became identified with specialized preparation and ingredients, known as *à la Bayonnaise*. By 1856 Bayonne had thirty-three chocolate factories, several of them using steam-powered machinery.[17] This supremacy of Bayonne may be seen in a review published at the end of the eighteenth century about the chocolate made in a Paris shop:

The city of Bayonne, France, home to early chocolate making by Jews.

> He employs Spanish, Piedmontese and Italian methods as though Madrid, Florence, Genoa and Turin were teamed up in his boutique and were vying with Bayonne with the supreme honor.[18]

Indeed, the hot chocolate Mark and I tasted in Bayonne had a distinct flavor and, as in the old recipes, had been whipped by hand, its *mousseux* (foam) topped by whipped cream. It percolated us into earlier chocolate history. The unusual flavors (was it cinnamon?) evoked in our taste buds a chocolate trail reaching from Mexico, to Spain, to southwest France.

Chocolate Complications Bubble in Bayonne

Bayonne's chocolate bubbles with complications. On one hand, we found repeated statements that Jews first brought chocolate making to France. This idea reappeared in many reputable research sources and in tour books. As Mort Rosenblum wrote in his book *Chocolate: A Bittersweet Saga*, the Jews of Bayonne "made the first French chocolate early in the seventeenth century."[19] *The Encyclopaedia Judaica* reads, "Bayonne Jewry helped to introduce the chocolate industry to France."[20] Jewish cookbook author Joan Nathan shares this view, writing, "These refugee Jews ... brought the traditions of chocolate making to Bayonne."[21]

In Bayonne itself we observed that many chocolate stores, several museums, and the city's tourist literature reiterate the Jewish origins of French chocolate. At the local Basque Museum, the instructional labels teach that Jews fleeing the Inquisition initiated the French chocolate industry. A few blocks away, the company-owned Le Choco Musée Puyodebat text panels mentioned again that Jews brought chocolate making to Bayonne. At a second company-owned chocolate museum, the Planète Musée du Chocolat in the neighboring town of Biarritz, the owner's daughter confidently touted this same idea to me. The Ville Bayonne city website restated this claim to visitors, as did local postcards. The map produced and distributed widely by the City of Bayonne Office of Tourism highlighted this message. Several historians of the Bayonne area argued that chocolate arrived in France as a result of the royal grant of refuge in southwest France to Iberian Jews escaping the persecutions in the sixteenth and seventeenth centuries. Without question, this account of Jews introducing chocolate making to France became quite popular in Bayonne.

Despite the frequency of this Jewish chocolate tale of Bayonne, things there were not always so smooth. From the beginning, the Jewish chocolate industry of seventeenth-century Bayonne encountered discrimination, jealousy, even anti-Semitism. Although in 1602 King Henry IV stipulated protection of the Jews by the local governors, Bayonne imposed restrictions on the Jews. Jews could not own or rent commercial or residential property outside of the St. Esprit suburb, and they could not live in Bayonne proper. Jews had to leave the city of Bayonne each evening by sunset and were prohibited from selling chocolate on Sundays or Christian feast days. This meant that Jewish chocolate makers had to carry their grinding stones to and from the retail stores and homes of customers in Bayonne each day. In 1681 Bayonne leaders implemented an ordinance to limit Jews' wholesale chocolate trade outside of St. Esprit, forbidding Jewish sales in retail shops or directly to individuals in Bayonne. In violation of that decree, the Jewish merchant Abraham d'Andrade, probably related to the Andrade of Martinique, rented an apartment in Bayonne for chocolate manufacture. Several later attempts to enforce these ordinances suggest that they had been ignored.[22]

Competition between the Bayonnais and the Jewish choco-late makers grew. The Bayonnais founded their own exclusive guild of chocolatiers in 1761, imploring the mayor and municipal leaders of Bayonne to recognize them as the sole chocolatiers of Bayonne while seeking to secure prohibitions against chocolate making by Jews. The city leaders favored the guild request, granting its eleven petitioners exclusive rights to run shops and sell chocolate. After the city of Bayonne and the Bordeaux law court registered these statutes in 1761 and 1762, the Jews appealed to the Count of Gramont, who instituted an investigation that led to the intercession of the king.

The resulting defense of the Bayonne Guild of 1763 complained that chocolate had become part of the daily Bayonnais diet. Its letter argued that extreme caution needed to be applied to chocolate preparation, since Jews "habitually falsify what they sell and should be prevented from making [chocolate]." It reasoned that Jews should work and sell only in St. Esprit. Fortunately, in 1764 a legal brief on behalf of the St. Esprit Jews was presented to the Bordeaux court. It argued against the guild statutes on the grounds that the Jews had long practiced the chocolate craft in Bayonne.[23]

Two Bordeaux lawyers who had been invited to write an opinion for the guild were ambivalent. They agreed with the mean spirit of the guild's argument, claiming:

> We certainly believe that the production of chocolates by the master chocolatiers of Bayonne will be of higher quality than that of the Jews.

However, neither did they wish to intrude on the "natural liberty" of "Bayonnais bourgeois" to choose their chocolate suppliers, reasoning that

> If a bourgeois from Bayonne cared so little for his own self interest and is such an enemy of his own stomach as to prefer the chocolate of a Jew, why should one prevent him from having the Jew come to his home to make it?[24]

Finally, after three years of these legal arguments, the court annulled the special status of the Bayonne Guild, permitting Jews to continue their chocolate making in Bayonne. French monarchs had intervened repeatedly to reaffirm the original rights accorded Jews in the southwest, rights that had been registered with the Parliament of Paris in 1550 and reconfirmed by Henry III in 1574, Louis XIV in 1656, and Louis XV in 1723 and 1754. Following the French Revolution, Jews were granted full citizenship in 1791. Ironically, records from the Jewish Consistory of Bayonne reveal that St. Esprit Jews were moving away from chocolate making by that time. By 1860 only two Jewish artisans practiced the craft, even as the chocolate industry of Bayonne employed 130 workers.[25]

Bayonne Features Jews in Its Chocolate Marketing Today

Despite this strained history, today's Bayonne chocolate makers and town leaders oddly have revived this notion about the link between Jews and French chocolate. In citing Bayonne as the original site of French chocolate preparation due to Jews, they have sought to reestablish Bayonne's authenticity and primacy in a revived French chocolate industry following World War II. Claiming Bayonne as the center of continuous chocolate manufacture in France in this contemporary marketing approach—a historical fudge—they overlooked the discrimination against Jews by Bayonnais merchants and nobles. This makes Bayonne essential to the French chocolate industry of today, though none of the chocolate companies functioning in Bayonne now traces its roots directly to the Jewish chocolate industry of the seventeenth century. The few Jews living in the Bayonne area no longer work in significant aspects of the local chocolate trade. Nevertheless, this story of Jews introducing chocolate to France pervades Bayonne. We may speculate about whether the first creation of chocolate in France occurred in Bayonne or whether that chocolate was made by a Jew. Clearly, Jews played a very real part in the chocolate of France in Bayonne. Someday one of the other narratives of the transmission of chocolate to France, via royalty or cleric, may be proven to be more accurate. Nevertheless, in this complicated reassertion of its chocolate heritage, Bayonne privileges the idea that Sephardi Jews introduced chocolate fabrication to France. This launches Jews firmly onto the chocolate trail.

Mexican Hot Chocolate

This version of Mexican hot chocolate roots the Jewish story of chocolate drinking in the Inquisition in New Spain or Mexico.

Ingredients:

4 ounces unsweetened chocolate
4 cups milk
2 cups heavy cream
¾ cup sugar
1 teaspoon ancho chile powder (or to taste)
1 teaspoon chipotle chile powder (or to taste)
1 tablespoon ground cinnamon
½ teaspoon ground cloves
1 tablespoon vanilla extract

Instructions:

Melt the chocolate in a large bowl over a simmering pan of water. In a separate heavy saucepan, heat the milk and cream on low until hot, but not boiling. Add 3 tablespoons of the hot milk to the chocolate in the double boiler and mix well. Stir the rest of the milk mixture, sugar, chile powders, cinnamon, cloves, and vanilla into the chocolate. Whisk chocolate briskly for 3 minutes, over the double boiler to thicken. (*Note:* To make it less spicy, use less chile.)

Quantity: 8 servings

Chapter Two

The Inquisition

Chocolate Outed Jews and Divided Christians

TO HUNT FOR FURTHER INFORMATION ABOUT THIS intersection of Jews and chocolate we uncovered in Bayonne, Mark and I traveled to Spain, the origin of Europe's age of chocolate discovery. While Spain identifies several tourist destination routes such as the Silver Route, the Route of the Caliphate, the El Cid Route, and the Way of St. James (*Camino de Santiago de Compostela*) Pilgrimage Route, we were disappointed that no route identified chocolate or Jews. We had no choice but to create our own *Camino Xocolata* (chocolate trail) of four chocolate museums, two chocolate factories, and countless chocolate stores ranging from the historical to the highly industrialized in Madrid, Barcelona, Valencia, and Astorga.

Our Spanish chocolate trail started with a café, Chocolateria San Ginés in Madrid, founded in 1894, with what some call the best hot chocolate in Spain—very warm, flavorful, chocolaty, and pudding-like. The typical Spanish chocolate thickening agent turns out not to be cream or chocolate but rice flour or, in some versions, cornstarch. No wonder this soothed my upset stomach. Spanish doughnuts, called churros, or ladyfingers, called *melindros*, customarily accompany hot chocolate in Spain, as in Mexico. Barcelona's Petrixol street

The many chocolate drinks and their accompaniments available in Spain.

hosts several chocolate drinking shops and numerous chocolate candy establishments. Granja Dulcinea Café offers a cold chocolate milk plus three hot chocolate options—a regular thick hot chocolate; a "French" hot chocolate, which is less thick; and the "Swiss" (with whipped cream, perhaps referring to white snow on top of mountains, though it is not customary to top hot chocolate with whipped cream in Switzerland). Our chocolate sampling definitely fortified us for our touring.

Spain: Many Chocolates, Few Jews

At the Barcelona Chocolate Museum we learned about Fray Aguilar, a Cistercian monk who shipped chocolate with the recipe to the Cistercian Monastery of Piedra (Monasterio de Piedra) and possibly also to the founding monastery at Poblet, shortly after chocolate's arrival in Spain in 1520. Since then, there has been a "Cistercian chocolate tradition."[1] Our spontaneous detour to see the still-functioning facility at Poblet, originally founded in the twelfth century, led us to the delightful medieval monks' "chocolate room" and the medieval kitchen display of chocolate-making accoutrements, including a copper

As seen near the chocolate room at the monastery at Poblet.

chocolate pot and a wooden chocolate stirrer. Imagine lounging in that chocolate room with a cup of nutritious, warming, energizing chocolate after arduous work in the fields and hours spent kneeling in prayer on cold stones. That's the life of a clergyman!

We gained a clearer under-standing of earlier Hispanic chocolate preparation and its use by the monks at Poblet from the Comes Chocolate Museum, owned by the fourth-generation Comes fam-ily patriarch, Pedro Melero, in Sueca, located in eastern Spain. Their Spanish-only

The quaint, family-owned chocolate museum and factory in Sueca, Spain.

video shows the period-costumed family grinding beans on a stone (*à la piedra*). In live time, Pedro tossed the cigar-like chocolate rolls pizza-style while animatedly lauding natural ingredients, denouncing preservatives, and extolling his minimal equipment. His textured drinking chocolate contains unrefined sugar with 80 percent cacao, similar to that of Mexico and Guatemala.

In contrast to Comes, the fully mechanized Valor Chocolate Factory and Museum in Villajoyosa, about fifty miles south of Sueca, produces most of Spain's chocolate. Valor uses very sensual, almost soft-core "adult"-oriented advertisements to pitch their chocolate. Cocoa beans from Ghana line the storage area. The business was started in 1881 by D. Valerian López Lloret—Valor was his nickname—and his was

Spain's largest chocolate producer, Valor.

one of at least thirty families in the area making chocolate and selling it by cart around the countryside.

About five hundred miles northwest of Villajoyosa, in Astorga, another chocolate center, many chocolate stores peddle multiple brands of the very thick chocolate bars seen throughout Spain. Tourists and priests frequently visited this stop along the Way of St. James (*Camino de Santiago*), the Christian pilgrimage route to the Cathedral of Santiago de Compostela in northwestern Spain. Tradition has it that the remains of the apostle James are buried there. This historic city hosts yet another chocolate museum, where we learned that the clergy's fondness for chocolate created significant demand for it in Astorga. The exhibit highlights a chocolate "guillotine"

Thick chocolate bars are common throughout Spain; these are made in Astorga.

used for cutting through those local slabs of chocolate. Also, the *maragatos* (muleteers), who dominated the transportation system in this area in the seventeenth century, easily delivered the chocolate to other regions of Spain. Because Astorga's weather is cool and dry, chocolate could be ground quickly and stored appropriately.

Our DIY (do-it-yourself) delectable Spanish chocolate circuit, however, left an unappealing aftertaste, because Spain provides minimal markers identifying the historic role of Jews. Former synagogues have become restaurants or gift shops. The Golden Age of Spain and the Inquisition are barely noted. Jews were not permitted to live in Spain from 1492 until 1950, and the current Jewish community is a small immigrant population composed primarily of North Africans, Israelis, Argentinians, and Americans. I wondered whether it could really be that Jews of Spain would have completely missed out on chocolate. After all, Jews were expelled from Spain at about the time Columbus discovered chocolate in the New World in 1502.

It took decades until the Spanish court even tasted chocolate, and then more time for chocolate recipes and skills to spread to the populace. Admittedly, the Spanish enjoyed the privilege of the exotic chocolate import in significant quantity only after Seville welcomed its first chocolate cargo in 1591, though there had been smaller, private imports prior to that.[2] These shipments of cacao ultimately achieved such renown that they voyaged with what was called the "chocolate wind," or *viento chocolatero*, the name given in Mexico for the favorable northern breezes.

As we poked further into that history, however, it became clear that Sephardi Jews were probably riding those chocolate winds as well, furthering the chocolate trail. When Spain annexed Portugal in 1580, some Jews of Portugal, fearing an even more virulent Inquisition, ironically sought safety back in Spain, where the Inquisition had become dormant and they were less well known.[3] As a result of the kinship and economic ties between Spanish and Portuguese Jews along the commercial trade routes, Jews probably knew of chocolate as soon as most in Spain did and indeed played a significant role in chocolate's diffusion throughout the Western world to places such as Amsterdam, Bayonne, England, and New Spain (see chapter 1).

Surprisingly, it was New Spain's Inquisition records that revealed that Jews there actively traded chocolate and used chocolate in religious rituals. The New World offered freedoms unknown to Jewish communities of prior periods and knew nothing of earlier restrictions such as ghettos or requirements for wearing distinctive badges.[4] The Inquisition, however, hunted practicing Jews.

Judaism Persists Despite the Inquisition

The public Catholicism and private Judaism of these Jews varied. Crypto-Jews may have met secretly for prayer in New Spain in the homes of leaders such as Simón Váez Sevilla and Tomás Treviño de Sobremonte. Because they could not always

The Inquisition

Generally, the Spanish crown sought to keep Jewish riches in Spain, prohibiting Jews from taking money, gold, or silver with them when expelled or confiscating these precious materials from them.[a] The tribunals of the Holy Office of the Inquisition were royal institutions, and they worked independently of Rome, though sanctioned by the pope for theological purposes. The Holy Office eventually had branches throughout Spain and then, after 1571, in the New World as well. The Inquisition pursued these conversos all the way to New Spain, centering its work in Mexico City. In 1571 the Holy Office appointed an inquisitor for New Spain, Dr. Pedro Moya de Contreras, who arrived that same year.[b] Accused Judaizers were only 16 percent of the total number of people investigated or tried by the Inquisition in New Spain. Other offenses included fornication, bigamy, blasphemy, Lutheranism, and sexual misconduct. However, unconverted Jews in New Spain were required to leave or be deported, their property confiscated under the rules established by the Inquisition.[c] Jews, though not many of them, were the first of the Inquisition targets to receive the formal sentence of burning at the stake. Hundreds of people were tried for the crime of *Judaizante* (Judaizing or behaving as a Jew).[d] Had the Mexican Inquisition pursued *Judaizante* activities more intentionally, it might have benefited financially from the loot they could have confiscated. Indeed, a number of local writers used Jews as leading characters.[e] While the Inquisition was inconsistent and slow moving, any rumor warranted investigation, with punishments in an auto-da-fé (public imposition of sentence) ranging from stripping of rank/honor, to confiscation of property, to imprisonment, to wearing of Inquisition clothing (*sambenito*), or in rare cases, to death by fire. Joseph de Olmo witnessed such an auto-da-fé in Madrid in 1680 where King Charles II presided over the day-long proceedings. Chocolate and other refreshments were provided for the high-ranking officials. At this same event, Marie de Villars, the wife of the French ambassador, decried the tortures and executions of Jews by the Spanish Holy Office. She later wrote to a friend commending the Spanish custom of chocolate for its health advantages.[f]

be sure about the Jewish calendar, the observance of holy days and festivals was a challenge. For some, avoiding pork and praying for the coming of the Messiah adequately expressed their secret Judaism. Others believed that only the knowledge of and intention to follow Mosaic laws were enough to keep Judaism alive. On Fridays they bathed, prepared special foods, and changed linens in preparation for the Sabbath. Almost all married other crypto-Jews. Generally children were raised as Catholics until the age of thirteen. Sometimes they circumcised themselves as adults. Bizarre circumcisions included cutting a piece of flesh off of a left shoulder, a custom observed by females as well. Many abstained from food and drink on the traditional Jewish fast days of Monday and Thursday as a form of penance for their outward observance of Catholicism.[5]

Chocolate Bewitches New Spain

Chocolate's desirability generated financial controversies and also concerns about propriety and mores. Several cases before the Inquisition in Guatemala and in New Spain argued that chocolate had been used in sorcery to seduce, craze, or control. In pursuing these suspicions, the Roman Catholic Church essentially swallowed pagan beliefs about the powers of chocolate. It apparently believed, along with the indigenous Indians, that the unfamiliar texture and unusual color of the popular drink could conceal witchcraft additives and the church therefore prosecuted several bizarre, non-Jewish cases. In Yucatán toward the end of the sixteenth century, Sánchez de Aquilar reported that Indian women put spells in chocolate to bewitch their husbands. Juana de Sossain Tlaxcala used chocolate to ensure carnal success as she plied at least a couple of men with doctored chocolate. The "famous" sorceress María de Rivera, a *mulata* (of mixed ancestry) in Puebla, Mexico, told her client to grind cacao and add certain powders to captivate the man she desired. Thirty-year-old

Cecilia de Arriola was charged with sorcery by her husband, Juan de Fuentes, in 1695. His bewitched behavior, he claimed, led him to rise early, allowing her to sleep in, and prepare her chocolate for her. In 1730 twenty-one-year-old Manuel Antonio Caldero accused his wife of causing his insanity. One night she, her mother, and her sister offered him a cup of hot chocolate. Noticing that it was heavier than usual, he asserted that when he looked more carefully, he found suspicious particles in the foam. Setting it aside, he later found it filled with white worms, the cup moving around on its own. Manuela Gutiérrez, a twenty-year-old *mulata* servant, was advised by a *mulata* sorcerer, Gerónima de Barahona, to wash herself, beat the water into a hot chocolate, and serve it to the man she desired to seduce. Similarly, Nicolasa de Torres, also a *mulata* servant, sought to attract her employer and was advised by an Indian woman, Petrona Mungía, to mix special ingredients into his chocolate drink. Such techniques were used by a Spanish woman named Doña Luisa de Gálvez in 1682 to end the abuse by her husband. The twenty-eight-year-old *mulata* slave of a nun, Rosa de Arrevillaga, served a priest (Padre Francisco de Castellanos) chocolate at confession during Easter in front of the other priests, as was customary. However, when she entered the confessional, he started to seduce her. She fended him off, and he accused her of "bewitching his chocolate with powders to gain his love."[6]

Inquisition records also disclose that chocolate drinking during church services had become customary in the New World. At least one priest protested that many of the *damas de sociedad* (elite women) disturbed the service as their entourage of slaves served steaming cups of chocolate. Furthermore, in approximately 1695, Pedro Rosuela, chaplain of the Santiago de Guatemala Cathedral, complained that the nuns drank chocolate in the pews, and he denounced them by name to the Inquisition. Ultimately, Santiago's city government enacted a prohibition against chocolate consumption in church.

The Jewish chocolate business, both trading and retail, also surfaced in the records of the Holy Office of the Inquisition. Many of those tried in the Mexican Inquisition for secretly practicing Judaism were cacao traders in the growing business with Caracas and Venezuela, importing and exporting cacao. That lucrative trade suffered due to the Inquisition trials. To supplement their earnings as seamstresses and embroiderers, Jewish women sold chocolate they had made.[7] When I asked scholar Stanley Hordes about these connections, he commented:

> I was not surprised to learn of the involvement of crypto-Jews in all stages of the importing and production of chocolate. Many of these folks pursued mercantile occupations of one sort or another.... Since chocolate was a much-sought-after commodity, it is not surprising that crypto-Jews, like other merchants, would have been heavily involved.[8]

Jews Make Their Cacao Fortune in New Spain

Indeed, from the Inquisition records we learn about several conversos on the chocolate trail in New Spain. In 1641 Manuel Álvarez de Arellano imported goods from Seville and distributed them throughout New Spain. That same year, he left for Spain with Mexican chocolate and other items, but he was arrested by Inquisition officials in 1642 and sent to Mexico for trial. Luis Núñez Pérez, a Portuguese converso and cacao retail merchant in New Spain, was arrested in June 1642, not long after he arrived. A vendor of cocoa beans, he was sentenced to reconciliation with the Catholic Church and life imprisonment at the age of thirty. Pedro de Campos became a successful cacao merchant in Campeche by the 1640s. In 1624 Francisco López de Fonseca, who spent his childhood in Portugal and Spain, sailed to Cartagena at the age of sixteen to help his uncle in his general store and then traveled to Venezuela, where he purchased a shipment of cacao and sailed for New Spain. Another Jewish cacao merchant, Duarte Castaño, operating out of Caracas, exchanged cacao for silver and products desired in Venezuela. During one expedition to Veracruz in 1645, he carried twenty-five *fanegas* (dry measure of about ½ bushels) of cacao belonging to Rabbi

Cacao in Central America

Mexican markets used cacao beans as coinage until Spanish currency became regularized. By the end of the sixteenth century, New Spain exported cacao to Spain, Mexican chocolate having become quite popular. Settlers in Guatemala shipped cacao for the American and European markets, with Oaxaca in southwestern Mexico serving as a transit point. Most of the Venezuelan cacao reached New Spain at Veracruz, in eastern Mexico, or Campeche, about 370 miles east of Veracruz, both along the Gulf of Mexico. From 1620 Venezuela exported large quantities of cacao to Mexico. Traders could double the value of cacao imported from Maracaibo and Caracas, reselling it in Mexico City. The success of the cacao trade invited controversies over taxing the lucrative commodity. King Philip IV sought to tax cacao to gain the income, while the viceroy in Mexico resisted, fearing that cacao taxes would generate an uprising from both local clergy and Indians, who were very fond of their chocolate. In the end, the local merchants succeeded in defeating a tax on cacao. Seeking to profit as well from cacao, Mexico City's Cabildo, the seat of colonial government, prohibited the import of Venezuelan and Ecuadoran cacao in 1624 and 1628. They prided themselves on their higher-quality Mexican cacao. The Cabildo further attacked a cacao monopoly in 1635, specifically targeting "a few rich *vecinos* [neighbors] of this city" for buying up all of the cacao at the ports and hoarding it to raise prices. In 1636 the Cabildo outlawed the mixing of cacao beans of varying quality because the practice confused purchasers.[a]

Benito Enríquez, eight *fanegas* sent by Pedro de Campos, as well as his own cargo of one hundred *fanegas*, all on consignment of converso Antonio Méndez Chillón. Francisco Franco de Moreira imported and distributed cacao from Venezuela. Manuel López Nuñez controlled the tax on cacao. Luis de Burgos, at age sixty-three or sixty-four, purchased a store that specialized in cacao, chocolate, and sugar. When he was arrested in 1645, his shop was sequestered by the Inquisition. They left its manager, Juan de Acosta, in charge. Even when Burgos was finally released, the Inquisition tribunal kept the store. The Burgos store inventory included cacao that had been sourced from Maracaibo, Venezuela; Guayaquil, Ecuador; and Soconusco, Mexico. Another crypto-Jew and chocolate retailer, Luis Núñez, acquired a chocolate store in 1642 and was shortly thereafter arrested. In the records of the auto-da-fé of March 30, 1648, we learn about a grower of cocoa beans in Zacatula, forty-year-old Melchor Rodríguez López, who had been born in Portugal and became a resident of Mexico.[9] Manuel Fernandez, whose father was accused of Judaizing by the Inquisition in Toledo in 1649, testified that a converso, Francisco Díaz,

> had a store of chocolate and luxuries on the plaza of Anton Martin.... Diaz brought him into a room behind the store, and being alone, offered him a *xic* (*jicara* [meaning "cup"]) of chocolate and then explained to him the rules of Moses.[10]

Antonio Méndez Chillón, one of the wealthiest Jews sought out by the Mexican Inquisition, carried on a very sophisticated cacao trade. He had come to Mexico from Angola in southern Africa in 1629 and settled in Veracruz, becoming a leading importer of Venezuelan cacao to New Spain. His crypto-Jewish agents and merchants in Gibraltar as well as Caracas and Maracaibo bartered for cacao and monitored the fluctuations in price, quality, and availability of the cacao beans.[11] Following his arrest, the Inquisition tried to confiscate a load of cacao from his manager, Orozco, but since it had not yet been transmitted into his ownership, the Veracruz *maestre* (master) would not turn it over to the tribunal, though the Inquisition kept trying until 1664.

When the Inquisition officials inventoried Méndez Chillón's home after his arrest, they found immense wealth, including 8,486 Mexican silver pesos, 349 gold Spanish doubloons, and trunks of silver, jewelry, tableware, gold, and pearls. Chillón had sought to protect his illegitimate children from the investigations against the Jews. He hid his seven-year-old daughter at the oldest convent in Mexico City, putting a house in Veracruz into her name to secure the payments to the convent. Perhaps because he had not been found to have networked with other crypto-Jews nor observed any Jewish rituals, his imprisonment was shorter than those of others. He was nevertheless deported to Cadiz, Spain, in 1647, and sadly, the Inquisition confiscated the monies he had set aside for his children.[12]

Jews Ritualize Chocolate

As I plunged further into these Inquisition reports about people such as Méndez Chillón, I saw that Jews not only took an active role in the cacao trade in the New World, but they also secreted it into their undercover Jewish ritual life. Mexican crypto-Jews used chocolate for welcoming the Sabbath because wine was scarce in New Spain. For Jews attempting to follow Jewish dietary laws, the pareve nature of the local chocolate drink prepared without milk lent itself to the separation of milk and meat; it could be enjoyed with a milk meal or a meat meal. Chocolate seeped into these important Jewish customs and celebratory meals for holidays and life-cycle events. Beatriz Enríquez and her sister would not even drink their daily chocolate until they had prayed each morning. The same Beatriz recalled that following the private negotiations for an engagement, the entire family joined together for chocolate drinking.[13]

This chocolate use extended to sad times as well. Holding vigil for the dying Doña Blanca Méndez de Rivera, her daughters and granddaughters spent a day in reflection and prayer, fortified by a special meal of chocolate and pickled fish brought from Veracruz by the merchant Mathias Rodríguez de Olivera, as Margarita de Rivera recalled for the Inquisition (1644).[14] The proceedings of the trial of Gabriel de Granada (October 1642) report his testimony about the period of mourning for his father, Manuel de Granada:

> Gabriel sent to her the hard boiled eggs and chocolate which was eaten by the said widow and her children. During the six days preceding the said seventh, ... sent chocolate one day of the said six.[15]

At funerals, the Mexican Váez family (1630s) ate chocolate, raisins, almonds, salad, and homemade bread, but never any meat.[16]

Chocolate even accompanied meals associated with the beginning and end of the fast of Yom Kippur (Day of Atonement). This may have been the most frequently observed of the holy days, so much so that many secret Jews even risked writing down the exact date. The theme of atonement resonated for them, as they felt themselves constantly sinning through their public profession of Catholicism. On the other hand, Rosh Hashanah (the New Year) was rarely commemorated,[17] it being easier to hide a day of deprivation than Rosh Hashanah's celebratory meals and rituals. Gaspar Váez broke his 1640 Yom Kippur fast with chocolate, eggs, salad, pies, fish, and olives.[18] Isabel de Rivera testified on October 7, 1642, that a year before, on Yom Kippur, Doña Juana, who was married to the wealthy Simón Váez Sevilla, sent "thick chocolate and sweet things made in her house."[19] Around 1645 Gabriel de Granada and his family washed down their pre-fast meal with chocolate, having dined on fish, eggs, and vegetables. Others reported that they preceded the Day of Atonement with fruit and chocolate and that they broke the fast with chocolate and similar treats.[20] Beatriz Enríquez, at the age of twenty-two, testified that when her husband left for long business trips, she took advantage of her sadness to hide her abstinence from chocolate and food on *día grande* (big day), or Yom Kippur:

> From the window she pretended to be crying over the absence of her husband and with this suffering she was able to hide from her *negras* (Negro servants) the fact that she ate nothing and did not drink chocolate that day.[21]

In order not to eat on fast days, Amaro Díaz Martaraña and her husband would stage a falling out with each other in the middle of the day. When chocolate was brought to them, they would pretend to be offended and spill it on the servants. They reconciled in the evening.[22] Isabel Duarte told the Inquisition that she had tested Diego Díaz to see if he shared her religious secret of Jewish identity by offering him chocolate at different times, including on some fast days. When he refused, she asked him why. His reply, she told the Inquisition, was that "it was stupid to ask him why." To offer chocolate at times when it was proscribed and to receive a refusal in response was to communicate through a coded language.[23] Jews developed such subterfuges to avoid being outed for drinking chocolate on Catholic fast days or not drinking chocolate on Jewish fast days.

Crypto-Jews who marked minor fasts and penitential fasts established by the Jewish calendar may have been aware of the discussions in the Catholic Church as to whether the Lenten fast permits chocolate. These debates centered on whether to define chocolate as food or as drink. While drinking was permitted in Catholic fasting, it was not in Jewish fast observances. Jews generally sided with those of the Christian view that drinking chocolate broke the fast and maintained the Jewish view that it broke a Jewish fast.[24]

Such fasts were also framed with meals that included chocolate. Attempting a fast, fifteen-year-old Símon de León confessed to the Inquisition in Mexico in 1647 that he ran away from home because he had broken a fast that his father had ordered him to keep. When he could not bear the hunger any longer, he asked his sister Antonia for some chocolate.[25] One Juan de León and his Mexican converso friends preceded their fasts with chocolate and broke the fasts with chocolate, among other foods. They also followed local colonial Mexican custom and finished their meals with a cup of the festive drink, chocolate.[26] When, two weeks after Beatriz Enríquez married Tomás Núñez de Peralta in 1637, he left on a trading trip, she did an *ayuno* (fast) for him for the first time alone at the age of nineteen. She could not complete the fast fully, taking "a little bit of chocolate."[27]

Family members testified against each other using chocolate in their accusations. Fernando Rodríguez, a successful Jewish merchant who traded in cacao and slaves, owned a chocolate service of small silver spoons, silver saucers called *cestillos*, and deep clay cups known as *tecomates,* which he and his wife used for their daily chocolate drinking except on Jewish fast days. On such fast days, he dissembled to his servants that the price of cacao was too high and that he could not afford to drink it. As one of his adult sons testified to the Inquisitors, there were days when his parents skipped their daily chocolate: "I didn't see them eat all day nor drink chocolate as they always did on other days." Another son, Francisco López, testifying against his brother, mentioned that "a day before Holy Week," the brother had not had his chocolate "as was his custom" but went off and spent the day by himself in his father's warehouse on the beach, suggesting that he avoided the chocolate in order to observe some Jewish ritual, perhaps Passover's ritual of the fast of the firstborn son.[28]

Chocolate Nourishes Inquisition Jails

Even once Jews were arrested by the Inquisition, chocolate continued to be part of the experience of Jews during the capture and in jail. Muleteers hired to transport suspected crypto-Jews to trial drank chocolate and listed it as a reimbursable expense. The muleteers who captured Rodrigo Serrano in Veracruz in September 1646 purchased chocolate in each place where they spent the night, planning ahead for the next morning's breakfast chocolate. The Holy Office mentions payment to Jesuits for "writing and occupying themselves with other internal business, ... they have been given some alms [for the purchase] of their chocolate."[29]

Chocolate lubricated jail life, according to Inquisition records, and was used commonly as a gift, bribe, barter, or jailhouse commodity. Jewish prisoners received chocolate, sometimes several times during each day, often delivered by servants or slaves. For some, this helped pass the time and broke up the boredom. Ana Suárez, who for a while shared a cell with her mother, Rafaela Enríquez, reported to the Inquisition that in the morning after their chocolate, Rafaela had carried on prohibited conversations with other prisoners. In other testimony, Simón Váez Sevilla repeatedly begged to see his son and his wife, Juana Enríquez, expressing grave worry about her. When called again to appear before the inquisitors for his twelfth hearing in April 1644, he first requested some chocolate with sugar and only then asked to see his son and his wife. A slave, Francisco de la Cruz, fingered a prisoner to whom he had secretly delivered messages, identifying him as the occupant of the cell above the chocolate room. Beatriz Enríquez gave a Congolese slave, Sebastián Domingo, two pesos, explaining that he should buy her chocolate but intending to really pay him to help her deliver messages to her husband in jail. Yet another slave entered an Inquisition cell to find the prisoner perched on a bag of chocolate.

Chocolate Bribes

Chocolate smoothed life outside of the Inquisition jails as well. Diego Correa and his wife, Catalina de Rivera, who knew many of Mexico's crypto-Jews and could identify them, owned a small stall selling chocolate in the Cathedral Plaza. When the Inquisition arrested Blanca Méndez de Rivera and her daughters (May 17 and 19, 1642) to get their testimony, the Enríquez women called upon Correa, hoping to enlist his help in preventing his wife, her sisters, and their mother from selling them out. Correa testified that Juana Enríquez had given him a gift of six *libras* (pounds) of chocolate. Another woman, also worried about being reported to the Inquisition by Correa's wife, gave him "a little chocolate and a loaf of sugar."[30]

Chocolate continued to be important even after the Inquisition sentenced Judaizers to return to Spain to be dealt with by the Inquisition there. When Simón Váez Sevilla and his family emerged from penitential cells (1649), they were commanded by the Inquisition officials to leave Mexico City immediately. They departed for Seville with a cargo of chocolate, 5,000 pesos, jewelry, and silver.[31]

While Mark and I found plenty of chocolate in Seville, Cadiz, Barcelona, and Astorga, our Spanish chocolate route led us to the complexities of Jews, religion, and chocolate in New Spain. Delving into the Inquisition records surfaced information about how chocolate both jeopardized the lives of Jews there and also enriched their businesses. It permeated their ritual observances and sustained them in jail. An authentic Spanish route of chocolate would explore the tensions between threat and nourishment for Jews represented by chocolate at this time. For Christians, chocolate pitted those who delighted in the treat against those who saw it as a source of pagan sorcery. This story of chocolate, Jews, and religion branched off into other destinations of the Sephardi migrations, including North America.

Chocolate Pudding

Based on the 1871 Esther Levy recipe from the first Jewish cookbook in America, this updated version transports our appetites to the American colonial period.[a] Warning: This is actually a cake.

Ingredients:

1 cup milk chocolate or dark chocolate, crumbled
5 large eggs, separated
1 cup sugar
1 cup graham cracker crumbs

Instructions:

Preheat the oven to 375°F. Lightly grease an 8-inch springform pan. Melt the chocolate in a large heatproof bowl set over a pan of simmering water; remove from the heat to cool. Beat together the egg yolks and sugar. In a separate bowl, beat the egg whites. Fold the egg yolks and sugar into the cooled chocolate. Fold in the graham cracker crumbs. Fold the egg whites into the chocolate mix. Pour the batter into the prepared pan. Bake for 30 minutes. Cool in the pan. To serve, cut into wedges.

Quantity: 6–8 servings

Chapter Three

Jews Dip into Chocolate in the American Colonial Period

Jewish shopkeepers specialized in cocoa and chocolate which they secured in large quantities from their co-religionists in Curaçao.... Chocolate in fact may have been a Sephardic Jewish specialty.[1]

THIS PASSING MENTION ABOUT THE SEPHARDI chocolate specialists in North America from the work of preeminent American Jewish historian, Jacob Rader Marcus, remained buried amid his many pages of writings. Perhaps no one in his time cared to pursue chocolate inquiries. Or perhaps it was because there was so much other fascinating material in Marcus's writings that drew attention. In previous decades, historical themes of assimilation and anti-Semitism were certainly more compelling. Yet as Marcus noted, the Jewish chocolate trail winds deeply through the North American colonial period, and chocolate was in fact a Sephardi Jewish specialty. Here again the Sephardi trading network imported and shipped cocoa beans, as well as manufactured chocolate.

Hunting for Chocolate Up the Hudson

To trace the Sephardi diffusion of chocolate to colonial North America, Mark and I packed our barely awake Brooklyn-based adult kids into a rental car for what our daughter called a "family fun day" of chocolate research. It was a stormy New York June day, and our plan included an outing to the Gomez Mill House, the oldest extant Jewish homestead in North America, which was built in 1714 as a trading post by the New York Jewish community's leading Sephardi family. In a perfect mix of history, chocolate, and family frolicking, we quibbled over the front seat, got lost, ate from each other's plates, and explored Gomez family chocolate roots in Newburgh, New York, about sixty miles north of New York City. The Gomez family members were among the several colonial and Revolutionary period North American Jews who engaged in the manufacture, retail, and consumption of cacao and chocolate, primarily in New York City and Newport, Rhode Island. Indeed, many of these pioneering Jewish chocolate endeavors preceded the beginning of the Baker's Chocolate Company, which bills itself as "America's Oldest" and "evolved into the first branded 'Baker's Chocolate' product in 1780."[2] However, there were certainly many others making chocolate prior to Baker, including Sephardi cousins Gomez and Lopez.

The fort-like stone cabin in Newburgh, now listed on the National Register of Historic Places, was intended primarily for trading fur. This first Jewish settlement up the Hudson River—established by patriarch Luis (Lewis) Moses Gomez— was probably run by his sons Daniel and David Gomez. Born in Madrid, Luis and his mother escaped the Inquisition to France, possibly even Bayonne. According to Gomez family tradition, his father, Isaac Gomez, a Spanish nobleman and a favorite at court, was warned by the king that the Inquisition was about to arrest him and confiscate his estate. He quickly sent his wife and infant son, Moses, to France to secure their safety, along with "money, jewels and plate." It is said that the "Luis/Lewis" was added to Moses's name in gratitude to the French king for allowing him refuge in France. In 1706 Luis obtained a letter of denization (bestowing some privileges of a British subject) now displayed at the Mill House, which enabled him and his family to live in New York, where he purchased land and became a very successful merchant.[3] Luis bought the Hudson River plot at the intersection of several Indian trails leading to a holy site near a spring, which came to be known as Jews Creek. He built the

The Gomez Mill House in Newburgh, New York— the oldest Jewish house still in existence.

house at least six miles from other habitations. The mill could have been used for grinding chocolate, although there is no direct evidence of such use.

The Gomez Chocolate Dynasty

At least five members within two generations of the Gomez family enjoyed chocolate connections in New York City: Mordecai (1688–1750), his wife, Rebecca (1713–1801), his brother Daniel (1695–1780), Mordecai and Rebecca's son, Moses (1744–1826), and their nephew, Isaac (1768–1831).[4] In particular, Rebecca Gomez stands out not only for her retail advertising but also as the only known woman to manufacture chocolate in the colonies.

The Gomez family's chocolate business was built on a granular chocolate, which was plentiful and commonly imbibed as a beverage. There were no chocolate ice creams, chocolate candy bars, chocolate truffles, chocolate cakes, or chocolate chip cookies at this time. The proximity of the colonies to cacao bean sources in Central America kept prices reasonable, although Britain levied high taxes on chocolate. Some countries, such as France, established monopolies on chocolate. By contrast, in the colonies there were fifty or more chocolate makers, with approximately twenty-four in Philadelphia by 1776. Surprisingly, America had more chocolate per capita than Europe did. Benjamin Franklin even sold chocolate in his Philadelphia print shop.[5]

Cacao beans first arrived in North America sometime in the seventeenth century. Colonial Williamsburg food specialist James Gay speculated that Jews may have brought chocolate to North America, arguing that conversos from New Spain, Brazil's Recife, or Amsterdam brought it.[6] Jews from these settings would have been exposed to chocolate, consumed chocolate, and traded chocolate. In Newport, Rhode Island, Aaron Lopez used chocolate at Passover and distributed it as *tzedakah* (charity) gifts. It was also thought that chocolate provided nutrition on a fast day during a cholera epidemic.

Jews Retailed Chocolate before Baker's

While the Baker's Chocolate Company counts its first recorded sale of Baker's-made chocolate in Boston on July 2, 1772,[a] there were many sales of chocolate by Jewish grocers and others prior to that, including by Nathaniel Abraham,[b] Hyman Levy,[c] Jonas Phillips,[d] as well as the following:

- [1752] Nathans and Hart included chocolate in the store price list for grocery items in their shop in Halifax, Nova Scotia.[e]
- [1760] Isaac Delyon, Savannah, Georgia, wrote to Barnard Gratz in Philadelphia requesting a number of items, including "25 lb chokolet."[f]
- [1761] Joseph Simon, Lancaster, Pennsylvania, ordered from Barnard Gratz "one barrel of good muscavado unrefined sugar, 24 lbs of chocolate, 25 lbs of good coffee."[g]

Dr. Daniel L. M. Peixotto argued in August 1832 that Jews in New York should not observe the fast day of the ninth of Av, Tishah B'Av, but rather "they should be permitted to take a light meal of coffee, tea, or cocoa with dry toast"[7] and thus build their immunity to the epidemic.

Jewish trading of chocolate began in New York. Since the first known business record of the Jew Isaac Marquez importing twenty-five pounds of chocolate in New York in 1701, Jewish merchants profited from this chocolate culture.[8] Originally from Denmark, Marquez died in New York in 1706. New York customs records in the decade following 1701 list their cargoes as consisting mainly of "cocoa, rum, wine, fur, and fabrics." The customs records for cargoes in New York include cacao for the ten years after 1715.[9] Another Jew, Nathan Simson, engaged in significant trade of cacao, shipping more than thirty-three thousand pounds between 1710 and 1721. As early as 1728, the Jew Rodrigo Pacheco imported thirty thousand pounds of cacao through New York's port, the equivalent of approximately one-third of the total annual import through New York in the late 1760s in the period of what has been called the New York chocolate boom.[10]

In this period Jews imported cacao from distant as well as nearby ports. At times they ran into legal difficulties. Sometimes they did business with family. The cacao came primarily from Caracas, Venezuela, as well as Curaçao, Jamaica, and Haiti. It was also sourced from other colonies. Jewish merchant Rachel Luis imported cacao from Curaçao. Simson secured cocoa that had been imported to South Carolina. In 1734 one of Rodrigo Pacheco's ships sailed from New York to Curaçao, where it loaded cacao that was exchanged for rice in Charleston, South Carolina. Then it continued on to Falmouth, England. He also traded to Jamaica, through New York, Lisbon, Genoa, and Barcelona. Between 1702 and 1704 the Jew Joseph Bueno, who was awarded his license to trade and traffic in New York in 1683, was buying large quantities of cocoa in Newport, Rhode Island, dealing with "24,000 wt (pounds) coko [cocoa]." Bueno shipped cacao to England from Newport on the sloop *Mary*. In at least one case, his captain attempted to circumvent the law. Claiming that his ship leaked, Bueno's captain unloaded in New York, storing the cacao in Bueno's warehouse rather than at the customs shed, purportedly awaiting an increase in the potential price of the cacao. Bueno was charged and fined. Another court case concerning cacao arose when Moses Levy sued Nathan Simson and Jacob Franks, executors of Samuel Levy's estate, claiming that Samuel Levy had sold him spoiled cocoa with salt in it in 1722. In 1753 Daniel Gomez wrote from New York to Aaron Lopez in Newport inquiring about the price of cacao and at the same time notified Lopez of the death of his wife. Gomez's business with Lopez's father-in-law, Jacob R. Rivera, included chocolate.[11] Jews enjoyed a far-ranging, intercolonial, and intercontinental chocolate trade that was also familial.

Colonial Chocolate Habits

This trade supported a daily chocolate habit throughout the colonies. Hot chocolate made from "cocoa nuts" or "chocolate nutts" (cocoa beans) dressed up breakfast or supper, sometimes composing the full meal.[12] Coffeehouses and chocolate houses were as fashionable in the colonies as they were in England.[13] Ships' crews savored chocolate provisions on board, whether purchased by individual sailors, or the captain for his use, or provided for the crew. While the governments of England and Holland sentenced people to hang for stealing one pound of chocolate, it was so reasonably priced in North America that it was frequently dispensed to soldiers, prisoners, and poor people.[14] Chocolate drinking became even more popular in America around the time of the 1773 Boston Tea Party as an accessible and obvious alternative to politicized tea. James Green's advertisement reads, "Coffee and chocolate ... instead of tea, to which article we have bid farewell."[15] An English traveler reported in 1775, "Last Night [Twelfth Night] I went to the Ball.... A cold supper, Punch, Wines, Coffe [sic] and Chocolate but no Tea. This is a forbidden herb."[16] Philip Fithian, traveling in West Virginia as a Presbyterian circuit rider in December 1775, wrote, "Tea is out of the question; it is almost Treason against the country to mention it, much more drink it."[17] And, "Mr. Aaron Lopez, owner of the ship *Jacob*, Capt. Peters, has assured us in writing that said ship has not India TEA on board and that he thinks himself happy in giving such assurance."[18] In 1797,

Colonial Chocolate Recipes

Mars sought to reproduce the taste and look of colonial American chocolate in its *American Heritage Chocolate*, "Handmade chocolate inspired by an authentic colonial recipe."

To Make Chocolate: [1796]

Take six Pounds of cocoa-nuts, one of anise-seeds, four ounces of long pepper, one of cinnamon, a quarter of a pound of almonds, one ounce of pistachios, as much achiote as will make it the colour of brick, three grains of musk, and as much ambergris, six pounds of loaf-sugar, one ounce of nutmegs, dry and beat them, and searce [sift] them through a fine sieve; your almonds must be beat to a paste and mixed with the other ingredients; then dip your sugar in orange-flower or rose water, and put it in a skillet on a very gentle charcoal fire; then put in the spice and stew it well together, then the musk and ambergris, then put in the cocoa-nuts last of all, then achiote, wetting it with the water the sugar was dipt in; stew all these very well together over a hotter fire than before; then take it up and put it into boxes, or what form you like, and set it to dry in a warm place: the pistachios and almonds must be a little beat in a mortar, then ground on a stone.[a]

a group known as the Manufacturers of Chocolate appealed to the United States Fourth Congress complaining about the high duty laid on the import of cocoa. As a result, Congress repealed the additional two-cent duty on the cocoa.[19] This kept chocolate inexpensive and accessible to all as a common household item.

Our colonial chocoholics did not simply toss a packet of chemicals, sugar, and processed cocoa into boiling water. Painstaking preparation of this early American chocolate began with the import of the beans, which were then generally purchased at local dry goods stores.

James Gay explained the multistep, tedious process to me when I interviewed him in 2008. The task of tending and roasting the cocoa beans over a fire, shelling each one individually, grinding the chocolate nibs with sugar (sometimes along with cinnamon and/or other spices) while warming them over a chocolate stone with a roller, and then cooling the chocolate into hard tablets was often relegated to servants or slaves. It resulted in a drinking chocolate similar to that found elsewhere at that time and today in Mexico and Guatemala.[20] The solidified chocolate, wrapped in used newspapers or in rags of questionable sources, was often stored randomly, likely absorbing the smells of sometimes fetid foodstuffs or rancid products. Larger fifty-pound chocolate quantities were generally sold in boxes.[21] Some households kept twenty-five to fifty pounds of chocolate on hand, which would have supplied a family of four with a customary daily hot chocolate for about a month. Before indulging, the hardened chocolate required further mixing with water and sugar using a special stirrer (*molinollo*, or mill) while heating in the chocolate pot, with its special opening in the top for the stirrer. The hot chocolate might have then been served in unique cups especially for drinking chocolate. Such specialized tools also were available at local dry goods shops. Colonial chocolate was very slow food.

These colonial chocolate experiences also leaked into religious life for better and worse. A vignette from this period relates that in 1690 Pilgrims traveled to Plymouth Rock via Amsterdam and stayed in a house near the city's biggest chocolate houses. The Pilgrims termed that chocolate "the Devil's food." Later, a chocolate cake became popular in Amsterdam that the local bakers named "Devil's Food." In this early American religious mind-set, chocolate represented evil, perhaps because it indulged the senses and distracted from work and worship.[22] At least one New England moralistic ascetic charged "Serious Christians in the Professing Country to think of forgoing amongst other Things, Chocolate."[23]

An American colonial pantry boasts a chocolate pot.

Domestic colonial chocolate imbibing seeped happily into other ecclesiastical settings, perhaps influenced by the reports of British royal chocolate piety, as in this dispatch from London, 1761, about King George III:

> His majesty riseth at five o'clock every morning, lights his own candle ... dresseth himself, then calleth a servant to bring him bread, butter and chocolate. At six he goeth to chapel where he hath morning prayers in the most religious manner.[24]

Several ministers enjoyed their chocolate. Chocolate bolstered the daily routine of Thomas Prince (1687–1758), reverend of Boston's Old South Church and a historian of New England. After his graduation from Harvard and his wedding, the reverend's daily routine included rising at 5:00 a.m., reading the Bible in his study, waking the rest of the family at 6:30 a.m., gathering all for family prayers, and enjoying "only the Porringer [pewter dish] of chocolate for Breakfast."[25] Military chaplains were rationed a certain amount of chocolate: "Chaplain of a brigade shall be entitled to draw only six galons of Rum, either four pounds of Coffee or Chocolate ... monthly."[26] The diary of Samuel Sewall—who studied for the ministry, became a chief justice of Massachusetts, and was a judge at the Salem witch trials—noted that his pastoral ministrations bundled visits and sermons with gifts of chocolate.[27] Sewall himself drank chocolate on occasion.[28] Chocolate was used in houses of mourning as well. When Poulis Freer died in 1802, his heirs served chocolate at the time of the funeral.[29] Another minister complained that he could not maintain his standard of living, including his customary chocolate drinking. His protest to the *Boston Evening Post*, signed by "Your humble Servant, T.W.," lamented:

> Upwards of 40 years ago I was ordained Pastor of a Church in ... and by the unanimous Vote of my People had settled on me ... with which I could buy ... Chocolate.... You will readily perceive by comparing these Accounts together that the same Articles one with another have risen more than seven and an half for one since my first Settlement with my People, whereas they could never yet be prevailed on to raise my Salary more than three for one.... And I may venture to say, this is the Truth of the Case with respect to most of the Ministers throughout the Province.[30]

For these religious leaders, financial challenges and shortages were identified through the ability to buy daily chocolate supplies.

Chocolate nourished these men of God and seemingly enhanced their ministries. These chocolate customs were enabled by the significant cacao trade and chocolate manufacturing of people such as Aaron Lopez and the Gomez family members.

The Gomez family led the Sephardi and secular community of New York. The state assembly met at Mordecai Gomez's house.[31] Mordecai and Daniel served as Spanish interpreters to the admiralty and supreme courts, Daniel serving for some twenty years at this post.[32] The house of Luis Gomez was taxed at nearly ten times the value of the Jews' rented house of worship.[33] At New York's Congregation Shearith Israel, the Gomez family enjoyed the most prestigious seats. Isaac bequeathed silver ornaments for the Torah (scroll of the Five Books of Moses) to his eldest son, Mordecai.[34] Moses Gomez laid the first stone of the new synagogue, and Luis Moses Gomez, along with his son Mordecai, signed the contract with the mason. The affluent Gomez family's donation was the highest from any single family.[35] Lewis Moses Gomez also contributed the highest gift from a Jewish community member to the Trinity Church steeple. Of the twenty-five Sephardi members of the leadership committee of Shearith Israel, twenty were part of the Gomez family.[36] Mordecai, Daniel, and David, along with father Luis Moses Gomez, appeared in the title for the Jewish cemetery in 1729. The northwest gallery of the synagogue's women's section, called the *banco,* was reserved for the Gomez family women, symbolizing their wealth and stature.[37]

Daniel Gomez engaged in a large and lucrative business in New York, trading with the West Indies, Madeira, Barbados, Curaçao, London, and Dublin, and sending 133 ships to Curaçao between 1739 and 1772. He corresponded and traded with Sephardi Jews in these locales.[38]

Jews Traded Cacao from Philadelphia

[1801] Simon and Hyman Gratz worked as commission merchants, as real estate brokers, and in the very successful shipping trade out of Philadelphia. In their trade with Brazil they imported fifteen thousand pounds of St. Domingo cocoa.[a]

In addition to retailing chocolate,[39] Daniel Gomez imported more than 20,860 pounds of cacao to New York via Curaçao between 1728 and 1747.[40] In 1759 Gomez advertised boxes of drinking chocolate for sale at the corner of Bruling's Slip in New York City.[41]

When Mordecai Gomez died in 1750, he left several chocolate accoutrements in his estate inventory, including "16 chocolate cupps, whole and broken, 1 chocolate pott; 2 boxes Chocolate 50 lbs each and 6 Surnis (840 pounds) Coco [Surinam],"[42] suggesting his personal use in addition to his commerce.

For many years Moses Gomez earned his living as a chocolate maker. In 1788 he announced his hunt for his runaway "indented servant" who was "used to chocolate making."[43] Moses Gomez and company also advertised the private sale of "1 ton of Carracas cocoa."[44]

In 1815 Isaac Gomez's advertisement for smaller quantities of chocolate, "Isaac Gomez Jr. and Co 6 boxes chocolate," ran at least forty-three times.[45]

Rebecca Gomez sold chocolate, as did other women of the day. However, she was the only woman known to manufacture—this, despite the fact that she was left property and a significant portion of her husband Mordecai's estate and may not have needed the income. The youngest child of Abraham Haim Lucena, she married Mordecai in New York on May 4, 1741.[46] Rebecca Gomez plied her wholesale and retail chocolate made at the "Chocolate Manufactory" through newspaper advertisements.[47] Rebecca used promotions such as these to further her endeavors:

[1779] Rebecca Gomez at the Chocolate Manufactory
Corner of Ann and Nassau-Street
HAS FOR SALE ...
Own manufactured Chocolate, warranted free from any
   sediments and pure.
Great allowance made to those who buy to sell again.[48]

[1780] Rebecca Gomez
Has for sale at the CHOCOLATE Manufactory
No. 14 upper end Nassau-Street between ...
SUPERFINE warranted CHOCOLATE, wholesale and
    retail ...[49]

[1781] Chocolate
Manufactured in the best manner, warranted fine and
    good, to be sold wholesale and retail,
by REBECCA GOMEZ at the Chocolate Manufactory,
    No. 57, Nassau Street between Commissary Butler's
    and the Brick Meeting ...[50]

[1781] CHOCOLATE
WARRANTED fine and good, wholesale and retail,
    at reasonable rates, by REBECCA GOMEZ, at the
    chocolate manufactory, No. 57, Nassau Street ...[51]

She reflected a mid-eighteenth-century interest in quality and increased focus on one product: "superfine, free from any sediments and pure."

Rebecca Gomez's business savvy led her to advertise about her unique chocolate, reflecting a growing sophistication about marketing. Using her family reputation and name to good effect, she not only ventured into business but also participated in a trend to specialization. Rebecca's manufacturing marked shifts in commerce toward industrialization in the decades of the 1770s and 1780s, perhaps using Mordecai's snuff mills and houses on Ann Street.[52] Overall, the Gomez family endeavors in chocolate trade, retail, and personal consumption exemplified the general popularity and availability of chocolate in the colonial period, as well as Sephardi interests in this market.

Aaron Lopez Sips, Sells, and Ships Chocolate

From his British wallpapered, wood-timbered office overlooking the Newport, Rhode Island, wharf, Aaron Lopez used labeled pigeonholes in the rafters to monitor his many vessels and related businesses, including that of chocolate.[53] There the multigenerational Gomez gusto for all areas of the chocolate business in New York mingled with that of their Newport cousin through their Sephardi roots, marriage vows, religious ties, and financial interests. Though Lopez's chocolate business differed from that of his New York coreligionists, he too was steeped in chocolate manufacturing, retail, and trade.

This prominent Sephardi Rhode Island trader of the eighteenth century was born in 1731 in Portugal. Known as Duarte in the Old Country, he and his family lived publicly as Christians and privately as Jews. Aaron abandoned Portugal to live a full Jewish life in America. He traveled to Curaçao to learn the sperma (whale sperm) process and introduced it to America for the purpose of candle making, arriving in Newport, where his older half-brother, Moses, was already living and setting up shop in 1750. Another Newport merchant, Jacob Rodriguez Rivera, became Aaron's father-in-law in 1763. Although he was refused citizenship in Rhode Island, Aaron became the first Jew to be naturalized in Massachusetts. Until 1765 Lopez's trade was mostly coastal, between Boston, New York, Philadelphia, and Charleston. He expanded across the Atlantic, importing from Bristol, England, to satisfy the American desire for British products while avoiding London prices. By 1767 Lopez had sent at least nine vessels to the West Indies, shipping livestock, poultry, pickled oysters, candles, naval stores, bricks, lumber, and even silverware; return cargoes brought cocoa, molasses, rum, coffee, and sugar. In 1768 he ran thirty-seven coastal voyages.[54] Lopez's success boomed so that by the time of the American Revolution, he had financial interests in nearly thirty of the one hundred sailing vessels associated with Newport and the transatlantic trade. By the middle of the 1770s, Lopez was the highest taxpayer in Newport and the richest man there.[55] His trading ventures and volume put him on par with the Browns of Providence, benefactors of Brown University.[56]

Even with all of the demands of his business, Lopez maintained his Sabbath observance. He "rigidly observed ... Saturday as holy time," closing from Friday afternoon to Monday morning. Over a three-year period none of his ships left port on a Saturday. He customarily ended his letters, "Sabbath is coming on fast."[57] When he died prematurely in a freak drowning accident, Reverend Ezra Stiles, the president of Yale University, wrote about him:

> In honor and aptitude of commerce there was never a trader in America to equal him. In business he dealt with the highest degree of seriousness and clear-sightedness, showing always an affability in manner, a calm urbanity, an agreeable and sincere courtesy of manners. Without a single enemy, no one is known who was more universally loved.[58]

Lopez's expansive business interests included the cacao bean trade and chocolate manufacturing. As historian Jacob Rader Marcus put it:

> Aaron Lopez ... saw food-processing as ancillary to his involvement in the coastal and West Indian traffic.... The chocolate he secured through outwork was destined for local and North American consumption.[59]

Captains and agents represented Lopez in these endeavors, selling chocolate on his behalf, paying off accounts in cocoa, and buying chocolate from others. Lopez also often sold chocolate at his dry goods shop on Thames Street in Newport. His Jewish and non-Jewish customers bought chocolate there every few months, purchasing periodically in small quantities of about one or two pounds and paying about two pounds sterling.[60] Lopez was also buying larger quantities of chocolate, perhaps for his personal use. After the American Revolution, Samuel Wallis of Boston received from Mr. Ezekiel for the account of Mr. Aaron Lopez "five boxes of Chocolate weighing 110 pounds, 110 pounds, 110 pounds, 102 pounds, and 108 pounds totaling 540 pounds ... forty pounds of Chocolate over to fill the Boxes."[61]

There were some Jewish connections to chocolate for Lopez as well. In Newport the reasonably priced chocolate made its way into *tzedakah* gifts, which Lopez distributed on behalf of the Jewish community. In March 1765 he organized "*sedakah* ... delivered [to] Mrs. Lazarus towards her support 14 pounds of rice, a pound of tea and 2 pounds of chocolate."[62]

Again in 1770 the Aaron Lopez account against the synagogue's treasury itemizes "Sedakah Sunries for Judah Abrahams, 28 pounds of bread, an iron pot, a pound of tea, and two pounds of chocolate."[63]

Also, Lopez may have been the first to connect chocolate with Passover. In April 1772, Lopez paid Joseph Pinto for "6 lb Chocolate for Pesah."[64] Maybe he dunked his matzah in it!

Jewish Estate Inventories: Personal Chocolate Usage

[1708] Jacob Bueno, New York: One hundred bags of cocoa worth as well as chocolate grinding stones.

[1709] Isaac Pinheiro, New York: Thirty pounds of chocolate, a copper chocolate pot, and ten chocolate cups.

[1725] Abraham de Lucena, New York: One copper chocolate pot.

[1750] Moses Louzada, New York: Four "baggs cocoa."

[1750] Mordecai Gomez, New York: One chocolate pot, sixteen chocolate cups, two boxes of chocolate of fifty pounds each, and six "srunes [British measure of approximately 140 pounds] coco."

[1782] Aaron Lopez, Newport: Fifty pounds of chocolate, eight brown china chocolate bowls, eleven turtle-shell chocolate bowls, and four and a half dozen chocolate and cake pans.

[1813] Michael Gratz, Philadelphia: Plate chocolate pot.[a]

The American Revolution caused Lopez significant business losses. In 1779 he described the wartime hardships of the inhabitants of Leicester, Massachusetts, and Newport to a Captain Anthony, noting that they lacked basic food but at least had chocolate:

> The Jews in particular were suffering due to a scarcity of kosher food. They had not tasted any meat, but once in two months. Fish was not to be had, and they were forced to subsist on chocolate and coffee.[65]

Newport and Providence Compete Over Chocolate

Lopez competed in the chocolate manufacturing business with Obadiah Brown of nearby Providence, Rhode Island. Figuring that he could make some extra money by grinding chocolate for his grocery customers, Brown built a water mill in Providence to increase his production and quality, as well as to lower costs. It may have been the first of its kind in Rhode Island or even in America. Brown's mill preceded Dr. Baker's 1764 water mill on the Neponset River by twelve years. When Brown announced this "chocklit" processing to his customers in 1752, he noted his competition in Newport:

> I have been at considerable charge to git a chocklit mill going by water which have now completed. I am advised ... that you have occasion for a considerable quantity of chocklat in your way. I shall be glad to supply you with all you have occasion for at ye cheapest rate you can have it at New Port or any whair else.[66]

Lopez also had difficulty keeping up with the chocolate makers of Boston. He was warned in 1780 by Joseph and William Rotch, his contacts in Boston and Nantucket, that his chocolate was inferior: "Massachusetts folks not buying Rhode Island Chocolate as Boston's is better and cheaper."[67] This may have been because Lopez's chocolate, never branded as uniquely his, had been hand ground for him by slaves and others in Newport, resulting in a less finely processed chocolate than that of machine milled. While the Gomezes and others advertised, neither Lopez nor Brown offered their chocolate in newspapers. Nor did they seem concerned with quality or with branding.

Jews and "Negroes" Grind Chocolate

In Newport, several people ground chocolate for Lopez, some of them Jews and others "Negroes," probably grinding by hand. Lopez paid local Jews such as Joseph Pinto and James Lucena to grind his chocolate. Lopez also hired "Negro chocolate grinders" Prince Updike, Cornelius Casey, and Abraham Casey,[68] paying them four to five shillings per pound of ground chocolate.[69] These Negroes were probably freed slaves or possibly were working to purchase their freedom, as was customary in Newport.[70]

Rhode Island merchants controlled a significant portion of the slave trade, though a very small segment of Lopez's trade was in slaves.[71] Lopez's chocolate grinder, Prince Updike, derived his name from the family for whom he worked, the Updikes of Wickford (also known as North Kingstown), Rhode Island. In 1744 the Updike family may have owned eleven slaves; one of them, Prince, died in January 1781 and was buried in the God's Little Acre section of the Common Burial Ground of Newport.[72]

Chocolate grinders Abraham and Cornelius Casey took the Casey name from a family located in South Kingstown. The Casey chocolate makers were occasionally reprimanded by Lopez for inferior work. Lopez withheld payment to Abraham or Abram for one batch of chocolate in 1768 "as it was only melted over." In 1768 "chocolate grinder" Cornelius Casey was fined by Lopez because he short delivered a couple of times, he absented himself on occasion, and he was one day "being drunk and put in gaol [jail]."[73]

"Negroes" working for Aaron Lopez probably ground chocolate in this manner.

Jewish Chocolate Grinders Working for Aaron Lopez

[December 1770–August 1771] Joseph Pinto paid off his debts for clothes and food by grinding chocolate.

[1770] Pinto's Negro Cezsar ground in twenty-five, fifty, and one hundred pound amounts.[a]

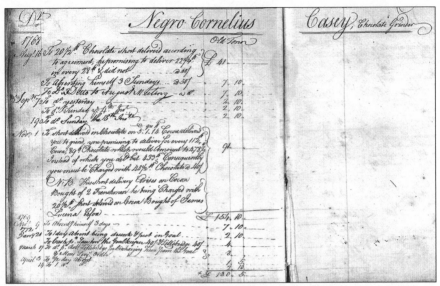

"Negroes" specialized in grinding chocolate for Aaron Lopez and others in colonial Newport, Rhode Island.

The easy access to slaves and cheap labor in the port of Newport meant that the use of hand grinding prevailed there, while in other communities, such as New York and Providence, alternate milling technologies took over. Newport's few mills served primarily for grinding corn. Had Lopez been using more advanced equipment, he would have probably generated larger quantities and higher quality. Increased opportunities for mechanized manufacture of chocolate in this period paralleled the industrialization that occurred after the American Revolution and accompanied the focus on quality of the product. Nonetheless, chocolate grinding, retailing, and shipping made up a part of his business and apparently his own daily pleasure.

Jacob Rader Marcus was quite correct in calling chocolate a "Sephardic Jewish specialty." Jews of North America's colonial period joined Sephardi Jews in other locales along the route of chocolate's dispersion. These eighteenth-century North American Jewish entrepreneurs dipped deeply into the chocolate concerns of their day. They benefited from cacao, enjoying the personal consumption of the beverage and economic profit from it as a commodity. Long before the Baker's Chocolate Company, these merchants and others, including religious leaders, made and relished their chocolate. Overall, these Jews reflected the commercial interests and technological advances in chocolate of the day, contributing to the pioneering cacao and chocolate enterprises of the colonial period in North America.

Peanut Butter Gelt Cookies

This easy recipe incorporates and maintains the shape of the gelt on top of the cookie. Not only is the cookie delicious with the chocolate, it also highlights the gelt.

Ingredients:

1 cup peanut butter (crunchy or smooth; do not use old-fashioned or freshly ground)
1 cup sugar
1 large egg
Approximately 35 chocolate Chanukah gelt (preferably organic, fair trade)

Instructions:

Preheat the oven to 350°F. Lightly grease two baking sheets. Beat the peanut butter, sugar, and egg together. Shape the dough in rounds with flat tops the size of the gelt. Bake for about 12 minutes. Remove the cookies from the oven, cool slightly on the pan, then gently press one piece of gelt into the center of each cookie. Cool the cookies on the baking sheets for 10 minutes before transferring to a wire rack to cool completely.

Quantity: About 35 cookies

Chapter Four

Chanukah and Christmas Chocolate Melt into Gelt

HAVING FOUND SECTIONS OF THE TRAIL OF CHOCOLATE, Jews, and religion in France, Spain, Newport, and New York, we hoped to catch more of it in the chocolate haven of Belgium. We would have been satisfied just to eat chocolate and visit Belgian chocolate museums, yet we suspected that with all of the chocolate there had to be something Jewish and/ or religious. We just had no idea what that might be.

To find one of the four chocolate museums in Belgium, Mark and I drove from Brussels about fifty miles southeast to Liege, Belgium, in early December. As we descended the hilly road into downtown, we stopped at a red light, where several young adults wearing plasticky white jackets covered with handwriting in many colors of marking pen approached the car window, jiggling cups at us. They said a few words in Flemish, shrugged, and walked away. We did not understand a word, but we were in Europe so we were, perhaps mistakenly, not frightened. As we wandered in town later that night, we were approached repeatedly by similar groups, again wearing the white jackets, again shaking the cups. This time we heard coins clinking in the cups. Perplexed by what was happening, we inquired at the tourist office the next day. The clerk

Chocolate molds of St. Nicholas for the celebration of the festival of St. Nicholas.

patiently explained that we had arrived during the feast day of St. Nicholas, December 6, when college students customarily roam the streets begging for gifts to buy beer to observe the holiday.

Throughout Belgium we had noticed, in both the best and the junkiest of chocolate stores, chocolate molded in the shape of the tall, lanky St. Nicholas in his Episcopal robes. That made sense. We knew that St. Nicholas provided the prototype for Santa Claus. To find either one in chocolate did not surprise us. After all, we had seen, and probably eaten, our share of chocolate Santas over the years. Something else clicked for me. I began to wonder about coins in December, students collecting coins for the St. Nicholas feast, and how these might relate to Chanukah coins, especially given that Chanukah and Christmas usually coincide in December. And, most importantly, what about the gold-covered chocolate for Chanukah, also known as gelt, the Yiddish word for money?

Chanukah's Money

As I dug further into the literature about Chanukah's connection to coins, I found many associations. Chanukah recalls the victory of the ancient Maccabees over the Syrian Hellenists and renewed access by the Jews to their ancient Temple in Jerusalem (165 BCE) after its desecration. The gelt of Chanukah recalls the booty, including coins, that the Maccabean victors distributed to the Jewish widows, soldiers, and orphans, possibly at the first celebration of the rededication of the Jerusalem Temple.[1]

In ancient Israel, striking, minting, and distributing coins expressed Chanukah's message of freedom. The Maccabee's descendants, known as the Hasmoneans and who ruled Judea, started to strike coins. As the book of 1 Maccabees records, Syria's King Antiochus VII said to Simon Maccabee, "I turn over to you the right to make your own stamp for coinage for your country" (15:6).

Unfortunately, few Jewish coins were produced between the time the Romans destroyed the Second Jerusalem Temple in 70 CE and the establishment of the modern State of Israel in 1948. Since 1958, Israel has minted commemorative Chanukah medals, reforging this connection of coinage, freedom, and the holiday, most appropriately because Chanukah celebrates political independence and religious freedom.

Money and Chanukah go way back in other ways as well, including the very observance of the holiday. As early as the sixth century, the legal text known as the Talmud taught that the poor must light Chanukah candles even if they had to wander door to door to beg for the money to pay for the lighting materials, which in those days were probably oil, clay lamps, and wicks. Later, in Sephardi (following the customs of Jews descended from Spain) and Oriental (following the customs of Jews from North Africa and the Middle East) Jewish communities, people walked through their neighborhoods burning special grasses to ward off the evil eye in exchange

Ancient Israelite Coins

One of the early Israelite coins, produced during the rule of Antigonus Matityahu (40–37 BCE), the last in this line of Hasmonean kings, portrays a seven-branched menorah (candelabrum) on one side and the shewbread (offering) on the other, each symbol a reminder of the centrality of the ancient Jerusalem Temple to the Jewish people and the victory of the Maccabees over the Hellenists.

for gifts or money at the Chanukah season. Yemenite Jewish children were given coins to purchase sugar and red food dye to make a special Chanukah wine.[2]

With time, additional customs evolved related to giving coins at Chanukah. The Hebrew word *Chanukah*, which refers to the rededication of the Jerusalem Temple after the Syrian Hellenists had desecrated it, came to be associated with the Hebrew word for education, *chinukh*. The gelt or money for Chanukah supported Jewish learning. In the days of the Chasidic leader, the Ba'al Shem Tov (1698–1760), rabbis often traveled to distant villages to give instruction to impoverished and illiterate Jews, generally refusing payment. However, at Chanukah time, the instructors accepted coins and food as tokens of gratitude. Chanukah gelt signified appreciative, though modest, compensation for dedication to Jewish education.[3]

In addition, coins came to be an expected part of the Chanukah festivities in the home. One such custom involved giving gelt on each night of Chanukah, except for Friday evening, the Sabbath, when the use of money is prohibited. The normative legal code, the sixteenth-century *Shulchan Aruch*, stipulated that the light shed by the Chanukah candles may not be used for benefit, not even for counting money. It therefore became customary to play games, some of them using money, while the candles burned (*Shulchan Aruch, Orach Chayim*, chapter

Gelt and Gold

Gelt and gold are also connected linguistically. With the development of the Yiddish language, the Judeo-German dialect of the eleventh century, we first find the word *gelt*, meaning "money." This word is related to the Dutch and German *geld*, which also means "gold." The first recorded appearance of the word *gelt* may have been in 1529, gelt coming to be identified with Chanukah money.

46; *Chanukah* 671:5, 673:1). In dreidel, the popular children's game of Chanukah using a spinning top, the winner is also sometimes paid in coins.

In recent years, some Chasidic rebbes have given gelt to their followers, a much-cherished Chanukah gift for the recipient. Rabbi Chaim Soloveichik, a contemporary Jewish scholar, ruled in 2000 that the biblical requirement of tithing, which is still observed today in some Orthodox settings, applies also to Chanukah gelt. Gifts are counted into the income of the 10 percent that is given away as the tithe. Many older people today remember receiving no gifts at all at Chanukah, only a few coins of gelt, suggesting that gift giving has only recently become customary.

Money Grows on Cacao Trees

With so many ties between coins and Chanukah, it would not be surprising to find chocolate in the mix. After all, there was an early and fundamental joining of money and chocolate, as cocoa beans served as currency for the pre-Columbian peoples. Columbus and his crew soon learned that those mysterious-looking "almonds" they first saw in the bottom of a canoe were used by the indigenous people of the Americas as coinage. For example, in 1513, Hernando de Oviedo y Valdez paid one hundred cocoa beans to purchase a slave. So valued were cocoa beans that counterfeiters were known to fill empty shells with clay or earth.[4] In the New World, cacao was gelt and it grew on trees.

Why Chocolate Coins?

Opinions differ, however, as to how chocolate came to be associated with coins for Chanukah. According to Tina Wasserman, food writer for *Reform Judaism* magazine, eighteenth- and nineteenth-century Jews became prominent in European chocolate making and started the Chanukah chocolate coin custom. Jenna Joselit, in her book *The Wonders of America*, notes that with the increased purchasing capacity in the American Jewish community in the 1920s, two chocolate companies, Loft and Bartons, began producing Chanukah chocolate. Gelt may have roots in a Polish custom that informed Israel's Elite's production of chocolate coins.[5]

Certainly, gold foil chocolate coins unfailingly appear every December in many commercial and residential Chanukah displays. My mother used to put bags of chocolate Chanukah gelt into large plastic dreidels. Some people scatter gold Chanukah gelt on the holiday table. While President George W. Bush's White House chief of staff, Joshua Bolten shared chocolate gelt at senior staff meetings in December. An online search yields comparisons of quality and costs of chocolate Chanukah gelt. A rap song lauds Chanukah gelt.[6]

St. Nick's Coins Save Family

I realized that this St. Nicholas miracle tradition we happened upon in chocolate-suffused Belgium may explain Chanukah gelt. As we continued to savor Belgium, we learned that St. Nicholas, the patron saint of sweets, journeys from distant Spain to reward children with gold-covered chocolate coins! The festival associated with his birthday, December 6, 270 (approximately), has been relished in Western Europe since the thirteenth century. One of the several St. Nicholas *Golden Legend* miracle stories, written in 1275 by Jacobus de Voragine, archbishop of Genoa, records that Nicholas tossed bags of gold coins to an impoverished father in order to provide his daughters with dowries, thus saving them from lives of prostitution. Rituals related to the celebration of the feast day of St. Nicholas in Belgium, the Netherlands, Germany, and the United States use gold-covered chocolate, *geld*. Youngsters collect chocolate coins from their shoes on the morning of December 6, following the previous night's visit by St. Nicholas, or as the Dutch call him, Sinterklaas.[7]

While Chanukah chocolate initially seemed pretty remote from Liege that night in December, St. Nick's *geld* surprisingly

Chocolate coins of St. Nicholas for the holiday of St. Nicholas.

and sweetly flowed right into Chanukah's gelt. Gold-covered chocolate coins for the Christmas season commemorating the miracles of St. Nicholas may very well be the basis for the gold-covered chocolate gelt celebrating the amazing events of Chanukah, or possibly the other way around. These Christian and Jewish golden coin stories, each originating from the Mediterranean area, each of them centuries old, each with inspiring accounts of courage and liberation, also indulge and nurture a love of chocolate. Jewish and Christian customs melt together on this fork of the chocolate trail.

Cognac Truffles

Refugee Lisa Hoffman, whose story is featured in this chapter, fled Germany in 1939 with this recipe. Her chocoholic assessment of it: "These truffles make a wonderful present and are the ultimate in chocolate richness. When making them, always use the finest ingredients."[1]

Ingredients:

2 ounces unsalted butter
3 tablespoons superfine sugar
1 pound bittersweet or dark chocolate, broken into pieces
½ cup heavy cream (fresh, not ultra-pasteurized)
½ cup quality Cognac (or rum or a liqueur)
Cocoa, finely chopped nuts, or powdered sugar, for rolling

Instructions:

Line a baking sheet with waxed paper. In a large heatproof bowl set over a pan of simmering water, heat the butter and sugar until melted and dissolved. Add the chocolate and stir continuously with a wire whisk until it starts to melt. Add the cream and continue to stir with a whisk until the chocolate is completely melted. Add the Cognac. Stir until thoroughly integrated.

Cool in the refrigerator overnight, or set a bowl over an ice bath and continue whisking until cool (this technique creates a lighter truffle and allows you to complete them sooner). Use two teaspoons to form chocolate balls, and roll in cocoa, finely chopped nuts, or powdered sugar. Place the chocolate balls on the prepared baking sheet. Store in a cool place in a covered container.

Quantity: About 30–35 truffles

Chapter Five

Chocolate Revives Refugees, Survivors, and Immigrants

AS I DELVED FURTHER INTO THEMES OF JEWS AND chocolate, I began to hear various stories about the potency of twentieth-century wartime chocolate for refugees, survivors, and immigrants. These accounts spanned from deprivation to comfort, from degradation to rescue, from despicable to artful, from Europe to America. For some, chocolate soothed and fortified refugee and immigrant passages and evoked sweet opportunities, loving reunions, renewal, and hope. For others, chocolate-making skills meant survival. On a business level, chocolate companies launched some chocolate workers into leadership of their wartime Jewish communities and beyond.

Immigrants Pave America's Streets with Candy

Jewish immigrants have a long history of succeeding in the chocolate and candy business in the United States, dating back to the late 1800s. Immigrant Louis Auster developed the chocolate egg cream in his candy store in New York's Lower East Side in 1890. He made the drink using his secret recipe, including a chocolate sauce that he developed, and sold it for three cents a glass, averaging three thousand sales on a summer day. Ultimately he opened four additional locations, until his business closed down in the 1960s. In 1895 Herman and Ida Fox, also New Yorkers, developed Fox's U-bet Chocolate Syrup in Brooklyn, offering a kosher-for-Passover version as well. The Fox family–owned company is still located in Brooklyn.[2]

In New York City in 1896, Leo Hirshfield started a small candy shop, having learned the confectionary business in Austria from his family. His special taffy-esque formula of Chocolate Tootsie Rolls—named for his daughter—avoided the cost of actual chocolate by using cocoa powder instead. This, plus the individual wrappers separating the candies, made them easily portable even in the summer.[3]

David Goldenberg immigrated to Philadelphia from Romania in 1880 at the age of eighteen, the youngest of seven children. He changed his name on the boat, having heard that it would be preferable to be a Goldenberg than a Seltzer. He developed a chocolate ration bar for the army using molasses and peanuts as a substitute for more expensive almonds. This candy bar came to be known as Peanut Chews. His children, Sylvia and Harry, introduced the individually wrapped Peanut Chews for retail sale in 1921, and the brand was sold to Just Born in 2003, yet another immigrant candy story.[4]

When he was twelve years old, Edmond Opler Sr. went to work in the Runkel Brothers Chocolate Company to help support his seven siblings after the death of his father just a year before. He worked his way up to salesman. After World War I, he and his brother Arnold moved to Chicago and opened a bulk cocoa packing company that ultimately became World's Finest Chocolate, Inc.[5]

A number of sweets makers and appetizing stores were located on Franklin Avenue in Brooklyn, including JoMart Chocolates, which was founded on April 15, 1946, by Martin Rogak with his cousin Joe. Their grandfather had made candy in Brownsville, Brooklyn, in the 1920s. Martin explained that he started the company after World War II seeking a business that would focus on life after so much sadness and suffering. Martin's son, wife, and family still run the company.[6]

Koppers Chocolate, now in its third generation of family ownership, was founded in 1937 in New York City by Fred Stern and claims to be the "first U.S. chocolate officially certified Kosher."[7] Morris Cohen opened Economy Candy in New York that same year. One of many typical candy stores of the time, it survives today on the Lower East Side. Carl Mondel arrived in Ohio from Hungary in 1923. He said, "When I first started out, all I knew about candy was how to eat it. I've always loved candy and I always wished to have a candy shop."[8] As his experiments with chocolate improved, he sold to his friends and relatives. In December 1943, he opened his store, Mondel Chocolates, in New York at Broadway and 114th Street, where his specialties were, and still are, handmade.

Refugees Make It by Baking It

Candy making wasn't the only sweet opportunity awaiting immigrants to the United States. In two American cities, refugees from Europe's war were hired in bakeries specially created to give them jobs. The Window Shop Bakery on Brattle Street in Cambridge, Massachusetts, was started by Bostonians to help German refugees during World War II. The Bake Shop in Cincinnati was started by the Jewish community specifically to assist refugees.[9] Holocaust refugee Ernest Weil opened his own bakery, San Francisco's beloved Fantasia, in 1948.

Weil, born in 1924, learned to bake and work chocolate from his mother in Landau, Germany. The proudest aspect of his Bar Mitzvah, he recollected, had nothing to do with the Hebrew, the Torah portion, or his speech. It was instead that he baked all of the pastries himself. When he was only fifteen, he escaped Germany and ended up in a French orphanage. There he won a scholarship to study at Le Cordon Bleu Culinary Arts Institute in Paris. Finally in the United States at the age of sixteen, he worked in a New York bakery. He hoped to have his mother's affidavit papers signed by a senator in Washington, to allow her to enter the United States, but the owner of the bakery would not allow him the day off. Only when the rest of the crew threatened to walk off the job on Ernest's behalf did the boss permit him to go. When Ernest's mother finally arrived in America, the two joined his older brothers in California. There, through one brother who knew someone who knew someone, Ernest landed a job at the elegant Blum's restaurant and café, which was decorated completely in pink. After his release from the U.S. Army, Weil launched his Fantasia bakery using many family recipes, including those of his mother and mother-in-law. When his longtime sweetheart and later wife, Margo, was confirmed, he made her a box of marzipan-filled chocolate, called Mozartkugeln. Fantasia made those, as well as Sacher torte and chocolate truffle roulade, among many other international treats. While Fantasia did not have a formal plan to hire refugees, they did hire several. Their first pastry chef was born in Germany and studied in Switzerland. They also employed an elderly German-Jewish man from Shanghai who had difficulty finding a job and who had been a manager in a department store in Shanghai.[10]

World War II and Chocolate's Dark Side

While sweets and chocolate shops were opening and, in some cases, thriving in the United States, wartime Europe cast some darkness over chocolate. European Jewish businesses, including a number of Jewish chocolate enterprises, were forced to shut down during the Nazi period of World War II. Nestlé's chocolate subsidiary, Maggi, employed thousands of war prisoners and Jewish slave laborers in its factory in Germany near the Swiss border. As recently as 1997, it refused to open its Nazi-era records.[11] Nazis used chocolate bars to lure Jews onto cattle car trains to concentration camps.[12] German saboteurs designed a chocolate-covered, sleek, steel bomb intended to explode seven seconds after breaking off a piece.[13] Other Nazi schemes sought to poison Allied officers through chocolate.[14]

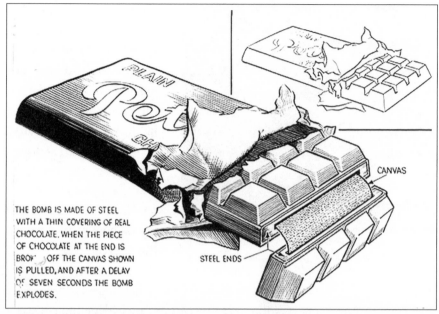

THE BOMB IS MADE OF STEEL WITH A THIN COVERING OF REAL CHOCOLATE. WHEN THE PIECE OF CHOCOLATE AT THE END IS BRO''' OFF THE CANVAS SHOWN IS PULLED, AND AFTER A DELAY OF SEVEN SECONDS THE BOMB EXPLODES.

CANVAS

STEEL ENDS

Booby trap chocolate bar developed by the Nazis during World War II.

Israeli author Haim Gouri's fictionalized chocolate's bitter layer in *The Chocolate Deal*, a depiction of the ruin, revenge, and recovery of post–World War II Europe. The main character, Rudi, a Holocaust survivor, paid his prostitute with chocolate. Rudi hatched a scheme premised on the abundance of surplus military chocolate, conspiring to spread rumors that the chocolate contained tranquilizing ingredients that were intended to pacify military men. Prices would drop, the false reports about the tranquilizer would be denied and corrected, and a fortune would be gained from the increased value. Rudi predicted, "You take what's yours and go far away."[15]

World War II Spurs Chocolate Innovation

While its dark side is very dark indeed, chocolate also played a positive role in World War II, sparking innovation, heroism, and the development of survival skills for citizens, the military, and business. Chocolate companies accommodated to

Camille Bloch developed these bars using hazelnuts
to save the cost of chocolate during World War II.

restricted food supplies and the severe rationing of the period by modifying their products. For example, to make up for the shortage of cocoa in Italy in the 1940s, Pietro Ferrero developed Nutella spread, using the abundant local Piedmont hazelnuts. Similarly, the Swiss company Camille Bloch created its popular Ragusa line, replacing unattainable chocolate with hazelnuts. Cadbury Dairy Milk, which depended heavily on fresh milk, could not be produced during the war, so the company substituted powdered milk in what came to be called Ration Chocolate. Home recipes were modified to accommodate chocolate shortages as well.[16] To satisfy government orders for chocolate in wartime, companies helped each other out. For instance, Nestlé would produce a bar for Cadbury, or Cadbury would make a Nestlé product.[17]

While many chocolate companies and civilians were chocolate deprived during World War II, the U. S. military put chocolate to good use in rations. Hershey developed its Ration D Bar to very clear specifications at the government's request. These bars needed to be nutritious, portable, and temperature resistant, yet not so appealing that soldiers would devour them as snacks.[18] The final ingredients included chocolate mass, sugar, skim milk powder, cocoa butter, oat flour, and vanillin. Sugar was decreased and chocolate mass increased to give the bar a less pleasing taste than normal chocolate bars. The formula created a heavy paste that had to be pressed rather than poured into molds. A four-ounce bar contained six hundred calories. The original formula and shape of the ration bar were altered slightly when thiamine hydrochloride was added as a source of vitamin B^1 to prevent beriberi, a disease likely to be encountered in the tropics.

While the calories and nutrition from chocolate helped sustain members of the military, the skills of chocolate making and homemaking helped sustain Jewish civilians under the deprivation of Nazi rule. In the late 1930s in Frankfurt, Germany, at the age of fifteen, Lisa Hoffman and two other classmates were told they could not return to school because they were Jews. Lisa had already been forced to greet the teacher with the Nazi salute and had been required to sing Nazi songs, which spoke of murdering Jews. When the Nazis closed her father's department store, her mother, Elsa, took boarders into their large apartment. Hoping to send Lisa to England as a domestic, Elsa trained Lisa along with other young Jewish women, some of whom were her lodgers, in homemaking skills. Unemployed Jews who had worked as waiters, cooks, and bakers also gave lessons.

The person who was to serve as chocolate instructor was arrested by the Nazis just days before he was scheduled to teach his specialty. Since Lisa had only weeks before begun an apprenticeship with a famous chocolate maker, she coached the group instead, staying one week ahead of the group's lessons. Lisa, a self-diagnosed chocoholic, taught them about chocolate fillings and how to use special dipping forks to form perfectly shaped and delicious truffles, including the truffle recipe included in this chapter.

Finally with a visa in hand, she departed Germany for England on August 18, 1939. Only two weeks later, war was declared between Germany and England. Looking back on that time when she was without family and classified as a foreign alien, she wrote:

> I carried inside of me all of the lessons my mother had worked so hard to get for me. I could make chocolate, cook

for large families and carry soup without spilling. But more importantly what she'd given me was a belief in myself. It's stood me well through the years, this gift from my mother Elsa Hoffman.[19]

An Even Sweeter Freedom

Chocolate's role in the war extended to the liberation of the concentration camps, serving as a symbol of the caring world beyond the walls of the camps as well as nourishment for friendships forged by chocolate.

Soldier Harry J. Herder Jr. connected with a very young survivor through chocolate at the liberation of Buchenwald concentration camp. Herder pulled a chocolate bar out of his pocket, but the child had no recognition of what it was. While the child practiced the pronunciation "candy" and "chocolate," Herder removed the chocolate wrapper. As he watched the youngster's puzzlement, Herder realized that he had probably never tasted chocolate! Herder showed him how to break off a piece, put it in his mouth, and chew it. He slowly ate the entire bar "with wonderment" in his eyes. They drank hot cocoa from Herder's K rations. At the end of his tour, Herder emptied his pockets of all of his candy bars for his new friend.[20]

Mike Jacobs tasted his first Hershey bar at the liberation of Mauthausen. Born in Konin, Poland, and named Mendel Jakubowicz, he was nineteen and a half years old and weighed seventy pounds in 1945. Having been sent to Mauthausen when Auschwitz was evacuated, he saw tanks approaching the camp and wondered why the Germans had switched the customary swastika to a star. Hours later, more star-studded tanks arrived, and a soldier tossed him a little package. "I grabbed it and run [sic] into the barracks and say, 'Hey, guys, look—I got a bar of chocolate. And can you imagine! The name of the chocolate is Hershel!' [Hershel is a common Yiddish name.] I didn't read the wrapper properly, so the first American food I eat is a Hershel bar."[21]

Chocolate Pilot Wiggles His Wings

Children in the ruins of postwar West Berlin were deprived of chocolate and candy. The Berlin Airlift sent in 1,535 tons of food, only enough necessary to maintain the city at minimal nutrition during the Soviet Union's blockade.[22] In 1948, after his first airlift flight into Berlin through Templehof airfield, U.S. Air Force pilot Gail S. Halvorsen, a Mormon, glimpsed a group of children gathered at the fence watching the flights of the airlift. He was impressed that they did not beg. Unsure how to distribute the two sticks of gum he had, he divided it for the four children who had translated for him and then decided to share the wrapper with the others, as he had nothing else to give them. They happily pocketed the scraps. On the spot he promised them that he would drop goodies for them the next time he flew into the field. As they questioned how they would know which plane was his, he promised to wiggle the wings of the plane, thus becoming known as Uncle Wiggly Wings, the Chocolate Uncle, or the Chocolate Pilot. He quickly enlisted his teammates to donate their rations of chocolate and gum, as well as their handkerchiefs to serve as mini-parachutes to ferry the chocolate to the waiting hands on the ground. Many successful drops followed in what came to be known as Operation Little Vittles, and the children began to write heartwarming and funny letters to Uncle Wiggly Wings.

One youngster, Peter Zimmerman, hoped that the pilot would aim the chocolate right into his backyard. He wrote, "Fly along the big canal ... at the second bridge turn right. I live in the bombed out house on the corner. I'll be in the backyard every day at 2:00 PM. Drop it there." When his packages did not arrive, he wrote back, "You are a pilot? I gave you a map. How did you guys win the war anyway?"[23]

The Chocolate Pilot received a letter from Elly Muss on October 15, 1948: "For days and days, four small brothers without a father have run to the airport in vain to get their hardworking mother a piece of chocolate. Is there another way to fulfill this request for five hungry souls?" And it was fulfilled when Halvorsen sent them a package of treats by mail.

Another child marveled:

> Suddenly out of the mist came a parachute with a fresh Hershey chocolate bar from America. It took me about a week to eat that candy bar. I hid it day and night. The chocolate was wonderful, but it wasn't the chocolate that was important. What it meant was that someone in America cared.... It represented hope.[24]

Based on her Berlin Airlift experiences, Mercedes Simon became the focus of a recent children's book about this chocolate operation. Mercedes was only seven and could not go to the airfield unless accompanied by her mother. When she finally did get there, a bigger boy grabbed the closest chocolate bar before she could. Instead of trying again at the airfield, with her mother's help she too wrote a letter to the Chocolate Pilot. In return, Halvorsen mailed her a package of candy and chocolate with a personalized note signed, *Dein Shokoladenonkel*, "Your Chocolate Uncle." Years later, Halvorsen and Mercedes met at her home, where she still kept the handwritten letter, which she had savored over the years as much as—or possibly more than—the chocolate.

When Halvorsen was sent to New York in 1948 on a tour that celebrated "Operation Little Vittles," which was headquartered at Westover Air Force Base in Chicopee, Massachusetts, he met with "John Swersey, a Jew," of the National Confectioners Association, which had sent thirty-five hundred pounds of chocolate and gum for the operation. These chocolate missions alleviated the bitterness of these war-torn children's lives.[25]

Chocolate Fuels the Fight after the War

While chocolate sweetened the lives of children affected during the war, it played a vital role in healing for Jews long after the war was over. The Swiss chocolate company Camille Bloch is soaked in the Swiss Jewish and Holocaust story, and today it is also one of the very few third-generation Jewish-owned chocolate companies. As explained to us in an interview with company CEO Daniel Bloch, the company's founder, Camille, Daniel's grandfather, was initiated into the chocolate business at a very young age. As a teen, he apprenticed at Tobler, another famous Swiss chocolate maker and creator of the patented Toblerone bar. He eventually went into sales for the company. At the same time, he began experimenting with his own private-label chocolates at home in Bern, Switzerland. When Lindt was bought out by Sprüngli, Camille bought their chocolate-making equipment. In 1929 he started his business, principally serving the Bern area, and business went well.

Needing more space, Camille moved the factory from Bern about twenty-six miles northwest to the farmlands of Courtelary, taking over a former paper factory in a depressed area of significant unemployment in 1935. During World War II, Camille's son Rolf was expelled from the Scouts, and his friends stopped speaking with him because he was Jewish. However, the factory continued to function, and Rolf focused all of his energies there, rising to become a leader of both the business and the Jewish community.

Rolf later became president of the Swiss Federation of Jewish Communities, an eighteen-thousand-member Jewish organization, from 1992 to 2000.[26] During his tenure, information leaked out about Swiss deceit and theft during World War II. While Switzerland had claimed neutrality, it actually profited in several ways from collaboration with the Nazis during the war through sales of Swiss products to Nazi Germany, purchase of Nazi gold, stockpiling of art stolen from Jews, investments of approximately $3 billion in Nazi Germany, and secret Nazi holdings in Swiss banks. Worse, Switzerland closed borders to thousands of Jews seeking refuge beginning in August 1942. After the war, accusations surfaced of Swiss profiteers who committed fraud through the disappearance of accounts belonging to families of Holocaust victims and the refusal to pay insurance policies to beneficiaries of deceased Jews. Counterclaims from some Swiss bankers that the Jewish community was blackmailing and seeking ransom money from them generated a backlash of anti-Semitism, including hate mail, graffiti attacks, and verbal harassment.[27] Subsequent investigations of the dormant Swiss accounts in the names of Holocaust victims raised doubts about the integrity of Swiss banks, insurance companies, and government policies as they repeatedly claimed no responsibility.

When Rolf Bloch noticed a change in the mood of Switzerland on these issues with the collapse of communism and the publication of a new study of Swiss attitudes toward Jews during the war, he encouraged Edgar Bronfman Sr., then president of the World Jewish Congress, to fly to Switzerland in 1995 to pressure the Swiss government to investigate. Kaspar Villiger, then Swiss president, called upon the country to apologize to its Jewish victims, pleading, "We can only bow our heads in silence before those whom we led into suffering and captivity, even death."[28]

Jewish leaders prior to Rolf Bloch had been reluctant to push and had made no progress. Rolf Bloch's very Swiss manner—reserved, very formal, always in suit and tie, nicknamed the "Ball" by his staff because of his build—was able to move things forward.[29]

> He is the perfect incarnation of a Swiss Jew, committed to Judaism in private and blending in publicly. When the Holocaust assets debate broke out, Swiss Jews could not maintain this peaceful dual identity. The fact that they were Jewish had become a public matter. Many felt anti-Semitism for the first time or felt uneasy in the boards, country clubs, and other societies they were part of. Bloch managed to walk on that tightrope quite brilliantly. He looked and sounded Swiss and did Swiss "things" (chocolate, which

was better than banking in those days). He was Jewish, but not a "visible" Jew.[30]

"Justice for the victims and fairness for Switzerland," a phrase Rolf Bloch coined before a hearing of the United States Congress Banking Committee in December 1996, captured this simultaneous resolution and discretion.[31] Later Bloch chaired the Special Fund for Holocaust Victims established by the Swiss government and funded by Swiss companies. Bloch's leadership furthered post-Holocaust healing.

Bartons Founder Flees Vienna

While Camille Bloch was upholding Jewish ideals and seeking justice for Jews in Europe, Bartons Bonbonniere was doing similar work in the United States by creating refuge for those seeking to flee the ravages of the war. Stephen Klein fled Vienna the day after the 1938 Nazi march into Austria known as the Anschluss. His soon to be vastly successful American company, Bartons Bonbonniere, in turn assisted other World War II refugees seeking to immigrate to America.

In Vienna, Klein had owned one of the city's largest commercial suppliers of chocolate. A Nazi competitor marched into Klein's offices and seized ownership of Klein's company the day after the Anschluss. To escape likely arrest, Klein hurriedly left his two children and pregnant wife behind, spending five months in Belgium before arriving in the United States. A few months later he brought the family to New York via Belgium, later to be joined by his five brothers and two sisters. From the small New York apartment that he shared with about ten family members, he prepared chocolates, which relatives then sold from pushcarts, catering to the varied tastes of the ethnic neighborhoods. Commenting on his product, Klein claimed that he knew which chocolates to blend and how to control taste. As he put it, "All the pieces should look good—no *chazerei* [junk]...."[32] Bartons sought to produce excellent bonbons, using the best Swiss and Belgian chocolate. The Viennese style in the product as well as in the décor mixed with the Orthodox values Klein held dear.

As his enterprise grew, so did his aid to numerous Jewish immigrants, refugees, and Holocaust survivors. For instance, Klein supported Jack Gold and Henry Kaye, survivors from Poland, in opening their own shop to make boxes for chocolate on West 18th Street in Manhattan. Gold and Kaye started working in chocolate on their own in 1949 at Madelaine Chocolate Novelties. Madelaine is still family run and thriving thanks to the boost they received from Bartons. The Gold and Kaye families, also adherents of Orthodox Judaism, affiliated with local synagogues, making seasonal mold confections with the Orthodox Union, or OU dairy *hechsher* (certification of kashrut, Jewish dietary requirements).

Never forgetting his European community of origin, despite his success in America, Klein helped to further the work of the American Orthodox relief agency Vaad Hatzala, a body originally established to rescue rabbis and yeshivah students and eventually expanded to assist all Jews during World War II. Initially the Vaad sent packages of religious articles, food, clothing, household goods, and Bartons chocolate via a loophole through Tangier to Nazi-occupied countries. After the war this Jewish charity continued its support of the religious rehabilitation of Jewry through educational and religious endeavors.[33] Klein also volunteered to do a six-month stint in 1946 in Europe with the United Nations Rescue and Relief Agency (UNRRA). Klein's Bartons headquarters housed an office of immigration for assisting with the technical details of bringing over displaced Jews. His company hired many of those approximately fifteen hundred individuals he had assisted. While the payroll included Orthodox Jews, it was a very pluralistic, multi-ethnic work line. No strikes disrupted the flow of chocolate, and there were no complaints about closing on Saturdays. Perhaps this was because employees were allowed to eat as much chocolate as they wanted.

Klein's commitment to Orthodox Judaism began very early in life and was apparent at every turn thereafter. In 1923 his father, Reb Simcha Klein, had taken Stephen to meet the illustrious rabbi and ethicist known as the Chofetz Chaim. The esteemed rabbi pronounced this blessing on Stephen: "May you be successful and in all of your endeavors, sanctify the Name of *Hashem* [God]." Klein seemed to embody these words in his workplace, in fulfillment of the Jewish law to rescue the captive and also in his inclusion of Jewishness in the workplace. As he once explained, "I am a devoted and conscientious member of the Orthodox Jewish community."[34] At least six hundred organizations, several of them Orthodox, benefited from Klein's generosity, including Young Israel and Yeshiva University.

While he had a broad customer base, Klein saw the Orthodox population as a niche market and proudly declared, "The competitors are just sitting around kicking themselves for having overlooked it." In order to cater to this traditionally observant clientele, he had to follow particular business practices that cohered with Jewish law. For example, he had the chutzpah (courage) to close his offices and all stores on Shabbat and Jewish holidays. This meant that in the fall Jewish holiday cycle, the operation might have been shut down for ten working days. With time, Bartons even publicized Shabbat and holiday closings in newspaper advertisements. Some think that doing so strengthened the Jewish identity of others to prioritize Shabbat observance over the workplace. A Brooklyn Catholic priest was reportedly so taken with this piety that he urged his flock to be as observant of Sunday's Sabbath as Bartons was of Shabbat. Still, calculations of the financial benefit or loss due to Bartons' Orthodox practices were never made and perhaps could not really be calculated.

Klein used his business to further educate Jews in their faith, albeit in a very sweet way. Bartons produced Jewish-themed chocolate, including Hebrew letter *aleph-bet* shapes. Other special Jewish products included chocolate matzah;

matzah balls, which were chocolate covered coconut or marzipan; chocolate-covered hamantaschen; and chocolate-shaped
latkes, which were chocolate disks with candy fillings. Advertising emphasized education, with materials such as games and
stories about the various Jewish holidays included in the boxes.
Approximately one million of these informational resources
a year were published, half of them for the boxes of candy.
Jewish subject matter often filled the full-page ads in major
newspapers.[35]

The commitment to Orthodoxy also meant a dedication to
kashrut. Bartons' supervisor for implementing kosher requirements was Rabbi Nachum Kornmehl, the brother-in-law of
Stephen Klein. Rabbi Kornmehl traveled once a year from
Albany to check ingredients, to review suppliers, and to
oversee the two-week closing for thorough cleaning prior to
Passover. Until a vegetable gelatin could be developed for use in
marshmallows and Klein had approval from his rabbi, Bartons
did not use marshmallow. Even the seasonal Santa Clauses and
Easter eggs were kosher.[36] In fact, while business increased at
Passover, Christmas sales exceeded all. Though it is difficult to

Complex Kosher for Passover Chocolate

Kosher for Passover chocolate certifications promote the Ashkenazi
prohibition against eating beans (kitniyot) or leavened breads during
the festival. This also precludes the use of soy lecithin as an emulsifier, which is often added to make the chocolate smooth. In some
situations this certification unnecessarily divides Ashkenazim and Sephardim whose Passover approaches diverge. Sephardi custom permits kitniyot and would not prohibit the lecithin. In Israel, a culture war
sometimes boils at Passover between Sephardim and Ashkenazim,
each group adhering to a separate Passover certification system.[a]

I prefer to buy chocolate that does not use soy lecithin, though it
may not bear a formal certification. It is better quality chocolate, generally. What a shame that chocolate furthers that Passover dissension.

know exactly how much of the Bartons' client base was actually Jewish, estimates suggest that more than fifty percent of sales were to non-Jews.[37]

Bartons played a significant role in the kosher food industry. Not only did it initiate kosher-for-Passover lines and mass-marketed kosher chocolates, cakes, and ice cream, Bartons also actively engaged in discussions about OU (Orthodox Union) kosher certification, initially rejecting it as arbitrary and overly demanding. When the competing chocolate company, Barricini, attempted to acquire a *hechsher* from the Orthodox Union, Bartons tried to stop it. Bartons resorted to advertisements, claiming, "If it isn't a box of Bartons, is it right for a Jewish home?" In the end the OU certified Jewish-owned Barricini, even though its franchises were open on Shabbat, which was generally not permissible. To do so, the OU had determined that ownership was really held by a corporation. Ultimately, Bartons also used the OU certification.[38]

The family sold this immigrant start-up company in 1978, and since then Bartons has been owned by three companies. This proudly Jewish company contributed to the growth of the kosher food industry and aided many refugees.

Mark and I kept this chocolate survivor in mind as we passed a shabby Bartons storefront sign in our neighborhood on Second Avenue between Sixty-Third and Sixty-Fourth Streets. One wintry day we noticed the demolition of what we thought might have been one of the last, if not the last, extant Bartons sign. As the sign was hauled away to the junk heap, it felt as though an era of refugee and immigrant chocolate that had aided so many people battling loneliness, dislocation, and trauma had ended. However, remembrances of the liberating essences of World War II–era chocolate endure.

Israeli Chocolate Spread

Chocolate spread permeates Israeli meals and experiences as it is served on bread at teatime, eaten for breakfast, toted in a lunch bag, and packed in army supply bags. The original version from the *Tzena*, the period of food scarcity in Israel between 1949 and 1959, would have used margarine.

Ingredients:

1 cup unsalted butter
1 cup sugar
3 large eggs
1 teaspoon vanilla extract
5–6 heaping tablespoons unsweetened cocoa powder

Instructions:

Cut the butter into small pieces and put in a blender. Add the sugar, eggs, and vanilla, and blend well. Add the cocoa powder and blend well again. Put in a container and refrigerate. Serve on bread or toast, with fruit, or in a sandwich.

Quantity: About 1½ cups

Chapter Six

Israelis

Meshuga for Chocolate

THE RAIN FLOODING THE STEEP STREETS OF NAZARETH
could not deter us from reaching the pinnacle of Elite's factory
site to continue the chocolate *shvil* (trail) in Israel. We walked
into a fantasy come true, an office bedecked with volumes of
Talmud and piled high with boxes of chocolate. Haphazardly
teetering Elite bittersweet bars, packets of popular Israeli
candies Pesek Zman and Mekupelet, jars of chocolate chips,
an alcohol-preserved cocoa bean—just the right assemblage
for Haim Palgui, whose business card reads, "Chocolate
Chief." I jealously noted the title before catching the next line,
"Technologist." So it was that we met the affable Palgui, the
Elite Chocolate Factory's secular-minded, mezuzah-kissing,
Talmud-studying, shul-going chocolate expert, only one of our
several fun chocolate visits, west, east, north, south (Genesis
28:14). Chocolate establishments dot Israel's countryside as
abundantly as *sabra* (cactus) plants. Tourists soon discover
the impossibility of seeing all the sites, and the same applies to
chocolate shops. However, layering fun chocolate experiences
onto the serious menu of holy sites makes for a tasty mix.

Make It Milk Chocolate

As Janna Gur, chief editor of Israel's *Al Hashulchan* [On the
Table]—*The Israeli Gastronomic Monthly*, explained to me in

a phone conversation, Israelis love chocolate, with a distinct preference for milk chocolate. At Nona Chocolate located across the street from the King David Hotel in Jerusalem, the attendant noted that Israelis tend toward a sweeter Belgian or Swiss style. While Nona proudly uses only French Valrhona, most Israeli chocolate experts were trained in Belgium. At one time Elite licensed with Swiss companies Maestrani and Camille Bloch, which may explain that Israeli proclivity. Only one small Israeli chocolate company, Holy Cacao, currently roasts beans for single-origin bars. Gur also told me that for Israelis, local chocolate rates over imported chocolate, and chocolate remains the most popular restaurant dessert offering. Between 2003 and 2008, as the Israeli economy improved, chocolate eating in Israel increased 100 percent. Climate differences may explain why Israeli consumption (about seven pounds per person per year) remains significantly less than that of the Swiss (about twenty pounds per person per year). The desert temperatures in Israel's summer make transporting chocolate difficult and may make it less appetizing, while Switzerland's more moderate climate would keep chocolate appealing all year long. Nevertheless, chocolate is a hot commodity in Israel, as may be seen from the theft of one hundred tons of chocolate from a factory in Haifa in 2008.[1]

Israel is a child-centered culture, so it is not surprising that the marketing of chocolate in Israel focuses on children. This is certainly evident in the playful kiddie menu at branches of Max Brenner, the Israeli chocolate shop chain, and the children's chocolate workshops at establishments such as Ornat, Galita, and De Karina. Strauss-Elite launched a milk chocolate confection named Etzbaot (fingers), aimed at children to compete with the Italian company Ferrero's Kinder (German for "children") line of chocolate. To entice Israeli children, Elite added popping candy, cookies, and Israeli-style "M&M's" (called *adashim*, or lentils).

As Israelis know full well, regarding taste and smell there is no arguing. In my experience, Israeli hot chocolate tends to be tepid, both in temperature and in flavor. With the exception perhaps of Nona's marzipan-laden hot chocolate, the local beverage falls short of an intense, thick, flavorful French or Spanish hot chocolate, though it is more frequently (happily for me) accompanied by whipped cream. Unusual local chocolate treats in Israel include honey and chocolate liquor (De Karina) and honey mixed with chocolate nibs (Roy), wonderful add-ons that could sweeten the first year of any newlyweds' marriage, following the custom of honey dripped onto the Shabbat challah bread.

Spread It, Bake It, Drink It

Israelis also adore chocolate-flavored spread. Around the time that Nutella unveiled its first modest version in 1946, Israelis developed a local formula, minus the hazelnuts.[2] Palgui at Elite explained its popularity to us: "It spreads easily on bread, it does not spoil, it is cheap and sweet." In the austerity period of the 1950s called the *Tzena*, his mother, *z"l* (of blessed memory), whipped up the spread using margarine, powdered sugar, and cocoa powder. One former Israeli army reservist recalled that chocolate spread was often served at meals in the army, its pareve nature making it an easy addition that caused no conflict with Jewish dietary laws. Also, night patrols fortified themselves with sweet tea, bread, and chocolate spread, both going out and returning, as my kibbutznik brother-in-law Jay recalls. In a sweet irony, our local Upper East Side, Egyptian-owned bodega sells the Hashachar brand of Israeli chocolate spread. Why? Isaac El Neggar says, "Just to have. Some people crave it because it relates to their childhood." He prefers the taste of Nutella.

Birthday parties in Israel often feature the evocative cocoa-based cake nicknamed *ugah kushit* (black cake). This un-PC name actually comes from the word *kushi*, referring to a black person, based on the biblical text mentioning Moses's wife's land of origin in the Kingdom of Cush in Africa, "And Miriam and Aaron spoke against Moses because of the Cushite woman whom he had married; for he had married a Cushite woman"

(Numbers 12:1). Some call it *ugat yomledet*, "birthday cake." Israeli-born Yigal Ben Aderet remembers his Turkish-born mother baking this "big deal," spongy, moist, chocolaty cake, sometimes frosted, sometimes with whipped cream, and not just for birthdays. This "incredible" treat was eaten with milk and/ or dunked in milk. Yigal Rechtman recalls that the class mothers responsible for the treats for special occasions who were expert bakers on his kibbutz occasionally made the very dark, unfrosted, somewhat coarse, round cake with a hole in the middle for very special occasions. Cheesecakes and white cakes were common enough, but this *ugah* was unusual, likely requiring a trip to Jerusalem to acquire the right ingredients. The last time he tasted it may have been when he became Bar Mitzvah in 1979. Winners of the Purim lottery might have won such a cake, as he recalls.

Black cake is not the only chocolate infused form of celebration. Another kibbutznik, now living in Cincinnati, suspects that her family birthday custom of creating a themed chocolate table for the early morning of the special day started at her kibbutz. For her daughter, it might be a seashore with chocolate seashells; for her husband's birthday, truffles with some erotic innuendos.

Surprisingly, we frequently saw private-label chocolate liqueurs in Israeli chocolate shops, especially given the stereotypes about Jews not drinking alcohol. While we enjoyed such liqueur in Italy and Belgium, it is not easily found in other countries; even in New York City our search yielded only a mediocre American brand. This Israeli affection for chocolate liqueur may have been inspired by Sabra, which was developed by Edgar Bronfman Sr. in 1963. Intended to be a unique Israeli product, the Sabra bottle resembled an ancient Phoenician flask. When the *sabra*-flavored recipe failed, chocolate combined with orange replaced it. For many years Sabra was readily available at duty-free shops and other stores. However, ask Israelis today about Sabra and many of them have no clue. While Sabra's popularity has waned, something in the Israeli psyche still demands chocolate liqueurs.

A Jerusalem chocolate shop shelf swells with chocolate liqueurs.

Chocolate Levels the Army

One fondly remembered line of chocolate made by Elite, Hayal-Hayelet, a fifty-gram milk chocolate bar, was sold to Israeli soldiers at subsidized prices at canteens. Since the great majority of the Israeli population served in the military, they would have experienced Elite this way, if not earlier in their lives. Chocolate eating in the Israeli army provided immigrants from Morocco, Yemen, and Ethiopia another means of engaging Israeli society. The antiwar song "Chocolate Soldier" (*Chayal Shel Shokolad*) sung by the High Windows, an Israeli group of the late 1960s, was rejected for radio play then but may be heard today. It speaks to the challenges of fighting and turning into a chocolate soldier, one who may melt in the heat of danger, dying in the battle due to lack of courage.[3]

Exploring Elite Firsthand

While Elite attempted to capitalize on the culture of the military, its Para brand captivated the general Israeli population. Israel's boutique chocolate purveyors of today compete with this long familiar taste.[4] Elite's pioneering Para (cow) brand, originally known as Shamnonit (fat), is wrapped in distinctive red paper imprinted with a cow. Israelis fondly identify it simply as Para or Para Adumah (red cow), or Shokolada Para (chocolate

cow). To find out more about Elite and its Para, I tracked down
a phone number for the Strauss Group (which merged with Elite
in 1996), expecting an ordeal to connect with the right person in
the chocolate department and hoping to confirm an appointment
during my limited time in the country. The receptionist responded
with typically hospitable Israeli informality and immediately
offered to gift me a book from her home about the history
of Elite. The next morning Mark and I drove to the company
headquarters in Petach Tikvah to find Tzila Gilbert at her desk
with the large commemorative picture book about the sixtieth
anniversary of Elite tucked carefully into a white envelope. Not
only that, but Gilbert then encouraged us to enjoy a drink at
the Elite café at the other end of the hall. As I downed my hot
chocolate with Mekupelet (bars of thinly folded milk chocolate
produced in Israel since 1935, originally by Elite, similar to the
Flake Bar of Cadbury, developed in 1920), Gilbert contacted the
director of the Chocolate Division for an appointment. Within
just moments we were chatting with a very pregnant Hila Elad,
director of the Chocolate Division of the Strauss Group, and her
assistant, Lior Offer. They, in turn, referred us to Haim Palgui
in Nazareth. We managed to squeeze a meeting in between his
international travel and our remaining days in Israel.

As we sat in his office perched over the chocolate plant,
Palgui explained, "The Israeli customer likes more [sic] the
Elite product. They are used to it and it is more *amami* [for the
people]." He elaborated that foreign chocolates, such as Valrhona or Godiva, are of a "different class and more expensive."
Since its introduction in 1934, Para has cornered 80 percent
of the market. Hila grew up on Para, having often lunched on
a fifty-gram slab of Para chocolate on a roll. Twenty to thirty
years ago all they had was Para, she recalled nostalgically.
When David Ben-Gurion was prime minister, his wife, Paula,
entertained guests with Elite chocolate.[5]

Palgui started working for Elite in 1987. He and his team
develop new products using engineering, chemistry, biochemistry,

thermodynamics, micro-
biology, and food science.
They sometimes eat the
chocolate straight from
the machines, generally
preferring bittersweet, the
higher the chocolate con-
tent the better, around 70
percent. Over the years,
the basic Elite milk and
dark chocolates have not

The Para brand of Elite decorates chocolate coins, gelt.

changed much. However, Israelis are increasingly interested
in the dark version because it is thought to be healthier. Also,
the growing religious market prefers pareve. Oriented to their
customers, Elite constantly runs tests and focus groups. When
Elite first developed a 70 percent chocolate over a decade ago,
they tested it using Lindt as a benchmark; Palgui boasted that
Elite rated higher in the blind tests. The seasonal nature of
chocolate in Israel recognizes the very hot summer as a low
season and launches new products in the fall. Elite imports
quality chocolate from the Swiss company Callebaut and the
Belgian company Cargill.

Sacred Sweets

Holy Cacao owners and chocolate makers Jo Zander and
Zev Stender work from a religious perspective out of a small
workshop in the Hebron Hills. They are possibly the only Israeli
company that works bean to bar, meaning that they start making the chocolate with the bean rather than importing chocolate.
Their website boasts the appropriate Hebrew blessing recited
before eating chocolate and transliterates the company name
into traditional Torah-style Hebrew letters. As Zander put it:

> As religious Jews we live a life in a constant state of refine-
> ment that every day should be better than the day before;
> and for us, chocolate making is an excellent parallel to this

concept ... the next batch and all the steps in between will be even better.[6]

Diaspora Influences Both Bar and Business

Holy Cacao's founder, Zander, grew up in New Jersey. Mainstay Elite and Para flavors started in the Diaspora as well, in Riga, Latvia. Janna Gur, who grew up in Latvia, notes the similarity of Elite's bonbonnieres (chocolate boxes) and their contents to the Laima Chocolate she remembers from her childhood. Russian candy maker Eliyahu Fromenchenko (also spelled Fromchenko) fled to Latvia and founded Laima Chocolate in Riga in 1922.[7] With the Nazi rise to power, he sold Laima in 1933 and immigrated to Palestine, having explored chocolate opportunities in Palestine the year before with his partner, Yaakov Arens. They had met with Lieber (which Elite bought in 1970), which was at that time one of the very few sweets and chocolate companies in the pre-state Yishuv settlement. With several partners, Fromenchenko bought property in Ramat Gan and opened Elite. Production began in 1934, with distribution reaching stores in time for Passover. Fromenchenko hawked new products—such as waffle cookies covered with chocolate and sesame encased in chocolate—on the streets. As it grew, Elite located plants in then outlying areas such as Ramat Gan, Sefat, and Nazareth in order to develop Israel's economy. Poet and songwriter Jonathan Geffen captured this pioneer Israeli chocolate scene in his lyrics, "At the edge of Ramat Gan, there's a special place where you can stand and smell chocolate in the air."[8]

In those early years, Elite shipped products to Iraq and to Beirut by train. Based on Polish custom, Elite made chocolate coins in 1958 for export to the United States. In the tradition of the utopian Quaker chocolate companies of England (see chapter 9), Elite built a *beit havraah* in 1941 (a vacation retreat center) for employee use on vacation. In 1945 the company built apartments to sell to workers at special prices. It also provided a medical clinic and an orphanage in K'far Saba, in the Central District of Israel.[9]

The official Elite website and other publications vary the founding narrative from the one I learned from "Gingy" (redhead), Rabbi David Wilfond, former rabbi of the liberal synagogue in Riga. He recalled a woman known as the "Chocolate Princess," a descendant of the Laima Chocolate Factory creators. She was also an original member and leader in the Reform Synagogue of Riga. In this version, Laima was co-owned, years ago, by her family, two Jewish brothers with the family name Moiseyvich (or Moshvitz), meaning "son of Moses." They argued and their partnership dissolved. One brother made aliyah to Israel and, using the Laima chocolate recipe, started Elite. Meanwhile, with the socialization and nationalization of the company under Soviet rule, the Laima company in Riga was confiscated from the remaining Moiseyvich brother, and the chocolate recipes were altered by the new regime. After the collapse of the Soviet Union, older folks in Riga, remembering the original taste of their beloved Laima chocolate, discovered that Elite had replicated it. Thus, Gingy says, a lot of Israel's Elite chocolate is now imported to Riga. Chocolate Princess Vera Moiseyvich reported to me that she also sees Elite in her local Riga markets.

While Elite had its roots in Riga, it prospered in Israel. Max Brenner, which since 2001 has been owned by Strauss-Elite and uses its own chocolate formulas, had its start in Israel in 1996 and has now seeded chocolate throughout the Diaspora in Australia, the Philippines, Singapore, and the United States. A highlight of our trip and a must-visit shop, Chocolate by the Bald Man: Max Brenner, bears the combined names of its founders, Max Fichtman and Oded Brenner. Claiming to create a "new chocolate culture worldwide," Max Brenner tempts with its creative marketing and out-of-the-box chocolate menus for adults and for children. Supreme self-control would be required to bypass the hot chocolate options served in specially designed cups called "Hug Mugs" or "Suckao" cups, the

"Choctail" cold drinks/smoothies, and other chocolate treats such as the "Aphrodisiacs" (the liquor-added drinks), the "Max I Scream" (ice cream) options, the crepes and waffles, or the "Sweet Icons" (sundaes). Chocolate continues to go forth from Zion to the entire world as Oded Brenner recently opened Little Brown Chocolate Bakery & Coffee in New York City.

Old-New Chocolate

To explore the old-new chocolate of De Karina and its immigration from the Diaspora to Israel, Mark and I made a pilgrimage to the Golan Heights. Driving past numerous army installations, we saw the tiny De Karina factory at Kibbutz Ein Zivan finally emerge out of the morning fog. De Karina may be among the newest chocolate businesses in Israel. Karina Chaplinsky made aliyah from Argentina with her husband and two young children in 2002 through a program that absorbs new immigrant families in a kibbutz framework. Initially, Karina says, she cried a lot, missing her family and friends.

Having sought a change from the economic challenges in Argentina, Karina and her husband were not sure what to do once in Israel. They explored *confitura*, making jams from the local stone fruit. Seeking to make a unique contribution, however, they soon shifted focus to her South American family business, chocolate. At first they started in her home kitchen, then expanded to the former infirmary, and then moved to the current larger factory location. Now they import high-quality chocolate from Spain and Belgium to the Golan to make the finished product, which is then trucked from the Golan to duty-free shops and stores all around the country. Because only twenty-five miles separate Ein Zivan from Damascus, the factory sits on top of bomb shelters. Local customers include United Nations officials.

While deeply rooted in her Argentinian family's chocolate history, Karina fetes her new Israeli home in the names of her lines, drawing on the local mountains such as Hermon, Avital,

Bental, and Gamla. A version of folded chocolate is also hand-made at De Karina. Karina's grandfather, Jacob Lechtman, had worked in a chocolate company in Germany before fleeing Europe with only his immediate family after World War I. Not

The truffles named for the local mountains at De Karina in the Golan Heights.

able to afford chocolate in the early years in Buenos Aires, he made candy. With increased financing, he slowly developed his chocolate company, Juego Real. The Lechtmans supported the Jewish community there, particularly the Conservative synagogue, Comunidad Bet-Am Medinat Israel. Karina also attended youth group there and traveled to Israel as a youngster.

The De Karina factory is inspired by her father's factory. She treasures his smudged, worn, handwritten recipes at her home, using them with some modification. Karina's father, Louis Alberto, worked by hand in his chocolate company, as she does. In Argentina, Juego Real produced seasonal items. At Easter this meant chocolate chickens, fish, rabbits, and eggs as big as eighteen pounds. At Christmas they made turonis/marzipan with dried fruits. They produced no seasonal Jewish chocolate, because there really was no local Jewish market. Karina lamented that her father did not know that she has built on his legacy.

Local Israeli chocolate experiences and unusual confections entice, whether with honey and marzipan, produced as liqueur, formed into cocoa spread, baked into *ugah kushit*, or devoured alone. Chocolate's aliyah to Israel accompanied new immigrants such as Elite's founding partners and Karina. Paralleling the growth of the state, it mirrors a heritage of determination and adaptability. From Riga, Argentina, Belgium, and Switzerland, it has transitioned from generation to generation into the Israeli palate and psyche. Today, the Holy Land chocolate trail also extends out to the Diaspora—to Europe, North America, the Far East, and Down Under.

PART TWO

Other Religious Chocolate Revelations

Mark's Cocoa Nibs Citrus Salad

Mark created this delicious and appealing fruit salad. Though citrus was not known to pre-Columbians, the cocoa nibs harken back to the most basic form of the roasted cocoa bean of Mesoamerica.

Ingredients:

1 grapefruit, peeled (membrane removed, optional)
2 navel oranges, peeled
3 blood oranges, peeled
4 clementines, peeled
Pomegranate syrup (optional)
Several tablespoons cocoa nibs, to taste
Pistachios, roasted and chopped

Instructions:

Cut the fruit into bite-size pieces and place in a large serving bowl, preferably glass. Add the pomegranate syrup to taste.

When ready to serve, sprinkle the cocoa nibs and roasted pistachios over the fruit salad.

Quantity: 10–15 servings

Chapter Seven

Pre-Columbian Peoples Idolized Chocolate in Mesoamerica

AFTER THE LONG FLIGHT FROM NEW YORK CITY TO Mexico City, to prospect for chocolate's earliest religious heritage, my energy spiked as I meandered into an Oaxacan-based chocolate shop named Mayordomo at the airport. Inhaling the recently ground chocolate and marveling at the piles of cocoa beans, I aimed directly for several small dishes filled with a dark, thick chocolaty pudding set out on the counter, mini-spoons jutting straight up as if intended for my mouth. Perfect. My first taste of Mexico would be chocolate soufflé. I eagerly picked up the little bowl and happily, yes, greedily, stuffed a spoonful into my mouth. Within seconds I spit it out. Instead of the sweet, warm, chocolate mousse I had expected, I had bitten into a hotly spiced mole cooking sauce. I hastily replaced the little container on the display case and quickly backed out of the store. Out of the corner of my eye, I spied the attendant inserting a new mini-spoon, as she positioned the uneaten remains of my bowl for the next customer!

I had time to browse again, more cautiously, in another Mayordomo outlet at the bustling bus station in Oaxaca as we waited for our family friends, Miriam and Luis. It was close to midnight after our eight-hour bus ride. My sleep-deprived brain

A stone metate used for grinding cocoa beans and other local foods.

conjured doubts about the trip. Would we find anything on this chocolate trail that would fill in the mysteries of chocolate, Jews, and other religions? What kind of religious heritage of chocolate, if any, might there be in Mexico? Was this exhausting trip worth it?

Finally arriving at their home, Luis, a Mexico City native, whipped up a comforting bedtime Mexican hot chocolate—a mixture of sugar, cocoa beans, cinnamon, and almonds that had been milled for him at his favorite chocolate purveyor. That soothed the start of the investigation, and despite that first mole, Mark and I enjoyed several more delectable chocolate moments.

True, we found very little eating chocolate except at the Ferbach store next to our hotel in Mexico City; at L'Atelier du Chocolat, which only took orders; and at the Sanborns department store, which showcased truffles. Despite that deficit of eating chocolate, every restaurant and café in Mexico compensated by offering drinking chocolate. We resisted the local custom of dunking a yummy pastry or a chunky churro into each cup of hot chocolate on this pilgrimage to Mexico's chocolate center of Oaxaca, where chocolate perfumed the downtown and Christmas processions tossed brightly colored tissue–wrapped chocolate balls our way.

Chocolate for Breakfast

Multiple stalls in and around the food markets ground cacao beans to order. The larger, local *tiendas de chocolate* mills such as Soledad, Mayordomo, and Guelaguetza also sold packaged bars prickly with sugar and primitively ground chocolate—to be used mostly for drinking chocolate, mole sauce, and chocolate-covered coffee beans. Patchworked on Mina Street, the Soledad and Mayordomo companies each boast multiple storefronts, with Guelaguetza's shop just around the corner. On our first day Luis whisked us to the small town of Tiacolula and his favorite chocolate grinder, Molinos Y Chocolate, from which every few weeks he orders his custom ingredients for hot chocolate. Owner Florentine Antonio Andres filled Luis's spe-

cial request by pouring one kilo of cacao beans from the Mexican cities of Chiapas or Tabasco, two large sticks of cinnamon, and a few almonds into an annoyingly noisy electric grinder.[1] Within seconds, the warm, liquid chocolate oozed into the sugar waiting in the bowl below. Most locals use much more sugar, probably four pounds of sugar to two pounds of cacao. Florentine, who admits to drinking chocolate only a couple of times a week, mixed all of this together with his bare hands, scraping every drop into a Styrofoam container. He promised to crush the

Murals at Café Tacuba in Mexico City recall early chocolate making.

cacao with peanuts for the following week. Back at the house several hours later, we poured the still warm chocolate muck into a cookie pan, cooled it, and scored it into tablets.

At last we were contentedly supplied for a week or more of breakfast hot chocolates. Mark and I agreed that our favorite hot chocolate was homemade by Luis, with second place going to the elegant Café de Tacuba in Mexico City. Tacuba's colorful murals, memorializing the role of chocolate in Mexican and Old World culture, authenticated that delectable drink for us.

Grasshoppers and Chocolate

Sunday found us at the immaculate, orderly, and immense market called Tlacolula de Matamoros (place of abundance). We sampled strange, bright-orange fruits in the footsteps of Hernando Alonso, one of the Jews in the group that accompanied Hernán Cortés in the conquest of Mexico.[2] As we tossed back flavorful *mezcal*, an alcoholic beverage made from a form of agave, I recalled how Jewish cacao traders escaped the Spanish Inquisition only to face it again in New Spain.[3] Continuing through the market's stalls we bought hand-carved gourds for chocolate drinking, measured two-foot-long sticks of cinnamon, and admired the varied designs on the chocolate stirrers known in Spanish as *molinollos*. As we stared down the market's piles of roasted grasshoppers, I mused about how Jews of the colonial period in Mexico learned chocolate-making skills from the locals and incorporated chocolate into Jewish customs.

We meandered back to Florentine's shop for the anticipated peanut-based batch of chocolate. This time Florentine not only added peanuts but he also ran the goo through the grinder several times to create a finer powder. He confessed that he paid approximately fifty to sixty pesos per kilo of cacao beans, selling the chocolate ground with sugar at 50 percent profit. To add flavor, sometimes he threw cocoa bean shells into the mix. In the busy Christmas season, Florentine needs to replace his grinding stones once a month. The Oaxacan *Posada de Cacao* (procession of cacao) would keep him especially busy. Before Christmas, the procession, representing Mary and Joseph seeking shelter, wanders from home to home singing while the carolers are refreshed with special treats of cacao.

Chocolate Heritage of Mexico

Digging into the very basic and early entwining of chocolate and religion in this region of the world framed the context for the later Jewish commercial and personal use of chocolate during Mexico's colonial period.[4] Just outside Oaxaca this cacao history hovers over the expansive archeological ruins of Monte Alban, host to cultures preceding Columbus and the Spanish discovery of the New World in 1492. Cacao beans and the chocolate beverage were soul food for the people living in Central America, countries we now know as Mexico, Belize, Guatemala, Honduras, El Salvador, Nicaragua, and Costa Rica. We joke that we will die without chocolate. For the peoples at settlements such as Monte Alban, chocolate symbolized life: cacao pods represented extracted hearts, and chocolate signaled blood. They depicted this notion in icons of bleeding cacao. These concepts of enlivening chocolate suffused every life transition. Traditions idolized chocolate and the cacao tree as powerful bonds between humans and gods for hundreds of years. Chocolate in cultic contexts escorted infants as well as aged, dying parents over the thresholds of life. Chocolate drinking solemnized political allegiances, noted civic agreements, and marked religious occasions. Divination rituals, human sacrifices, life-cycle offerings, and agricultural rites used cacao. Throughout these occasions cacao flowed thick and strong, sustaining the life force of the community as well as the individuals within it.[5]

Cacao's popularity and potency carried it hundreds of miles from its source. Aztec royalty in Mexico so desired cacao that to attain it they conquered the lowland of the region of Soconusco, along Mexico's border with Guatemala, transporting the beans via canoes or on the backs of porters along intricate systems of trails. Royal females prepared the cacao in formalized rituals at state banquets. The arches from ancient Mayan ruins depicted cacao alongside the god of abundance and wealth, identifying cacao with affluence, a message that the nobility and others certainly drank in.[6]

The plateau of Monte Alban whispered to us of religious tales about the cacao fruit's part in the creation of the world and how it sustained the gods. The biblical narrative focuses on the singular apple as the symbol of sin and exile; this differs greatly from the pre-Columbian elemental first food, cacao. Grown on a sacred tree, cacao was coveted among the supernatural beings and was the very substance of humanity. Before European views and mores infiltrated the area, the Mayans learned cacao stories from their *Popol Vuh*, "The Book

Generations of Chocolate Lovers

Aztec: These Native American people and cultures dominated large parts of Mesoamerica in the fourteenth, fifteenth, and six-teenth centuries, when the Spanish conquered the area. They created a significant empire in the fifteenth century and founded what became Mexico City. They learned about cacao from other peoples nearby. They spoke the Nahuatl language, which some say provides the basis for the word "chocolate," from *cacaoatl*, mean-ing "cacao water," or *xoco*, meaning "sour water."

Maya: Native American peoples who flourished in Mesoamerica since approximately 2000 BCE and possessed the only written language of these pre-Columbian peoples. The languages and cultures of the Maya still exist in Central America.

Mesoamerican: Area and culture of Mexico, Belize, Guatemala, El Salvador, Honduras, Nicaragua, and Costa Rica prior to the Spanish colonization that occurred in the fifteenth and sixteenth centuries.

Pre-Hispanic and pre-Columbian: The era before Europeans and European culture influenced the area and peoples, particularly before Christopher Columbus's voyages of 1492 to 1504.

of Counsel." It taught that cacao ensured a balance among the earth, sky, and underworlds.[7] In these legends the gods created humans from chocolate and maize. For them, the cacao tree was a "world tree," the first tree, the center of the universe, and the primordial source of life. These ideas were reinforced in depictions of the flower god, Ahaw Nik, who clutched a cacao tree as if it were a staff that supports life itself, as well as in images of ballplayers feeding cacao pods to a god.[8]

Gods Eat Chocolate

From the misty past of high places such as Monte Alban, these peoples would have heard and recounted the Aztec tales of the gift of cacao to humans bestowed by the Aztec god Quetzalcoatl, also called the "Feathered Serpent" or the "Gardener of Paradise." Quetzalcoatl secretly smuggled cacao beans, the food reserved exclusively for the gods, and delivered it to humans, patiently instructing them in cacao cultivation. Out of love for humans, Quetzalcoatl betrayed the other deities. Quetzalcoatl planted a cacao tree, collected its pods, toasted the beans, and then showed women how to beat it with water in gourds to produce the chocolate. When the gods saw how happy the people were, they became envious. They swore vengeance on Quetzalcoatl and banished him. To punish humans, they transformed cacao trees into thorny mesquite bushes, and Quetzalcoatl's last seeds could flourish only in remote Tabasco, in the southeast of Mexico, making cacao harder to enjoy. As a result of this gift of the godly chocolate, "the god of light, the giver of the drink of the gods, the giver of chocolate,"[9] Quetzalcoatl was adored in Mesoamerican villages at impressive gatherings. At an event in his honor, an effigy with a human body and a red-beaked bird face sat in a long, wide chamber decorated with gold, silver, jewels, and fine cloth. Forty days before the feast, a male slave, "flawless of hands and feet, without stain or blemish" was purified twice with water, dressed exactly as the god, shut up in a cage at night, served good food, and decorated with garlands. Portraying the god, the poor man sang and danced and was greeted by women and children. If he became sad or stopped performing, they forced him to drink an elixir of chocolate mixed with blood scraped from sacrificial knives. He was sacrificed at midnight as the price paid for the human enjoyment of chocolate, which should exclusively belong to the gods.[10] Thankfully, our chocolate indulgences today only require sacrifices of calories and dollars.

Chocolate Is Life

In the pre-Hispanic days of Monte Alban's activity, cacao nurtured many potent and sacred moments of agriculture and fertility. Supplications for abundant maize, rain, cacao, and good weather reveled in chocolate. In a harvest ritual, gourds of chocolate and other assorted foods were used to appeal to the god Tlaloc. To wheedle rain from Cac, the cave-dwelling rain god, the moon goddess, IxChel, negotiated with him for chocolate over a large pot decorated with two depictions of cacao. In a New Year ceremony, the opossum god carried the rain god as he ate cacao. When the cacao flowers first sprouted, people offered blood from their ears and arms to the earth deities to ensure good weather for the cacao crop. The cacao harvest festival hosted by cacao plantation owners included sacrificing a dog spotted with the colors of cacao, burning incense to their idols, and presenting each of the officials the cacao fruit. To mark the end of the cacao harvest and to honor the cacao god Cacaguate, the Pipil-Nicarao peoples of Nicaragua performed a ceremony of rapturous dancing, with humans leashed to a tall pole flying around the image of the god. The planting of cacao trees deserved blessing as well. Chocolate drinking also embellished the rite of *Xochipaina*, which marked the first flowers of the season.[11] Chocolate smoothed the cycles of the agricultural year at harvest and planting.

Rituals of chocolate eased the goings and comings, the departures and returns of traveling merchants in this pre-Columbian time. Banquets extended divine protection to the merchant, which included cacao drinking songs of the gods and for the gods. Chocolate's support of the most frightful of all journeys, death, also hovered over Monte Alban's steep steps. Chocolate fed the dead, escorted the soul's travels, and promised the possibility of rebirth. It anointed the transition from one world to the next, blurring life and death and easing the sadness of mourners. Mayan funerary implements for food and drink, particularly for chocolate and maize, supplied and decorated the graves of the honored dead. Marking the portals to the underworld, cacao beans represented the bodily organs of new gods. Offerings of chocolate-filled gourds emerging from the underground are depicted at the Temple of the Owls in Yucatán. A supernatural howler monkey holding a cacao pod marched alongside the death god. An incised vessel portrayed a dead man being reborn as a cacao tree, sprouting

History of Cacao

This rich chocolate tradition dates back three millennia. Traces of a chemical component of chocolate, theobromine, have been found in ceramic vessels of Belize, and historians believe that cacao cultivation began around this time as well. The earliest iconography of cacao may be seen on a twenty-five-hundred-year-old Peruvian vessel decorated with cacao pod elements. Many more tall vases and spouted chocolate pots (air blown through the spouts foamed the chocolate) depicted cacao gods and goddesses, cacao trees, cacao pods, and the word *cacao*. Fronds and pods of cacao, emblematic of the source of the community's wealth, sprouted from the bodies of gods and humans. Jaguars were seen as protectors of cacao as they stalked their monkey prey, preventing the monkeys from eating the precious pulp of the cacao pods.[a]

from his earthly grave. The dependence on cacao in death settings may be seen from the placement of a chocolate vase next to a dead king's head.[12]

Chocolate's connection to death profoundly reflected the pre-Hispanic sense of it as a precious life force full of sacred energy. Those who lost blood were treated with chocolate. Chocolate and cacao were fed to Aztec sacrificial victims before their hearts were extracted. Birth festivities started with the purchase of chocolate and the spices often paired with it, such as pepper, cayenne, and achiote. At a Mayan banquet for a new-born, every male guest received chocolate in a *jicara*, a special gourd for drinking chocolate. Children draped in white cloths were decorated with feathers and cacao seeds. The holy water for anointing a newborn was made from "certain flowers and of cacao pounded and dissolved in virgin water."[13] A presenta-tion of cacao would have occurred twelve days from the birth, at the time of the baby's naming. Mothers, when bathing in the river after a delivery, also offered cacao to the river to divert evil. Only young children were considered "pure" enough to serve the "*Kakaw*" drink at such occasions. Ideally, there would have been leftovers of chocolate and other foods from the feast, a good omen that the host would be blessed to offer similar plentiful feasts in the future.[14] The planting of a cacao orchard and the first fruiting of those trees commemorated the growth of a royal child. Chocolate spiced up those first days of life for the baby, the family, and the community.

Cacao and chocolate also sweetened marriage negotiations and ceremonies throughout Mesoamerican culture. In a palace scene depicted on a vase from Guatemala, matchmakers stood above a vessel of chocolate decorated with ear flower, a popu-lar ingredient for wedding chocolate, as they haggled over the nuptial terms. Cacao beans were used as currency to pay the wedding dowry.[15] Cacao drinking sealed traditional marriage agreements between families. Contemporary wedding planners might note this efficacy of chocolate in marriage celebrations.

The ruins of the pre-Columbian settlement at Monte Alban, outside of Oaxaca.

Chocolate in Rituals Today

Today chocolate graces life-cycle occasions in Central America. A matchmaker is often paid in cacao. A gift of cacao goes from the groom's family to the bride's family via the matchmaker, and acceptance of the gift signifies approval of the match. In Yucatán, the bride and groom are feted with chocolate. At Catholic weddings and baptisms as well, the Yucatec Maya of Mexico drink chocolate. In the Kekchi Maya customs for the wedding ceremony, the groom bestows thirteen cacao beans upon the bride. In Guatemala and Mexico, cacao is served at birth ceremonies twenty days following the birth. It is also presented to godparents before and after the baptism. In Oaxaca, godparents bestow a gift of several kilos of chocolate on the parents.[16]

Chocolate also reigns in rituals for the dead. The pastel-painted graves at the cemetery in Chichicastenango, Guatemala, often bear chocolate, candles, herbs, and sugar laid out in circular configurations. Oaxacan Day of the Dead ceremonies feature chocolate at graves, and at home altars families feast on chocolate and other festive foods. As one local commented, "In this festival, chocolate is the main drink, for the living and for the dead.... When I die, maybe the living will put out chocolate for me, because I liked it."[17] Anthropologists in the 1930s even witnessed chocolate poured into the graves of the Oaxacan dead.

Chocolate also supports the agricultural cycle. Belize villagers still appeal to the cave gods with cacao for good weather. In May, as the dry season and cacao harvest end in Comalcalco, a city within Tabasco, Mexico, the town celebrates the Fiesta de San Isidro Enrama, paying tribute to the patron of cacao, San Isidro, in a most colorful way. Cacao pods and beans are everywhere, tied to horse carts and to bicycles, and made into costumes. Cacao branches line the church steps and the pews. Necklaces of cacao beans decorate the statue of the Virgin Mary and of San Isidro. Priests bless all of these with holy water; some of the income from the local chocolate-processing plant benefits the church, so the factory is included in the blessings as well.[18]

Current Guatemalan Lenten customs also connect to chocolate. During the days leading up to Easter week, they drink chocolate rather than coffee. On the Wednesday of Holy Week, the week prior to Easter, known as Semana Santa, young men customarily pilgrimage from Santiago to the coast's ancient cacao groves, to gather cocoa pods and cocoa branches to decorate the town.[19]

I had only grazed the surface of a very deeply embedded and rich chocolate culture of the local peoples when I sought energy from that chocolate nibble at the airport in Mexico City. No wonder Carl Linnaeus's eighteenth-century clas-sification of plants labeled cacao *Theobroma*, the "food of the gods."[20] Pre-Columbians such as those at Monte Alban revered this miraculous, primordial, elemental cacao fruit, which they understood to blend innately and inherently into the sacred essence of humanity and existence. They celebrated, perhaps better than we do, an abiding love of chocolate. This amazing fruit of the divine world was, and remains, essential to the sacred moments of human life in Mesoamerican celebrations. Jews, who arrived in this area in the seventeenth century, confronted these chocolate customs as well. The European clerics who followed Columbus to this region struggled with how these deep and enduring sanctities could, or should, be molded into their Catholicism. These tensions along the chocolate trail span the distance from Central America to Spain.

Mendiants

This easy-to-make confection recalls the mendicant orders of the Catholic Church and embodies the Christian chocolate connections discussed in this chapter.

Ingredients:

4 ounces dark or bittersweet chocolate, broken into pieces
¼ cup cocoa nibs, almonds, or hazelnuts
¼ cup candied ginger
¼ cup dried blueberries or raisins
¼ cup candied orange peel

Instructions:

Line a baking sheet with waxed paper. In a large heatproof bowl set over a pan of simmering water, stir the chocolate until melted.

Remove the chocolate from the heat. Drop tablespoonfuls of chocolate onto the prepared baking sheet, using the back of the spoon to flatten into disks. Place one of each of the four toppings onto each circle. Work a few *mendiants* at a time; they will harden as they cool. Cool on the baking sheet until hardened. Store in a cool place in a covered container.

Quantity: About 20 *mendiants*

Chapter Eight

Faith Diffused Chocolate around the World

UNDERSTANDING JEWS, RELIGION, AND CHOCOLATE required Mark and me to try the chocolate goodies (shucks) that memorialize early ties to Christianity while investigating the leads related to the chocolate appetites of sixteenth- and seventeenth-century Christian religious orders. When Catholic clergy first encountered chocolate use among the indigenous peoples in places such as Monte Alban and Central America, some became early chocolate adopters, some critics, and some salesmen. Chocolate delicacies such as the *mendiant* immortalize the mendicant (beggar) orders, those that serve the poor and rely only on donations for support—Augustinians, Carmelites, Dominicans, and Franciscans. Each nut and dried fruit in the *mendiant* treat symbolizes the color of the respective monastic robes: raisins for Dominicans, hazelnuts for Augustinians, dried figs for Franciscans, and almonds for Carmelites. We first noticed *mendiants* in Paris. Eyeing the several artful offerings in a crowded confectionary, I was intrigued by the flat, chocolate disks decorated with nuts and dried fruit. When I asked about it, the attendant muttered an indecipherable French word, which I now understand was *mendiant*. After that we saw them frequently in France and in the

The *mendiant* treat; dried fruits and nuts recall the mendicant orders of the Catholic Church.

United States as well. Though some customs associate *mendiants* with Christmas, we first saw them in the spring. In Provence, Christmas dinner customarily ends with *les treize desserts de Noël* (the thirteen desserts for Christmas), including *mendiants*.

Fishing for Easter Chocolate

Mark and I saw pre-Easter chocolate fare all over France that spring. We noted a lot of fish-shaped chocolates, which we were told are abundantly available and popular during that season in particular, though no one could explain why. I figured that Jesus and fish were associated through the miracles of the fish. Also, the Greek letters for the word for fish relate to an acrostic referring to Jesus as messiah. The French may not know the origin of the custom, but we enjoyed the miraculously yummy chocolate fish.

Geneva's Christmas Chocolate

We encountered another unique religious chocolate custom in Geneva, where December 12 every year is known as L'Escalade, or Fête de l'Escalade. Swiss chocolatiers fabricate soup pots out of chocolate and fill them with vegetables molded from marzipan. This commemorates the 1602 victory of the citizens of Geneva over the attempt of the Duke of Savoy to destroy the Reformation and reinstate Catholic order. Genevans forced the Savoyards to retreat when, according to the legend, a woman called Mére Royaume flung her hot soup cauldron out the window, killing an enemy soldier. To recall that providential triumph, the many festivities include a long-standing custom of the oldest and youngest in each family together breaking

Fish-shaped chocolate for Easter recalls Jesus.

the chocolate pot in victorious joy. A traditional song invokes these words: "God holds the victory in His hand; to Him alone our thanks we bring. May His holy name be forever blessed."[1]

Monastic Chocolate

Other chocolate delicacies with religious sources invigorated us in our travels. When we learned that many Spanish convents and monasteries specialize in chocolate and other *dulces* (sweets), we pulled on the bell of one such Toledo convent, located about forty-five miles south of Madrid, to sample their goodies.

We also sought out Barcelona's Caelum, a shop situated above what some say were Jewish ritual baths. Named for a heavenly constellation, this café features treats from convents and monasteries all over the country. The menu's "Monastic Sweet Temptations" tap into the centuries-old Catholic legacy of chocolate. In Ferrara, Italy, we devoured *pampepato*, "the bread of the pope," a spice, nut, candied-fruit concoction covered in chocolate. Known as a Christmas dainty created first at the monastery of Corpus Domini, it is baked in what the nuns describe as a skullcap shape. In a church square in Turin, Italy, we savored the distinctive *bicerin* drink, which certainly fulfilled its meaning in the local dialect as something delicious. We tried mole at dinner in Oaxaca. In the New World, the Convent of Santa Rosa in Pueblo de Los Angeles may have been home to the first mole. As the legends unravel, Sor Andrea de la Asunción, a nun, or perhaps it may have been the prioress of that Dominican convent, concocted and served a peppery sauce over turkey, adding bitter chocolate at the last minute for the visiting bishop. In another telling of the legend, some think that a nun, wishing to honor the archbishop for constructing a convent for her order, may have combined Old World with New World ingredients, including chocolate.[2] Little did Mark and I know that with these samplings, we had bitten into deeply embedded chocolate complexities and religious controversies.

Clergy Reports: Exotic New World Chocolate

Adherents of the mendicant orders, along with Jesuits and a host of others,[3] generated the first reports of cocoa beans and other New World exotica to the Old World. Some of these religious people treated chocolate's early European history with dismay, ambivalence, or disgust, while others did with co-optation, or with passion. Informants such as Bernardin de Sahagun and Diego de Durán may have had Jewish ancestry.[4] Clerics propelled chocolate's advancement into European awareness, discourse, popularity, and economy. Some sought to squelch pre-Columbian chocolate usage, while others attempted to assimilate it into Christian religious rites. They struggled with chocolate's pagan history, worried about its exoticism, debated its theological implications, and exploited its resources. How could they allow themselves to enjoy this nourishing and tasty substance given its roots in idolatry? Would their missionizing to potential converts fail if the locals were to see chocolate in Christian settings? Could they voice their appreciation of chocolate and also root out heathen rites? How might cacao finance the church?

Not surprisingly, when Columbus and Cortez introduced the drab cocoa bean to the Spanish court, King Ferdinand and Queen Isabella focused instead on the glittering gold, silver, and other New World treasures. The first legal shipment of cacao arrived in Spain in 1591, while smaller, private amounts had been sent earlier. Only in 1544, when Dominicans tantalized the court with prepared chocolate presented by a

Kekchi Maya delegation of New World natives, did it slowly gain popularity.[5] From 1585 to 1630 Spain attempted to maintain a monopoly on cacao. This was preceded by written accounts of chocolate. Chocolate lover and priest Peter Martyr d'Anghera's (1457–1526) official chronicle of the New World, which characterized chocolate among the luxuries at the court of Montezuma and the highly evolved culture of Mexico, would have intrigued the reader, especially his description of chocolate "as wine, a wonderful drink, fitte for a king."[6] Confusion may have resulted from Martyr's report that sacks of cacao served as currency. Our idiom about money growing on trees turns out to be about our beloved chocolate:

> Blessed money which furnishes mankind with a sweet and nutritious beverage and protects its innocent possessors from the infernal disease of avarice, since it cannot be long hoarded nor hidden underground.[7] ... For this groweth upon trees ... drinke is made from of them for rich and noble menn.[8]

Martyr's early report of chocolate reached the Vatican, informing Pope Clement VII of its existence. Sadly, the pope, like most of the recipients of these reports, possessed neither the beans nor the equipment for making it[9] and therefore must have been baffled by it all.

Franciscan Friar Bernardino de Sahagún (1499–1590) based his writings about chocolate on interviews of local elders in Mexico.[10] His story inspired Portland, Oregon chocolatier Elizabeth Montes to name her store of handmade chocolate after him. Franciscan Bishop Diego de Landa of Yucatán (1524–79) witnessed a Mayan baptism that used cacao in the anointing water.[11] He also detailed Mayan processing of cacao into what he described as a butter-like grease. Born in Spain, raised in Mexico, Diego Durán (c. 1537–88) entered the Dominican Order in 1556 and then served in Oaxaca. Durán recorded chocolate's use in pre-Columbian religious rites.[12] In his report on his 1730 mission to the West Indies, Father

Jean-Baptiste Labat depicted the popularity of chocolate in the New World, citing how Spaniards dunked toasted bread fingers and special biscuits into their chocolate. He also noted that the Creole population of Martinique drank "*Chicolade*," a daily morning beverage of the New Americans.[13]

Giovanni Francesco Gemelli Careri (1651–1725), a suspected spy for the Vatican, extolled the Spanish transformation of chocolate:

> The efforts of the Spanish have raised chocolate to perfection. Today it is taken so much in the Indies that there is neither Negro nor peon who does not drink it every day and the wealthier four times per day.[14]

A critique of the foamy chocolate was penned by Jesuit José de Acosta (1539–1600) in the 1590s. He named chocolate a cultural marker that differentiated locals from the elite Spanish, describing it as a

> crazy thing prized in that land and Spanish women born in that land would die for the black chocolate ... disgusts [those] ... not of the land ... [those] who had not grown up with ... [those] could not have a taste for it.[15]

To him, it resembled feces. He also mentioned that some drank it hot, cold, or lukewarm; for medicinal purposes it could be applied as a paste.[16]

Seventeenth-century chocolate lover and English Dominican friar Thomas Gage (1597–1656) captured church ambivalence in his account. Gage defined chocolate as nutritious and noted that Spaniards drank sweet chocolate in New World public establishments called *chocolaterias* in the 1630s. His work included an account of chocolate preparation. Impressed by the popularity of chocolate in Mexico among the Spanish, he enjoyed a dinner in Veracruz at the home of a clergyman where the first course was "the Indian drink called chocolate."[17] When fleeing his post in Guatemala, he stockpiled chocolate for his journey.[18]

Chocolate Poisons Bishop

In a gossipy passage, Gage reported about colorful chocolaty incidents in Chiapas, Mexico, where the bishop warned the women to stop drinking chocolate during the Mass. The bishop condemned these disruptions of the holy ceremonies and threatened to excommunicate violators, posting warnings on the church doors against eating or drinking in church. The women protested that they could not be in church without their chocolate. They ignored the bishop and continued to drink in church, until one day the priests rudely grabbed their chocolate cups out of their hands. The husbands gallantly pulled their swords against the priests to protect their chocolate-smitten wives. The chocoholics switched allegiance to a neighborhood church where the nuns and friars were not as demanding. The bishop then mysteriously fell very ill. All of his physicians agreed that he had been poisoned. Gage thought he knew that a particular woman was responsible. She argued against grieving for the bishop. She claimed that since he had so opposed chocolate in church, the chocolate that he had drunk in his own home had disagreed with him. Thus the proverb:

> Beware of the chocolatte of Chiapa! ... that poisoning and wicked city, which truly deserves no better relation than what I have given of the simple Dons and the chocolatte-confectioning Doñas.[19]

Chocolate's popularity seeped from pre-Columbian culture and custom into the Hispanic New and Old World popular palate due, in part, to these generally positive reports from clerics, despite the real ambivalence of some church leaders.

Christians Co-opt Chocolate

Church leaders struggled with what they saw as the theological threats and opportunities presented by chocolate. Some pre-Hispanic beliefs about cacao were folded into New World Christianity in a syncretistic mix. Chocolate leaked into acceptability as it offered a "visceral link to the feel of life and religion in a past era."[20] Early on, Spanish explorer Hernán Cortés (1485–1547) argued that pre-Hispanic religious traditions could be refashioned to serve the new rulers and religion. He insisted that Indians welcome missionaries with chocolate because this was already familiar as a customary sign of respect for Aztec priests.[21]

Chocolate could also entice respect for Christianity and Christian celebrations, as, for example, All Soul's Day, when offerings to the dead included cacao. One of twelve Franciscan friars baptizing thousands of Indians daily, Friar Toribio de Benavente (d. 1569), who was also known as Motolinia (the humble one), reported that in almost all the Indian towns mourners served chocolate to their dead kin. In 1743 Jesuits arranged a public drinking of the novel beverage in Guatemala City, a marketing technique for chocolate and Christianity at the same time.[22]

In his guide for the evangelization of the Indians of Central Mexico, Franciscan missionary Diego Valadés (c. 1533–82) fostered a Christian worldview of the centrality of chocolate. In keeping with his pre-Hispanic beliefs that saw the cocoa tree as central to creation stories, his book boasts an engraving of a cacao tree at the center of his faith's arboreal realm of the heavens.[23] This veneration of the cacao tree recalled earlier celebratory offerings, the paradise of Quetzalcoatl, and the Maya creation story of the *Popol Vuh*. Valadés digested earlier chocolate pagan notions. A similar example of such co-optation may be found in the representation of the Garden of Eden centered on the cacao tree in the murals of the sixteenth-century Augustinian Monastery of the Purification (*La Purificación y San Simón*) in Malinalco, Mexico. These didactic images and beliefs presented "a world of harmony of Indians and priests in 'perfect Christianity.'"[24]

Priests themselves relied on chocolate for energy and as comfort food in the New World as well as in the Old World. In Bartolomé Marradón's 1616 *Dialogue* concerning the use of tobacco, chocolate, and other beverages, it becomes clear that chocolate had so poured into the life of Catholic priests that his Indian "character" reports that he witnessed a Spanish priest so addicted to chocolate that he interrupted the Mass to drink it while missionizing to Indians. Marradón reported:

> I once saw ... a priest saying Mass who was obliged by necessity—being exhausted—to sit on a bench and drink a *tecomate* [a deep clay cup] full of chocolate, and then God gave him the energy to complete the Mass.[25]

Likewise, in words that Gregorio Mayans y Siscar (1699–1781) dedicated to the Jesuit cardinal Álavaro Cienfuegos, "[Chocolate] introduces life-giving sap ... restores the strength and gives new breath to the spirit."[26] In 1690 a chocolate fan noted with approval:

> Preachers find much good in taking chocolate before and after preaching, taking it before relaxes and gives them better vigor for their task and after it repairs the exhausted spirits, and they ascertain that in addition it gives them ideas and fortifies the memory.[27]

Chocolate took on powerful, sacral qualities. After her family and her church superiors convinced her to enter into a worldly marriage instead of the order, the devout Carmelite novice Isabel de Jesús requested a bit of chocolate to assuage her feelings of anxiety and revive her at a cousin's wedding. Locals also drank chocolate in church, the chocolate competing with the wine and wafer as divine. Chocolate came to embody the Eucharist, building on pre-Columbian linkages between chocolate and blood. The words *chocolate, ambrosia, manna*, and *eucharist* became interchangeable. Oaxaca nuns were famous for their cinnamon- and anise-flavored chocolate. The Concepcionista nuns of Regina Coeli of Mexico City so adored their chocolate that they were called *monjas chocolateras* (chocolate nuns). With time, a Catholic cacao god adorned the Metropolitan Cathedral of the Assumption of Mary in Mexico City. Cacao beans offered at the side chapel of the cathedral enriched the priests. Unlike the bishop of Chiapas, priests permitted chocolate drinking during Mass and sold it as well.[28] Chocolate insinuated itself into the faith.

As chocolate was absorbed into Christian rite, locals soaked up Christianity into their chocolate. A tale related by the Kekchi Indians described the crucified Jesus explaining and endorsing the cacao tree, even perhaps identifying it as the tree of his crucifixion:

> Jesus came down from the tree and lay down in its shade. Then he blessed the tree that it might serve for cacao. Instantly there was cacao. He told the people ... that the cacao should serve in *cofradia* [brotherhood] in marriages and for borrowing money and maize.[29]

Those who argued for chocolate would have looked at this Kekchi tale as proof of their success in adapting chocolate into Christian rites.

Church Condemns Chocolate

For some, this transformation of chocolate into Christian ideas and customs salved the boundaries between old pagan traditions and new Christian religion. Others, however, despaired over chocolate use in long-entrenched pagan heresies, seeing it as a threat to the true faith, as some natives secretly practiced their chocolate-based pagan rites. The first bishop of Mexico, Franciscan Juan de Zumárraga (1468–1548), sought to eradicate all nonconformity, including any related chocolate use. Bartolomé Marradón's *Dialogue* ultimately condemned chocolate due to the sorcery among Indian women to avenge jealousy and to kill people.[30] A 1629 play written by Francisco Gómez de Quevedo y Santibáñez Villegas (1580–1645), *Discurso de Todos los Diablos* (A Discussion among Demons), critiqued heathen chocolate rituals that seemingly imitated Christian practice: "Chocolate-bibbers idolize the cup that they raise on high and adore and go into a trance over [it]," treating it as if it were Communion wine.[31]

Seeking to squelch such unorthodox chocolate rites, one parish priest, Baltasar Herrera, uncovered secret gatherings at the home of Francisco Pech, a Mayan noble. Covert midnight-to-dawn sessions depended on donations of thirty to fifty cacao beans from participants. A *jicara* (cup) of chocolate was passed to each participant in rank order, the art of the *puyulcha* (sacrifice) preparation having been passed down from mother to daughter. A woman named Ana Quime and occasionally her daughter, Catalina, prepared the cacao formula with ground maize and one hundred cacao beans.[32] The rite also required "four new *jicaras* ... idolators of old called it ... a sacrifice sent to the heavens."[33]

The sentencing imposed by Herrera on Pech included a flogging of fifty lashes, exile for three years, with labor at the cathedral in Mérida. Ultimately, since Herrera could not eradicate the idolatry in his area, he in turn was dismissed from his position. In another instance of uncovering these clandestine chocolate rites, one cleric climbed a supposedly abandoned Mayan temple to discover "cacao offerings and vestiges of copal burned not too long before, that was of some superstition or idolatry recently committed."[34]

Also hoping to eliminate chocolate heresies, missionizing Franciscan monks found that the local rulers of Tlanocopan were not willing to give up their gods. Two of these leaders, Tacatetl and Tanixtetl, organized secret worship following the traditional older calendar in local caverns, even when Tanixtetl's son, who had been raised by Franciscans in Mexico City, pleaded that they stop. These rites were discovered by the local *encomendero* (a recipient of a royal grant that included free labor and tribute from the Indians) Lorenzo Suárez. Though the worshippers had escaped, they left behind cultic trappings, including "food, and cacao."[35] As punishment for this transgression, Tacatetl and Tanixtetl endured public flogging and years of labor at a monastery.

In yet another such case, a man named Cristobal and his wife, Catalina, publicly professed belief in Christianity but secretly prayed to their traditional gods in Ocuituco. Their wealth included diverse objects such as a golden crucifix, rosary beads, and "twenty-eight *xicaras* which are used for serving chocolate with eleven stirring-sticks."[36] Cristobal was said to have attended confession only once in ten years. The pagan customs occurred primarily in their home, at midnight, with only a few participants, weekly and monthly. These actions ultimately led to Inquisition inquiries and sentencing to public flogging and hard labor.[37] These attempts and others sought to destroy local pre-Hispanic chocolate religious customs.

Church Debates Chocolate in the Mass, the Fast, and Communion

The ambivalence of clerics also percolated into theological questions about the drinking of chocolate by laypeople and priests during Mass, while fasting, and before Communion. Juan de Solórzano Pereira (1575–1654), a lawyer and judge in Peru whose writings helped form the basis of Spanish law in the colonies for about 150 years, expressed his view that the use of chocolate by priests prior to Communion should be banned. Chocolate challenged the ecclesiastical fast as well as the Mass, and much depended on whether chocolate was classified as a food or as drink.[38] Catholic fasts banned nourishment between midnight and the time of Holy Communion the next day and during the fast days of the Lent period, during which only one meal could be consumed. Such fasts permitted drinking to allay thirst but not to provide sustenance. In those days, bread, ground nuts, spices, or eggs were often added to liquids, including chocolate, turning them into nutritional smoothies. This complicated the questions about chocolate. Also, fasts were undertaken to lessen lascivious desires, which further challenged the permissibility of drinking chocolate. Consider the myth associated with Montezuma, who supposedly drank chocolate as an aphrodisiac before visiting his mistresses.[39]

While the frequent local usage of chocolate made these inquiries pressing for those in the New World, the pope and his cardinals considered these matters inconsequential and did not pay attention; they had barely heard about chocolate, much less experienced it. Perhaps for this reason as well as the deep love-hate relationship that chocolate engendered among clergy, this debate about chocolate and fasting lasted for more than one hundred years. Those who opposed taking chocolate during the fast argued that it was a food intended to nourish. As further proof, they resorted to an argument based on the Mesoamerican fast to the gods as part of the festival of Quetzalcoatl, which prohibited chocolate.[40]

Others defined chocolate as a liquid with inconsequential nutritional effects, as its essential nature, since its first use in Spain, was to alleviate thirst. Further, this argument went, Christians drink wine during fasts, so chocolate drinking should be permitted.[41] It was argued that if one drank chocolate combined with water to alleviate thirst, then it should be allowed. However, if the chocolate was intended as nutriment, as when it is mixed with milk, it should not be permitted.[42] Dominicans tended to be against chocolate drinking during the fast. Finally, in 1666, the Holy Office ended the debate, determining that chocolate during Lent was to be strictly limited to that made only with water and without sugar or milk.[43] Such controversies stirred from the moment that the earliest sips of chocolate crossed the lips of observant Catholics.

Clergy Hunger for Chocolate

Despite these several theological ambivalences and controversies about chocolate, gustatory appreciation for it enrobed many members of the church in the Old World. For them, chocolate became an instrument of adulation, an offering for the greater glory of God. In Spain, monks made chocolate, drank it in secret, and hoarded their supplies and recipes. Alphonse de Richelieu (b. 1585), cardinal of Paris, was among the first there to experience chocolate, when his protégé Cardinal Mazarin brought a personal chocolate maker with him from Italy. In 1634 Mexican Jesuits were shipping chocolate to their brothers in Rome by way of Seville. At a party at his palace, thrown by the viceroy of Valencia honoring the seventh birthday of King Charles II on November 6, 1669, the winning poetry verses claimed chocolate as "manna" preparing one for heaven. For his submission to the contest, a Carmelite friar referred to chocolate as "that inspirational Ambrosia."[44]

Lorenzo Magalotti (1637–1712) imported Spain's chocolate tastes when he returned to Italy bearing a library of recipe books by Cardinal de Moncada. "Jasmine-flavored and citrus-flavored chocolate, the sharp and crackling taste of glacé chocolate, and the much softer one of chocolate flavored with frangipane enticed him."[45] For this Italian philosopher, author, diplomat, and poet, chocolate was "a holy and noble elixir of fresh life ... embellished with vanilla, orange zest, and drops of distilled jasmine, chocolate 'in *garapegra*' the Italians called it, based on the Spanish term ... iced chocolate."[46]

In 1688 Francesco Redi, court physician to the Grand Duke of Tuscany, sent twelve packets of jasmine-scented chocolate delicacies to Jesuit Father Tommaso Strozzi.[47] In 1689 a similarly precious package was sent from the Florentine palace to Jesuit Father Paolo Antonio Appiani of the Society of Jesus, conveying

> the chocolate that, in your note, you say you desire. It is contained in six packets of six different sorts, of which the amber-scented, the Spanish and the jasmine-flavoured sorts should be the best.[48]

Brillat De Savarin (1755–1826), lawyer and epicure, recalled that Madame d'Arestrel, superior of the Convent of the Visitation at Belley (France), taught him about God's part in chocolate preparation:

> When you want to have good chocolate, have it made the night before in a porcelain pot and leave it. The repose

of the night concentrates it and gives it a velvet quality which improves it greatly. The good God cannot possibly take offence at this little refinement, since he himself is everything that is most perfect.[49]

Clerics were very enamored with the New World chocolate delicacy and debated subtleties of preparation. For instance, Dominicans firmly opposed what they called the abuse of aromatic plants in the chocolate beverage from Mexico. In addition, Francesco Arisi wrote to Alessandro Litta, bishop of Cremona, warning of taking cocoa iced rather than boiling it. Benedictine tradition frowned on fancy sauces, which meant that the bishop of Imola's chef, Alberto Alvisi, did not use chocolate in a mole sauce.[50] By contrast, Ignatius Loyola's followers spread a love of chocolate, "securing a monopoly over its trade and distribution, for the 'greater glory of God and his Society.'"[51]

Such chocolate beatitudes flowed among church leaders from Spain to Italy, who often insisted on good quality chocolate. Jesuit Father Roberti treated himself to a drink of what he called the "Mexican nectar" at his morning meal. He also sought inspiration from a bowl of chocolate when writing. He noted that he once procured a six-pound supply made with a secret cocoa, a gift from Count Jacopo Sanvitali. When he was in Rome, the cardinal of York had some thirty pounds of chocolate delivered to his room. When in Bologna, Father Roberti received author

Early European chocolate depicted in tiles at the Santa Catalina Bakery, Valencia.

Dr. Francesco Zanotti with a large bowl full of chocolate. Roberti details how the toothless, older man first sucked the head of froth from the top of the bowl and then dipped his *savoyard* (ladyfinger). Roberti kept the *chocolatiére* (chocolate pot) boiling and steaming so that he could replenish the bowl immediately.[52]

Church Exploits Cacao

As church chocoholic addictions increased, the economic interests of the church in the growing cacao trade boomed as well. Clergy fanned the business of chocolate along with merchants and aristocrats of the period. Evidence of this chocolate trade is seen in a lawsuit brought against a ship's captain by a Jesuit in Seville for lost containers of his chocolate. Also a shipment of five boxes of cacao and chocolate spices from Father Andrés Gonzáles, rector of the Jesuit house in Veracruz to Rome, was routed in the name of the *procurador* (delegated by the rector to handle business matters) of the Jesuit order in New Spain. Thomas Gage also reported that the church hierarchy worked the chocolate route. In the Indies, clerics adopted the chocolate habit and imported the substance with them when they returned home, carrying "great wealth and gifts to the Generalls," perhaps intending to bribe the popes, cardinals, and nobles in Spain, with "some boxes of curious Chocolate" and other exotica.[53]

Religious orders, particularly Jesuits and Franciscans, were very involved in the cacao business of the New World, notably in Brazil, Paraguay, and Mexico. Between the sixteenth and eighteenth centuries they established many cacao plantations in Brazil. The local peoples were forced off their land to villages called missions, or *reductions*, where the church intended to educate them, work them, and convert them. It also imported black slaves into Brazil to aid in cacao work.[54]

In 1665 it was a Jesuit missionary who brought the first cacao cuttings from the Amazon rainforest to the Bahia and Salvador de Bahia areas of Brazil, both to satisfy the personal desire of the governor general for a reliable chocolate supply and to develop the industry. In 1674 Jesuit João Felipe Bettendorff, SJ, who had administered the Jesuit missions in Pará, traveled by canoe from Pará and transplanted cocoa seeds to Santa Lucia. That went so well that within three years the Jesuit college had more than a thousand cocoa plants. The Jesuits then distributed seeds to the locals for further cultivation. Jesuits experimented with hiring native laborers to gather cacao because they were thought to know how to find the most valuable plants and how to leave the green pods to mature for collection. Expeditions into the jungle often consisted of a mix of this skilled labor and slave labor. By 1749 slaves had systematically planted seven thousand cacao trees in lower Amazonia. This Jesuit involvement with cacao kept Europe well supplied while enhancing revenues.[55] They saw these missions as the "Jesuit Republic,"[56] part of a vision of a great Christian mission state in Brazil. As a Jesuit wrote in 1560, "If there is a paradise here on earth, it is, I would say, this Brazil."[57] Franciscans also anticipated the conversion of the entire world in order to bring about the imminent millennium. While this huge cacao endeavor was initiated and dominated by Christian orders with theological and entrepreneurial motivations, there were priests such as the Jesuit Manoel da Nóbrega in Brazil and the Dominican friar Bartolomé De Las Casas who challenged the enslavements and protested the appropriation of land during the conquest of the Americas.[58]

Similar exploits took place in Mexico, where Jesuits also ran cacao plantations and imported slaves to work on them. Again, Jesuits depended on cacao income to pay their obligations to the mother church and to sustain themselves. A 1693 letter from Jesuit priest Father Alfonso Avirrillaga to the Jesuit Provincial Father Diego de Almonacir described that the college of Chiapas had two cacao plantations, with more than seventy-five thousand trees. A third boasted twenty thousand new cacao trees. It was also equipped with a millstone, enabling processing of the cacao beans. From 1704 to 1707 the annual profit from cacao covered the costs of the college. Similar cacao plantations were located elsewhere in Mexico as well.[59] Through this perverse vision of a paradise on earth embodied in a theocratic state, whether in Brazil or Mexico, these religious orders forcibly converted and enslaved the native peoples to further their cacao revenues.

Chocolate Travels California's El Camino Real

Chocolate provided good road food as the church extended its mission to California, creating the six-hundred-mile mission trail that originated in Baja California Sur, Mexico, and ended in San Francisco. Known as the El Camino Real, or the Royal Road, it connected twenty-one Catholic missions. The excitement about cacao and chocolate journeyed there through Franciscans such as Father Junípero Serra.[60] Some forty-four of Father Serra's many letters mention chocolate, indicating its importance in the daily life of the missions. When Father Serra left Spain for his duties in the New World, he nestled chocolate in his personal belongings. One of Serra's reports about this trip complained that rationed water on the ship did not allow for chocolate drinking. When storms required them to make port at Puerto Rico and the captain reneged on his promise to feed them, a local Christian mission provided sustenance in the form of chocolate: "For eighteen days we ate better than in any convent, all drinking chocolate every day."[61] And then again, when the ship returned to Puerto Rico due to storms, Serra marveled at the chocolate provided by the locals, so much that they were also supplied for the remainder of the journey.[62]

In Mexico City for his first New World position, Serra created a set of administrative guidelines for the College of San Fernando, which included chocolate usage and concerns. His rules cautioned against giving women chocolate at any of the meals in the convent, perhaps to avoid possibilities of seduction or tempting distractions. The chocolate shop (*chocolatería*), at the hostel on church premises held hours from 4:30 in the morning until 3:30 in the afternoon. Later, during a terrible cold spell, while founding the second mission at the Monterey Presidio, Father Serra noted "chocolate that, Thanks God, we were not lacking up to now."[63] Serra sometimes tended to the sick with chocolate allotments and also used it to motivate hard work.[64] Arguing that the port at San Blas needed to stay open for supplies and commerce, Father Serra entreated the viceroy in 1773 "not only for the corn but for the chocolate loads."[65] In addition, mission hospitality to guests was extended through chocolate. When the church determined to turn over supervision of the Baja missions to the Dominicans, Father Serra bemoaned to the padre responsible for the provisions that chocolate supplies were completely diminished at the missions. One of the first records related to chocolate in California may have been composed by Father Visitor Joseph de Echeverría, who sought to acquire chocolate and chocolate equipment, including about ten dozen hand mills. Felipe Barri, governor of Loreto, complained in 1769 that the Franciscans had stolen chocolate. When leaving Loreta to establish the mission at Velicatá, the supplies left behind for the next settlers included chocolate.[65] Chocolate traveled the route of the California missions as it had in other expeditionary ventures of the church.

Our travel trail's treats guided us to this venerable clerical tradition of chocolate. Mark and I learned that faith indeed spread chocolate along routes, leading into new regions of the world, into new religious contexts, and into new appreciation. As Europeans slowly acquired a taste for it, celebratory chocolate enhanced many Christian settings and also unsettled others. Church leaders depended on chocolate for physical, economic, and spiritual sustenance. Catholic chocolate both affirmed and adapted pre-Columbian chocolate. It proved to be much more complicated than Jewish chocolate at this time. Later, Quakers brought new perspectives to chocolate as our chocolate trail progressed into England.

Forgotten Cookies

The chocolate bud, or "kiss," that tops each of these cookies created quite a stir among competing chocolate makers in the late 1800s and early 1900s. To ensure a good result, as our friend Rabbi Marianne Luijken Gevirtz said when sharing this recipe, "Don't peek while the cookies are in the warm oven!"

Ingredients:

2 large egg whites
⅔ cup sugar
1 cup chocolate chips, cocoa nibs, or both
1 cup pecans, coarsely chopped
Pinch of salt (optional)
1 teaspoon vanilla extract
30–40 chocolate buds or kisses

Instructions:

Preheat the oven to 350°F. Line two or three baking sheets with parchment paper or aluminum foil. Beat the egg whites until foamy. Gradually add the sugar and beat until stiff. Gently fold in the chocolate chips and/or cocoa nibs, and nuts. Add the salt and vanilla. Drop teaspoonfuls onto the prepared baking sheets. Cap each cookie with a chocolate bud or kiss. Place the pans in the oven; after about 1 minute turn off the heat. Leave in the oven for several hours or overnight. Carefully peel the cookies off the paper or foil using a spatula.

Quantity: About 35 cookies

Chapter Nine

Utopian Chocolate Saved Souls

From Cadbury to Hershey

OUR QUEST FOR JEWISH AND RELIGIOUS CONNECTIONS to chocolate had us traveling to London and then another 262 miles north to the beautiful, rain-soaked town of Kendal. We were excited to pursue the description we read online about "our 1657 chocolate house, ... discover the delights of chocolate in all its different forms." When we finally arrived, we learned that while the building dates back to 1657, it had no chocolate until very recently. That was not the way it had seemed on the website. The words from Gilbert and Sullivan's comic opera *HMS Pinafore*, "Things are seldom what they seem," began to echo in our heads as we traveled a circuit of England's chocolate in Oxford, Birmingham, and the York Lake District. In Oxford, we paid homage to the site of possibly the first chocolate in England, the Grand Café. Birmingham's Cadbury, and York's Rowntree's and Fry's seethed with Quaker chocolate.

A curious blend of chocolate informed by Quaker religious utopianism, industrial paternalism, and clever tourism all folded together in the British chocolate companies of Fry's, Rowntree's, Cadbury, and later in the American Hershey Company. In the eighteenth and nineteenth centuries, the then novel chocolate

Chocolate House in Kendal dates back to 1657 but only recently started selling chocolate.

business offered Quakers tempting new opportunities at a time when the government of England excluded Quakers from university, prohibited their entrance into the medical, legal, or other professions, and precluded them from apprenticeships and partnerships. Pacifist Quaker views eliminated military service as a career option. Quaker support of the Temperance Movement melded well with chocolate drinking as an alternative to alcohol. The success of such Quaker chocolate businesses benefited workers and their communities. Industrial advances in chocolate-making equipment, plus improved distribution via Britain's railroad system, afforded a perfect cauldron for companies with high ideals.[1] No doubt Quaker religion influenced the British chocolate businesses, which in turn inspired Milton Hershey.

Quaker Apothecary Fry Sells Chocolate: 1759

Quaker Joseph Fry started selling drinking chocolate in Bristol in 1759. His grandfather, Zephaniah, was an early and devoted follower of George Fox, the founder of the Religious Society of Friends, the Quaker movement. As an apothecary, Fry had disguised bitter-tasting medications in chocolate. He advanced the new chocolate industry in advertisements that read, "The best sorts of chocolates made and sold wholesale and retail by Joseph Fry, Apothecary, in Small Street Bristol."[2] Using newly developing factory systems, Fry's began selling "eating chocolate," or *Chocolat Délicieux à Manger*, in 1847.[3] This may have been the first widely available eating chocolate in England. Fry's became the largest manufacturer of chocolate in the world of its time, having acquired the right to supply chocolate and cocoa to the Royal Navy. Though Quakers do not observe Easter, Fry's saw a business opportunity in producing the first chocolate Easter egg in the United Kingdom in 1873. Having survived for 150 years, Fry's was bought by another Quaker-owned chocolate company, Cadbury, in 1919.[4]

John Cadbury Opens Coffee and Tea Shop: 1824

Cadbury's story begins long before any merger with Fry's. Twenty-two-year-old Quaker John Cadbury opened a coffee and tea shop in 1824 in Birmingham, where he proudly also sold cocoa: "John Cadbury is desirous of introducing to particular notice 'Cocoa Nibs' prepared by himself, an article affording a most nutritious beverage for breakfast."[5] In 1853, Cadbury obtained the royal privilege to supply chocolate to Queen Victoria. Cadbury imported cutting-edge Van Houten equipment from Holland in order to make its successful "Cocoa Essence," producing a higher-quality cocoa than had been previously available in England. John's son, Richard Cadbury, developed the first Valentine candy box, though Quakers were not observers of Valentine's Day. Between 1893 and 1899, the business grew dramatically, and the Cadbury workforce bulged from 800 to 2,600.

A hot chocolate at the site of the first coffee house in Oxford, England, opened by Jacob the Jew in the mid-seventeenth century.

The Cadbury family's deep religious belief in responsibility for others led them to ameliorate dangerous and unsanitary factory conditions and workers' slum housing. Influenced by contemporary writings about garden cities and labor reform, Cadbury implemented innovative benefits to workers such as granting a half-day off on Saturdays, closing completely on legal holidays, and providing medical and dental care at the factory. Eventually the workweek was reduced to forty-eight hours and savings accounts were provided, with an initial deposit by Cadbury. In 1866, daily Bible readings created a wholesome and proper atmosphere. Revivalist hymns were introduced into the daily routine a few years later.[6] Other factory amenities included heated dressing rooms, kitchens for warm meals, gender-separate gardens, sports facilities, and swimming pools. Women workers who married were dismissed from their jobs to raise their families but received flowers and a Bible.

Beginning in 1895, Cadbury developed a model town in Bournville, which was near the factory, partly to assist employees and also to prevent developers from accessing the land. With the first homes designated for the highest-ranked employees, Cadbury added cottages with gardens for workers and others. The town was open to people of all faiths yet informed by Quaker values, so alcohol was prohibited. Cadbury built an almshouse for retired employees in 1897. Members of the Cadbury family, especially George and George Jr., were interested in education and taught in the adult school movement.[7] Young employees were dismissed early for required night school. Visiting Bournville in 1933, novelist J. B. Priestley wrote about the Cadbury family that they

> have of course long been in the class of the school of the benevolent and paternal employers.... Here in a factory run for private profit are nearly all the facilities for leading a full and happy life.[8]

Cadbury and Hershey

In seemingly surprising ways, the Hershey and Cadbury companies paralleled their business approaches, religious backgrounds, and historical roots. Milton Hershey modeled aspects of his business after Cadbury when he started out. Today, in turn, the Hershey Company holds the license for manufacturing some Cadbury chocolate products in the United States. Hershey almost bought Cadbury in 2010.

George Cadbury also exhibited a special warmth for children. At bedtime on Sunday nights, he routinely visited the youngsters hospitalized at the Birmingham Cripples Union, bearing a large box of chocolates with each visit. Following World War I he took an interest in the children of Vienna, inviting some of the refugees to Bournville. Vienna's *Neue Freie Presse* called him the "Chocolate Uncle" after he sent three tons of chocolate for the Viennese waifs recovering from the stresses of war.[9] As he said, "If you can show that your life is happier by giving ... you will do more good than by preaching about it."[10] As we learned in chapter 5, the moniker "Chocolate Uncle" carried over to World War II.

In these personal and corporate actions, Cadbury reflected savvy business instincts and enlightened progressive reforms. Cadbury merged with Schweppes beverage brand in 1969, demerged in 2008, and was acquired by Kraft Foods in 2010.

Religious Rowntree Family Ventures into Chocolate: 1862

As with Fry's and Cadbury, Quakerism formed a primary ingredient in Rowntree's chocolate. In 1862, Quaker Henry Isaac Rowntree purchased the Tukes' cocoa and chocolate business (founded in 1725) and was joined by his brother Joseph in 1869 in York. Mary Tuke's grandfather had been one of four thousand people jailed for their Quaker beliefs in the 1660s. The Rowntrees grew up with Bible readings after breakfast, the required memorization of a Bible verse each day, regular Society of Friends meetings at their home, openness of inquiry, and tolerance of difference at the Friends school. It was a very orderly household, with father Joseph Rowntree issuing memos about mealtimes, behavior rules, and meeting attendance. Joseph Rowntree Jr. also engaged in good works, such as tracking statistics on poverty, writing five books about temperance, and teaching adult school every Sunday morning until he was sixty years old.[11]

The Rowntree Company also extended generous benefits to its workers, including a domestic school for young women, a widow's benefit fund, and the company village with housing

in New Earswick, near North Yorkshire, England. Joseph Rowntree's other son, Benjamin Seebohm Rowntree, conducted his own study of York's poor in 1899. Women workers who married were given a tray and a Rowntree's plaque. In 1906 the company board started a pension plan and later built gyms and schoolrooms, with compulsory classes for the youngest workers. The Joseph Rowntree Charitable Trust and Joseph Rowntree Social Services Trust were established in 1904. Veterans of World War I were given jobs, even if they could not fully accomplish the work.[12]

We found this Rowntree's Cocoa tin in Jerusalem bearing a Hebrew sales sticker.

The Rowntree's confectionery industry contributed much to the town of York as a source of employment and also as a model of social responsibility. Nestlé purchased the company in 1988.

Hershey Discovers Chocolate: 1894

Milton Hershey started his chocolate company in the Quaker state of Pennsylvania, sensing that his successful caramel company seemed to be declining and that chocolate would become more popular. His maternal grandfather was a bishop of the Reformed Mennonite Church (Anabaptist). Throughout her lifetime, his mother wore the traditional Mennonite fitted gray dress, white prayer cap, and black bonnet. However, Milton did not take to formal religion. When he was once asked about his religion, he said, "The Golden Rule."[13]

Visiting the World's Columbian Exposition of 1893 in Chicago, Hershey was taken with the several chocolate exhibits, especially with the chocolate-making machinery displayed by J. M. Lehmann Company of Dresden, Germany. Right there he bought the equipment and had it shipped by train to Lancaster, Pennsylvania. He immediately hired chocolate makers from Baker's in Massachusetts.[14] To learn more about the business, he traveled to England to visit Cadbury, Rowntree's, and Fry's and chocolate makers in other European countries as well. He presciently told his cousin that he intended to concentrate more and more on making chocolate, anticipating it to be a more substantial business in the long run. In the early years Baker's and Ghirardelli of San Francisco, the second oldest chocolate company in the United States, understandably sold much more chocolate than he did. However, the earnings from the first full year of Hershey's chocolate operations (1905–6) topped one million dollars. The challenge of creating a milk chocolate had been accomplished by Daniel Peter and Henri Nestlé in Switzerland in 1875. Hershey experimented with his own formula for milk chocolate in the 1890s. While he visited several European chocolate makers in Britain, Germany, Switzerland, and France, Hershey made a decision not to make milk chocolate the way they did. By the turn of the century, he had 114 different chocolate products. Less than a century

A chocolate set, including a chocolate pot and stirrers, displayed at the Fairfax House in York, England.

later, the 1964 World's Fair in New York featured the Hershey Company's own separate pavilion, the third largest at the fair.[15]

The Quaker chocolate companies Hershey had visited in England, as well his own background, inspired the way he molded his philanthropic efforts. He donated generously to his wife Kitty's Catholic church and to each of the other local churches in town. Factory profits were shared with the community through the development of the town of Hershey, Pennsylvania.[16] Hershey rejected the first "cookie-cutter houses" for the town built by his friend, Harry Lebkicher, desiring them to be more individualized. The amenities included indoor plumbing and electricity. The town provided a bank, a department store, new schools, entertainment, a subsidized trolley, and ultimately a community theater featuring Broadway shows. Monroe Stover recalled moving to Hershey in 1911, where his family rented a house with indoor plumbing and electricity on Areba Avenue, paying only fifteen dollars a month for rent:

> It was a small house for the nine of us but it was our first modern home and I'll never forget it. Moving to Hershey was like moving to paradise.... Everybody kept chocolate in their cupboards.[17]

Not surprisingly the press called Milton Hershey the "Chocolate Man," describing him as a good-hearted soul. He and Kitty founded the Hershey Industrial School for poor, male orphans. As he put it, "What good is one's money unless one uses it for the good of the community and humanity in general."[18] The boys were given clothes, one hundred dollars, and help finding a job at graduation or a full scholarship to college. Sunday school attendance was required. Childless, after Kitty's early death, Hershey in 1918 transferred all of his assets and his Hershey Chocolate Company stock—essentially all of the Hershey enterprise—to the school. Several Hershey executives graduated from the school, including William Dearden, CEO and chairman of the board in the 1970s. During the Great

Depression, the Hershey enterprise mounted a tremendous building project that continued to enlarge the town and also generated jobs for the community. Thus Milton Hershey's company and town prospered, unaffected by the devastating desperation elsewhere. In 1938 the Hershey Foundation endowed the short-lived Hershey Junior College, offering tuition-free higher education to all Derry Township residents (Derry Township being the governing municipality of Hershey) and all employees of the Hershey corporations.[19]

Chocolate Business: Not All It Seems to Be

Hershey, Cadbury, and the other chocolate moguls inspired by high ideals admirably sought to combat the terrible working conditions, poverty, illiteracy, and other social ills of their time. However, a closer look at these utopian chocolate companies reveals some "bloom" (discoloration) on the chocolate bar concerning ingredients, business practices, and shockingly, chocolate produced by child and slave labor. Despite the virtuous intentions of their business practices, these good people stumbled.

Adulteration of cocoa ingredients was pervasive in the nineteenth century. Cadbury and Fry's each admitted to adding impurities such as starch and flour and then launched intense advertising campaigns claiming the purity of their respective products. Cadbury put Fry's on the defensive, so that by 1897, Fry's had been vastly diminished in the thirty-year contest between the two companies over this issue. These companies also fought over claims about the production of the first chocolate Easter eggs. Fry's grabbed that distinction in 1873; Cadbury's website states that it brought out the first chocolate Easter egg in 1905.

Such adulteration is not a thing of the past. Just a few years ago British companies, Cadbury in particular, fought to gain acceptance of the use of less expensive cocoa butter substitutes such as dairy butter or vegetable oils (cocoa butter equivalents,

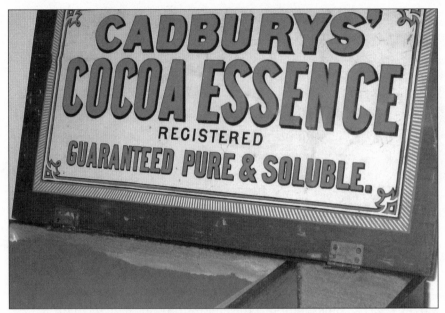

Accusations of adulterated cocoa flew between Fry's and Cadbury.

or CBEs) in eating chocolate. This reduced the price but also affected quality and taste. Due to the advocacy of Cadbury and others, the European Court of Justice in Luxembourg ultimately settled that thirty-year controversy, determining that candy companies could diminish the amount of chocolate content by up to 5 percent yet still label it chocolate.[20] Consumers should check the packaging of those European chocolates to make sure that the chocolate is really what it seems to be (see chapter 10).

In America, Hershey was not above shenanigans in business. Milton Hershey spied on Baker's company to learn more about chocolate-processing techniques in 1900. He was sued in 1905 for copying the packaging of Daniel Peter of Europe. He initially marketed a knockoff of Baker's Bittersweet to gain a foothold in that market. Moreover, his town of Hershey was motivated not only by altruism but also to generate revenue for the company. This may explain the lack of a mayor and city council there.[21]

Mark and I sniffed out some suspicions about the vastly popular Hershey's Kisses on our visit to Pennsylvania. The town of Lititz hosts a lovely chocolate café plus a museum at the Wilbur Chocolate Factory, replete with a beautiful collection of porcelain chocolate pots. The Wilbur Chocolate Company was founded in 1865 by Henry Oscar Wilbur and Samuel Croft and was purchased by Cargill in 1992. Browsing the Wilbur chocolate treats at the museum, we noticed that at least ten years prior to Hershey's introduction of the chocolate "kiss," Wilbur had been making "Wilbur Buds." These small, conical-shaped chocolate drops, initially available only in dark chocolate when first introduced in 1894, were individually foil wrapped. It turns out that at the time a number of companies were making candy kisses in varied flavors. However, very few of these kisses, if any, were made from chocolate. The bottom of the Wilbur Bud was molded into a flower with the letters "Wilbur" in each petal. Hershey introduced his "Milk-Maid Chocolate Kiss" in 1907, with a flat, undecorated bottom, making its manufacture less expensive than that of Wilbur Buds. As the chocolate turns, in 1906 Wilbur trademarked its name of "Bud" and went to court in 1909 to stop several imitators. With time, Hershey sought to secure its Kisses from encroachment through advertisements such as

These Wilbur Buds, with their floral decorations, were made in Lititz, Pennsylvania, about ten years prior to the Hershey Kiss.

"Insist upon having the 'Genuine' Sweet Milk Chocolate Hershey's KISSES. Be Sure They Contain the Identification Tag 'Hershey's.'" The Italian Perugina chocolate company developed a kiss with epigrams inside the wrappers in 1922.

Only in 2001 could Hershey gain the trademark on "Kiss," given the prior attitude of the trademark examiners that it was a general term. Today eighty million Kisses, in multiple flavors and combinations, roll off the lines from at least two factories daily, while Wilbur Buds may only be bought online or in Lititz, the original Wilbur Bud having been far surpassed by the Kiss.[22]

Cadbury's False Utopia: Slave Labor

Even worse than these commercial thefts and deceptions, cacao grown through slave and child labor cracked apart some of those Quaker principles. The Cadbury family had contributed to the British anti-slavery movement since at least 1893. Family members also subscribed to *The Reporter*, the publication of the Anti-Slavery Society.[23] Company founder George Cadbury belonged to the Aborigine's Protection Society from approximately 1900 to 1908.[24] In 1901 William Cadbury was told about the slave labor in cacao plantations in the West African island of São Tomé, which then supplied about half of the cacao beans used by Fry's and Cadbury. Those cacao harvests, some said, generated wealth comparable to that of the California Gold Rush.[25] Before beginning his journalistic investigations into the slave sources of chocolate in 1904, author Henry Woodd Nevinson contacted Cadbury company leaders to work with them in their research. They assured him they would run their own investigation. Nevinson offered to represent Cadbury in these inquiries, but its representatives wanted him to learn Portuguese first. They then selected Quaker Joseph Burtt to travel to São Tomé and to report to them about his findings. Before the journey, Burtt spent close to a year studying Portuguese.[26] Around the time that Burtt finally arrived in Africa in 1905, Nevinson was already publishing his exposé about cacao slavery in a series of articles for *Harper's Monthly Magazine* from 1905 through 1906. In 1906 it was published as a book titled *A Modern Slavery*. As Nevinson noted, slavery meant that England and America accessed chocolate and cocoa cheaply.[27] Overall, the Fry's/Cadbury/Rowntree's investigative process took almost a decade. Burtt's report, finally published in 1907, corroborated the Nevinson findings. Burtt concluded:

> Thousands of black men and women are, against their will and often under circumstances of great cruelty, taken away every year from their homes and transported across the sea to work on unhealthy islands, from which they never return. If this is not slavery, I know of no word in the English language which correctly characterizes it.[28]

Only after a number of years, the exposé, and a lawsuit did Cadbury finally boycott Portuguese cacao.

Cadbury and the other giant reformer chocolatiers poured much good into their communities and their workers over the years. They represent a significant stage of the chocolate trail. However, the combined ingredients of the theft of the concept of Wilbur's chocolate Wilbur Buds, the use of cocoa butter substitutes in some British chocolates, the history of earlier adulterations, topped off with serious human rights violations in chocolate sourced from slave labor, leave a slightly sour aftertaste. Sadly, though well intentioned and at times very progressive, this utopian-inclined chocolate was not all it seemed.

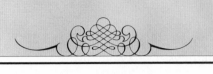

Cayenne Kicks

Hiker Steve Rock created these healthy chunks/balls and cautions that they will "kick you down the trail a bit." As they energize you for your day, they might also awaken your conscience to the best values to use when buying chocolate.

Ingredients:

1 pound dark chocolate, chips or broken into pieces
1 cup peanuts
½ cup raisins, dates, or other dried fruit
⅛ cup coffee beans
2 teaspoons cayenne pepper, to taste
½ cup unsweetened cocoa powder
Granola, dry cereal, or oatmeal (optional)

Instructions:

Line a large baking sheet with parchment paper, aluminum foil, or waxed paper. Melt the chocolate in a large heatproof bowl set over a pan of simmering water; remove from the heat. In a food processor with the chop blade, combine the peanuts, raisins, coffee beans, and cayenne. Pulse until coarsely chopped. Stir the cocoa into the melted chocolate. Once the mixture is even and getting stiff, add the chopped nuts and fruits; keep stirring. Taste to check the spice level.

If the mixture is too moist and sticky, add more nuts, granola, or chopped cereal, or wait until firm enough to handle. (Cooling in the refrigerator will firm the mixture faster.) Roll the mixture into balls and place on the prepared baking sheet. Cool completely. Remove from the baking sheet and store in a covered container.

Quantity: Approximately 20 chunks

Chapter Ten

Shopping for the Best Chocolate

Values and Ethics

It hurt my heart deeply to think about it.... They enjoy something I suffered to make. I worked hard for them but saw no benefit. They are eating my flesh.[1]

THESE WORDS OF A YOUNG MAN RESCUED FROM slavery on an Ivory Coast cocoa plantation reveal the sinister side of chocolate growing and production. From its very first discovery by Europeans up until today,[2] chocolate stirs up the basic ethics and values that support our spiritual and religious lives. The cocoa industry's transgressions—and perhaps ours, knowingly or unknowingly—result in bitter lives for individual laborers, in impoverished chocolate-growing populations, and in threats to the sustainability of the earth. People often ask me my opinion of the best chocolate. I suggest that the best chocolate derives from companies that seek to correct these transgressions through their business practices and from informed consumer purchases that satisfy our chocolate cravings as well as our human and religious values. There are other considerations as well, though none as profound as this.

147

The Cocoa Industry: Not Faring Well with Fair Labor

Demand for chocolate creates a great disconnect between the standard of living of most growers of cocoa beans and that of the manufacturers and consumers of these luxury products. Today's chocolate industry often obscures the tragic psychological and physical danger endured by children who grow and harvest the cocoa beans needed to satiate the developed world's chocolate addictions. The complexities of chocolate ethics both reflect and surpass the challenges of tea and coffee. While coffee and tea farmers do consume some form of those beverages in their own cultures, many subsistence cocoa bean growers have never tasted that final treat of chocolate.[3]

The wrongs perpetrated to produce chocolate began with its very discovery by Europeans. Cocoa beans were colonial extract products appropriated by Europeans through the conquests of Columbus and Cortés. Timothy Walker, writing about slave labor and chocolate in Portuguese-dominated Brazil, noted:

> Prior to the 1880's ... at every stage of Brazilian cacao production, coerced human labor played a role in the gathering and processing of this valuable commodity ... [which] included indigenous peoples, coerced work of free blacks, mixed race laborers and European convicts forced to emigrate to Brazil.[4]

Ironically, at about the same time that Cadbury created a utopian community for its workers in Bournville, it was embroiled in a controversy about purchasing cocoa beans from slave labor plantations in São Tomé and Príncipe[5] (see chapter 9). Novelist Jorge Amado captures the shame of the Brazilian cacao business:

> For cacao was money, cacao was power, cacao was the whole of life; it was not merely something planted in the black and sap-giving earth: it was inside themselves.

Growing within them, it cast over every heart a malignant shade, slaying all good impulses.[6]

Chocolate makers in colonial empires such as Holland, Belgium, and Germany reflected in their products both the exoticism of their black colonies and a repulsion of the indigenous populations. This may still be seen in the names of some European dainties. Chocolate-covered mounds of marshmallow are known as *mohrenköpfe* (Moor's head) in German-speaking Switzerland; in France, *negerküsse* (Negro kisses); and in Denmark,

negerbolle (Negro bun) or *negerkys* (Negro kiss). Today, we know them as Mallomars in the States and as Krembo in Israel. Powers such as Belgium, Holland, and Germany noted the blackness of chocolate to emphasize the conquest of natives in their colonial empires.[7]

Classic chocolate-covered marshmallows named Moor's king recall the colonial empire roots of European chocolate traditions.

Today, money and profit tempt farmers and producers into the child labor and child slavery market. Growers in places such as the Ivory Coast and Ghana claim that the low prices of cacao require labor of their own or enslaved children. The Ivory Coast law that workers must be at least eighteen is rarely enforced. Some twelve thousand children from Mali have been kidnapped from their families or sometimes sold by family members to work in the Ivory Coast or Ghana. They are not paid for dangerous work with machetes and are not allowed any personal possessions. They are imprisoned at night, denied schooling, forced to work long hours, and left with untreated wounds after beatings. Leaders of a Mali human rights association estimate that child slaves are found on at least 90 percent of the Ivory Coast cocoa plantations. Over half of the world's

chocolate may be defiled by the cruel treatment of children.[8]
This shame should melt away.

The 2005 Harkin-Engel Protocol, also known as the Cocoa
Protocol, written by Senator Tom Harkin (D-IA) and Repre-
sentative Eliot Engel (D-NY), sought to provide certification
to eliminate the worst forms of child labor. Eight chocolate
multinationals have signed on to the protocol, including Guit-
tard, Nestlé, Hershey, M&M/Mars, and Callebaut. However,
the protocol has not been fully implemented, and the initial
deadline has passed. Companies such as Cadbury, Hershey,
and Godiva "bulk" their beans, meaning that they buy from
middlemen and cannot accurately identify how much, if any,
originates in Ghana or the Ivory Coast, where child slave labor
is most prevalent. When cocoa comes from West Africa, and
about 80 percent of the world's supply does, then it is likely
that the bulked cocoa used by several major international
chocolate conglomerates uses child labor/slavery chocolate.
Mars has announced that it intends to certify its products as
fair trade by 2020.[9]

Some companies have attempted to ameliorate the harsh
realities of child slave labor by other means. Cadbury, for
instance, offers Green & Black's, its line of organic and fair trade
chocolate, along with other well-meaning initiatives. Indeed,
Green & Black's Maya Gold was the first product to go fair
trade in the United Kingdom in 1994. Through efforts such as its
"Cocoa Partnership," Cadbury donated five thousand bicycles
and over two and a half tons of books to the people of Ghana.
These symbolic gestures, along with its single line of fair trade
Dairy Milk bars,[10] may obscure darker chocolate ethics.

In order to provide fair compensation to cocoa farmers,
several fair trade systems seek to establish a minimum price
above market value. Chocolate producers such as Theo, Shaman, Divine, Zotter, and Dagoba claim fair trade credentials.
Massachusetts worker-owned co-op Equal Exchange sells fair
trade and organic coffee, tea, and chocolate, trading directly

with democratically organized small-farmer cooperatives, paying a guaranteed minimum price, and supporting sustainable farming practices.

These agreements establish criteria and standards for payment with the aim of providing increased gain to farmers. However, some analysts as well as chocolatiers question the success of these options, in part because fair trade chocolate makes up just about 1 percent of the global supply. Only one of these companies, Divine, is farmer owned. Several chocolate makers prefer to sidestep the costs of formal fair trade recognition, claiming that their farmers benefit more from their direct contact and superior financial arrangements.

There are continued efforts to bring attention to these issues. Almost sixty chocolate companies, social justice organizations, faith-based groups, labor unions, citizens, consumers, investors, and retailers signed the Commitment to Ethical Cocoa Sourcing (CECS): Abolishing Unfair Labor Practices and Addressing Their Root Causes. The pledge encourages the chocolate industry to embrace a more ethical cocoa supply chain by providing transparency starting at the farm level; committing to sourcing exclusively from farms and cooperatives that respect these core labor standards; paying farmers a fair and adequate price for the cocoa they purchase; implementing or maintaining structural practices so as to ensure farmers a consistently better price; supporting the drafting and enforcement of national and international laws that prohibit human trafficking, debt bondage, and the other worst forms of child labor; and committing to 100 percent fair trade–certified sourcing of cocoa or to financing the rehabilitation, reintegration, and education of children who have been exploited in cocoa agriculture, both in the growing countries and in the labor-exporting countries. Among the signers are Labor-Religion Coalition of New York State and the Unitarian Universalist Service Committee. The United Church of Christ and the United Methodist Committee on Relief also advocate for fair trade practices and purchases. Jewish tradition teaches of the value of fair wages and equitable treatment of laborers in an idea known as *oshek*.

I thought about this when one day a distinctive brown package arrived in my mailbox, as company owner and founder Shawn Askinosie had promised. Askinosie Chocolate exemplifies religious ethics permeating a chocolate business and the goals of the CECS. Cellophane swaddled a small "Noshie Bar," a crunchy, roasted cocoa nib–shortbread, topped with homemade caramel, flavored with a touch of salt, and coated in dark chocolate. The Yiddish-inspired name for the bar, from *nosh*, meaning "a bite" or "a snack," hints at the Jewish family background for Askinosie's chocolate endeavor.

As Shawn proudly explained, the Askinosie name links to Genesis 10:3 of the story of Noah, which became connected with Ashkenazi Jews, that is, those descended from Central and Western Europe. This, though Shawn's father had converted from Judaism to Christianity, raising Shawn in the Charismatic Episcopal Church, which teaches that the Holy Spirit may be available to contemporary Christians and manifest in signs, miracles, and wonders. Fourteen-year-old Shawn struggled with faith when his father became ill and died from lung cancer. Ultimately Shawn, like his father, became a criminal defense lawyer, winning high-profile cases featured in the national media. After working two first-degree murder cases back-to-back in 1999, he needed a break. Around that time he also started baking, considering a career in the cupcake industry. He experimented with high-quality chocolate. He

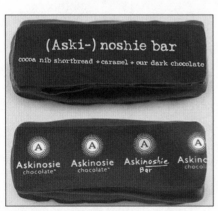

Noshie Bar: The name of this confection plays on the company name Askinosie and the Yiddish for snack, *nosh*.

prayed on it. Later that summer Shawn studied chocolate's secrets and intricacies in the Amazon and became reconciled to God as a Christian.

> God gave me this idea not so that my chocolate would be God's gift to the world or that it would be financially successful, but rather an undeserved gift to me to have another chance to try something different. In faith I went about trying to do that. [I often] pray for the wisdom to do the right thing, find the right people, close the right doors, listen carefully.[11]

Shawn runs his chocolate business in Missouri and gives back 10 percent of the earnings to his farmers in Mexico and Ecuador to enable them to participate in his business philosophy: "a stake in the outcome," based on the advice laid out in the management classic by Jack Stack and Bo Burlingham that promotes a new culture of ownership. Shawn knows the names of his farmers, thanks them directly, makes arrangements in person, and perhaps most importantly, introduces them to actual chocolate, which many of them have never seen or tasted. Shawn's religion-infused chocolate supports Askinosie's Chocolate University, a charitable endeavor from income derived from tours of the factory. Askinosie's partnership programs with Drury University, three local schools, and Missouri Hotel (Springfield's largest homeless shelter) all benefit the neighborhood, children, and his farmers. In doing so, he seeks to increase the quality of the cocoa bean and also improve the lives of the farmers.[12] The flavor of Askinosie's Jewish roots and his faith-based values permeate his products.

Taza Chocolate, based in Somerville, Massachusetts, also labels itself "ethically traded," meaning that it incentivizes quality, visits farmers at least once a year to inspect workplace standards, and conducts its business with each farmer transparently and publicly. It is also certified pareve—that is, prepared without milk, meat, or their derivatives—by the Orthodox

Union. Kallari Chocolate, with a U.S. office in Secaucus, New Jersey, takes another approach. Its cooperative of some 850 farmers in Ecuador reaps 100 percent profit from chocolate grown and processed there. This business plan, based on local and organic production, yields four times the income for the farmers. The Bolivian company El Ceibo aids the growers as well. Following yet a different formula, British Columbia's Terra Nostra's equitable trade label claims to go beyond fair trade by running a cooperative that collects and invests member fees for site-specific development efforts that "enhance and nurture vibrant, healthy communities and the ecosystems from which these traded materials are derived."[13]

While such fair trade and other certification systems assist the cocoa farmers, they cannot fully guarantee that these products are free of child labor or slave labor of children, as documented in recent reports. To avoid eating chocolate spoiled by corrupt, bulked beans from West Africa, a discerning chocolate lover might prefer to purchase bars of single-origin beans. However, sometimes even those single-origin products may include beans sourced from Africa, since the European Union requires that only 10 percent of the bar be from the origin, and the United States currently has no controls in this regard.[14] Lobbying for the full implementation of the standards sought by Harkin-Engel would help eliminate the crime of child slavery, as would protests directed at the relevant purveyors.

Kosher Chocolate: Looking Beyond the Seal

While unethically produced chocolate may be of greatest concern, other religious values may inform our chocolate diet as well. For example, conglomerates such as Hershey and Godiva adhere to Jewish dietary laws in some products. Kosher certification (*hechsher*) does not guarantee ethical standards, though some newer Jewish approaches look at worker justice and protection of animals. Generally, the seal certifies that the chocolate has not been contaminated with pork products, shellfish, or their derivatives and identifies whether the chocolate may be eaten with dairy meals or meat meals. I have been told by some smaller, artisanal chocolate purveyors that they would prefer to be certified but cannot afford it. A few chocolate companies generously demonstrate their dedication to social service by folding their earnings into good works to assist farmer communities. A Brooklyn company, Rescue Chocolate, supports rescue dogs by selling kosher-for-Passover chocolate in the shape of matzah called "Don't Passover Me Bark."

Adherence to religious values is not always as obvious as a printed seal of approval. The organic, fair trade–certified company Shaman claims that its chocolate sales support the Huichol Indians of the Sierra Madre mountains of Mexico. This enables the Huichol to keep their traditions alive, including their "healing and transformational shamanism." These and other admirable projects may delight our sweet tooth while alleviating our guilt about the great income gap between chocolate grower and consumer. However, supporting shamanism raises Jewish questions related to pagan worship. Therefore, this particular endeavor may not be appropriate for Jews.

Becoming Green Chocolate

Caring for creation is an ethical value for many faith traditions that can also be practiced through chocolate choices. For instance, Jewish ideas about not wasting that which has potential for future use resonate when considering recycling and sustainability in connection with chocolate. Original Beans, a chocolate and conservation company, commits to "restoring our planet's most valuable forests" with conservation training programs and buffer zones protecting old-growth rainforests. The use of fossil fuels in production is offset through monitored reforestation programs. Enter the lot number of your chocolate bar in order to see the trees planted in response to a particular batch of chocolate. Hershey's subsidiary Dagoba markets its chocolate as "good for people and for the planet" with its

Camel's Milk in My Chocolate?

Through the years of trekking along the chocolate trail—at many chocolate shows, festivals, and boutiques in several countries— I had perfected my rhythm of tasting and to avoid piggishness, when sated, dropped chocolate into my handy bag. At one New York Chocolate Show, I pursued the trail using that refined hand-to-mouth or hand-to-bag chocolate sampling. For the first time, however, I stopped short, arm poised, as my internal electric fence activated, just in time to avoid eating a piece of chocolate-covered bacon, forbidden to me because it is not kosher, from a huge pile on a display tray.

Turning away from the pig while trying not to appear to be one, I found myself at the Al Nassma chocolate booth. This brand claims to be the "first and finest camel milk chocolate made in Dubai." That may explain why Al Nassma had run out of samples.

The company was founded in 2009 by Dubai's ruler, Sheikh Mohammed bin Rashid al-Maktoum. With a flock of three thousand camels, it aims to produce one hundred tons of premium chocolate a year, according to the New York Daily News. The company touts that its chocolates are produced without preservatives or chemical additives and feature a variety of Middle Eastern spices, nuts, and honey. Purportedly camel's milk has health benefits over cow's milk—less fat, more vitamin C, for example—and it allows people allergic to cow's milk to enjoy even the milkiest of milk chocolates.

After a long search, Mark and I eventually found Al Nassma chocolate for sale at the American Museum of Natural History's exhibit "On the Silk Route." We hesitated just for a second when we saw the very pricey twelve-dollar label—it was expensive, especially since we didn't intend to eat it; like bacon, camel's milk is also not kosher. Of course we bought it and it still sits in my cupboard.

commitment to "Full Circle Sustainability," which seeks a positive change in "ecology, equity, community and quality." Its projects include reforesting Costa Rica's Upala Cacao Cooperative with thousands of seedlings and underwriting green space in several cities.

Certainly using recycled paper and low-impact inks in packaging, developing green factories, and implementing low-energy practices such as those claimed by some chocolatiers would be valuable. Companies such as Taza, Original Beans, Askinosie, Dagoba, and Honolulu's Malie Kai package with recycled materials. Taza and Askinosie also recycle cocoa shells into mulch. While organic, sustainable chocolate is not always packaged in recycled wrappers, the two do go together for Indianapolis-based Endangered Species Chocolate—fair trade, organic, kosher, and certified as a leader in energy and environmental design. This company donates 10 percent of its net receipts to protect endangered animals, habitats, and people. Organic authentication supports the resources of the rainforest, as does rainforest documentation.

Some cocoa companies boast rainforest designations such as that provided by Rainforest Alliance, which seeks to conserve the forest canopy in growing cacao, protects wildlife, and works toward sustainability. Between 2007 and 2009 these certifications doubled. Plantations Arriba Chocolate first carried the seal, joined by Newman's Own and others. Mars and Kraft have partnered with the Rainforest Alliance to train farmers in the Ivory Coast and Ghana about the standards. Chicago's Blommer Chocolate Company as well as Mars and Kraft have developed rainforest benchmarks for some of their chocolate lines.[15]

Processing the Local Angle

While such initiatives as organic farming, recycled packaging, reforestation, rainforest accreditation, and fair trade certifications apply to tea and coffee as well, additional sustainability issues foam up around chocolate. Coffee, tea, and chocolate challenge the popular admonition to eat unprocessed, local, fresh foods from the perimeters of the grocery store. Further, while coffee and tea require some minor modification of the plant product through roasting of the natural coffee bean or drying of the tea leaf, solid chocolate as we know it, love it, and devour it today requires intense processing. Chocolate customers living in the cooler, wealthier Northern Hemisphere import cocoa beans out of their equatorial habitat and transport them long distances, often by boat. The end product requires multiple energy-sapping steps, including fermenting, drying, roasting, winnowing, grinding, conching, and tempering. Only then is chocolate shipped to the retailer.

Given the intense usage of energy in most chocolate preparation, Taza's minimal stone grinding based on techniques from Mexico may make sense. Rather than importing chocolate from Belgium, France, Switzerland, or other distant countries, sourcing beans from Central or South America and processing them in the United States may diminish chocolate's carbon footprint. Buying chocolate from cocoa beans grown and processed in Hawaii from companies such as Hawaiian Vintage or Malei Kai may ameliorate these challenges also, since the chocolate is relatively "local."

The Raw Facts for Healthy Eating

Raw chocolate skips several production steps and may be an alternative as well. Makers of raw chocolate claim that after fermenting the beans, when temperature control is difficult, further preparation of the chocolate remains under 118°F. Vanessa Barg of Gnosis Chocolate imports pastes of stone-ground cacao from Ecuador, Peru, and Bali to fashion raw, organic, and hand-prepared chocolate. Nutritionist and author David Wolfe counts raw cacao as one of the world's superfoods: "The cacao bean has always been and will always be Nature's number one weight loss and high energy food."[16] He argues that it would be more nutritional to eat chocolate in its raw state, either the cocoa bean, the cocoa nibs, or other minimally processed forms.

Honestly, What's in the Chocolate?

Honesty is also a shared religious value that can be honored by consumer's chocolate purchases. Jewish teachings require honesty in business dealings and prohibit fraud (misrepresentation; literally, "stealing of the mind"). Jewish law rejects the concept of "buyer beware," placing the responsibility for any deception on the seller. American chocolate consumers, however, find themselves crunched between differing U.S. and European requirements for chocolate. Those purchasing from some European countries may not realize the importance of reading the label closely. I was surprised when I tasted an imported chocolate bar that contained the unusual ingredient of a cocoa butter equivalent (CBE) dairy butterfat, sensing something weird about the texture. Otherwise, the very politically correct company's wrapper carries its fair trade markings and kosher certifications. Furthermore, the company works with a farmer-owned collective in Ghana and receives support from Lutheran World Relief. I had missed the butter on the label. Similarly, an Austrian bar branded "Shokolad/Chocolate," which I purchased in the large chocolate section of my local market, contained cocoa butter but no cocoa mass, which actually makes it white chocolate; in the United States, a confection like this must be labeled "white chocolate."[17] While this Austrian company, too, meets the fair trade and organic ethical criteria, the labeling on both brands fell short for this American choco-foodie.

Confusion may easily occur when purchasing chocolate from England, Austria, Sweden, Denmark, Ireland, Portugal, or Finland. For several decades, European Union member countries fought over the proper composition and definition of chocolate. They differed over the appropriate proportion of milk to cocoa in milk chocolate and also argued over vegetable fat additives known as CBEs. Countries took sides, with France, Germany, Italy, Belgium, Luxembourg, and the Netherlands arguing against CBEs. Each side claimed that its preferred ingredients enhanced quality. Initially countries using CBEs were not allowed to use the word "chocolate" to describe their products. After pressure from Britain, in 2000 the European Parliament finally ruled in favor of adding no more than 5 percent vegetable fat.[18] This was affirmed in 2001. Because American chocolate eaters have different expectations, a close reading of ingredients may be important when purchasing European products.

Chocolate Challenges

Unless consumers pay close attention, they may unintentionally purchase chocolate that harms the environment, local populations, laborers, or themselves, souring the chocolate experience. Faced with a mélange of options when selecting chocolate, chocolate lovers might be informed by religious food limitations and, at the same time, informed by our ethics. We might take a very cautious approach to certifications, service projects, ingredient listings, type of processing, and country of origin. Such complexities include the following:

- Gas used in the drying process by some growers may mean that ostensibly healthy raw chocolate may be full of poly-aromatic hydrocarbons.[19]
- Beans sourced from Hawaii and Mexico may keep the carbon footprint low for North American consumers yet may not appeal to our palate.
- A fair trade, organic chocolate line owned by an international food conglomerate may mean supporting other company chocolate lines using beans bulked generally from West Africa and its attendant child slavery.
- Commitments to purchasing Israeli products may conflict with the desire for using fair trade and/or organic products.

- Beans from the Caribbean and Central America shipped to Switzerland for processing and then back to the United States for an otherwise politically correct chocolate company may raise questions about carbon footprint.

All of these ethical challenges complicate our path along the chocolate trail.

The earliest chocolate lovers, the Mayans and Aztecs, thought chocolate had heavenly grace. We, too, might savor our chocolate with a sense of the spiritual as we find our way on the chocolate trail. Ultimately, we hope to approach our chocolate intake with the wisdom of the sage Rabbenu Bachya ben Asher: "See how one's eating is considered a perfect act of worship like one of the forms of the divine sacrifices."[20]

Afterword

WITH ALL OF ITS ZIGS AND ZAGS, THIS SWATH OF chocolate's past is multifaith, multifaceted, and multinational. The many stories of Jews, religions, rituals, and the magic of cacao fashion a far-ranging trail of post-Inquisition migrations of chocolate and Sephardi Jews. These mark cultural, political, economic, and religious shifts. Divine and profane meet on this trail built on tensions of escape and exploration.

Had I listened to the advice of that cultural historian, *On the Chocolate Trail* would have resulted in a dead end. Thanks to my trusty choco-dar, our many sleuthing travel adventures, the prospecting in archives and libraries, plus the assistance of many people, this slice of religious and food history is no longer under wraps.

I recently received a note from a beloved congregant who shares my love of chocolate:

> Dear Rabbi,
> When I see chocolate
> When I eat chocolate
> When I read chocolate,
> I think of you ...[1]

I hope that the stories and values in this book accompany you when you see, eat, and read about chocolate and that you are now tantalized to keep only the best chocolate in your daily diet. Blessings as you explore the delights, magic, and complexities of the chocolate trail.

Additional Chocolate Recipes and Tips

Here are a few more chocolate tips and recipes that I hope you will enjoy.

TIPS

1. Raw eggs may be hazardous to your health.
2. Use Dutch-processed cocoa to provide the best taste.
3. Use the best quality chocolate available, preferably fair trade and organic or equivalent.
4. Do not microwave chocolate. Instead, use a large heat-proof bowl set over a pan of simmering water.
5. Try substituting matzah cake meal to transform the cake recipes, particularly the Basque Chocolate Cake and the Chocolate Pudding, into Passover options.
6. Use a *feuille guitare*, a sheet of smooth and thick plastic that makes it easy to work with melted chocolate, or a flat tray or platter that has been very lightly oiled, or parchment paper for laying out the warm chocolate goodie.

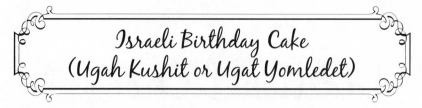

Israeli Birthday Cake (Ugah Kushit or Ugat Yomledet)

Israelis are *meshuga* for delicious chocolate cake such as this, especially at the time of birthday celebrations.

Ingredients:

CAKE:

1 cup milk
4 large eggs, lightly beaten
12 ounces butter, melted
1 teaspoon vanilla extract
3 cups flour
2 teaspoons baking powder
1 teaspoon baking soda
½ teaspoon salt
2 cups sugar
1 cup boiling water (optional: ¼ cup instant coffee for additional flavor)

¾ cup unsweetened cocoa powder

FROSTING:

½ cup whipping cream (optional: add 1 tablespoon instant coffee)
4½ ounces dark chocolate, crumbled
Sprinkles, for decoration (optional)

Instructions:

FOR THE CAKE: Preheat the oven to 320°F. Lightly grease a 10-inch springform pan or Bundt pan, or line a cake pan with parchment paper. Mix together the milk, eggs, melted butter, and vanilla. In a separate bowl, sift the flour with the baking powder, baking soda, and salt. Add the sugar and mix. Fold the milk mixture slowly into the dry ingredients. Mix the boiling water with the cocoa; stir into the batter. Pour the batter into the prepared cake pan. Bake for 40–45 minutes. Check with a toothpick to see how firm it is; bake until it is firm inside, perhaps another 20–30 minutes. Cool completely in the pan. Remove when cool.

FOR THE FROSTING: Warm the cream in a large heatproof bowl set over a pan of simmering water; do not let it boil. Add the chocolate and stir until melted. If you prefer to cover the entire the cake with frosting, double or triple the recipe. Once the frosting has cooled, apply it to the cake. Decorate with sprinkles.

Quantity: 10–15 servings

Flourless Chocolate Cake

This has been the favorite birthday cake of our son, Noam, for years. Because he was born during Passover, we make it annually.

Ingredients:

1 pound unsalted butter
Flour, almond flour, or matzah meal for dusting the pan
12 ounces dark chocolate
4 ounces bitter (or unsweetened) chocolate
3½ ounces milk chocolate with cappuccino filling (look for Perugina or Ritter)

8 large eggs
1 cup plus 2 tablespoons granulated sugar
3–4 heaping tablespoons espresso powder, dissolved in 1 cup boiling water
Confectioners' sugar, for serving
Whipped cream, for serving

Instructions:

Preheat the oven to 350°F. Butter and flour a 10-inch springform pan, and line the bottom with parchment paper. Set the pan on a square of heavy-duty aluminum foil, and bring the foil up around the sides of the pan. Set aside.

Combine the butter and chocolates in a large heatproof bowl set over a pan of simmering water and melt over medium heat, whisking until smooth. Transfer to a heatproof measuring cup. In the bowl of an electric mixer with the paddle attachment, beat the eggs and granulated sugar for 5 minutes at medium-high speed. With the mixer running, pour in the espresso and beat until blended; add the butter-chocolate mixture, beating until blended.

Pour the batter into the prepared pan and bake for 55 minutes. (The cake will crack around the rim.) Remove from the oven and cool on a wire rack for about 20 minutes. Cover with plastic wrap or aluminum foil, and refrigerate for at least 30 minutes. It freezes well.

Twelve to 24 hours before serving, take the cake out of the refrigerator. Remove the sides of the pan, slide a metal spatula under the parchment paper and slide the cake onto a serving plate. Sprinkle with the confectioners' sugar and/or serve with the whipped cream.

Quantity: 12–14 servings

Wacky Cake

This recipe represents another example of chocolate shortages during wartime. Author Mary Ann Rodman writes, "I grew up thinking that this WAS chocolate cake (my mom made it as a birthday cake every year, because she refused to use packaged mixes).... It was apparently a popular holdover from World War I rationing. It's a good cake, if a little on the heavy side. We called it 'Wacky Cake.'" A contemporary version could include ground ginger or ground black pepper.

Ingredients:

CAKE:
2 ounces unsweetened chocolate
1 cup milk
1¾ cups cake flour (or almond flour or matzah cake meal)
¾ teaspoon baking soda
Pinch of salt
½ cup unsalted butter (the original recipe uses cooking oil)
1 cup sugar
1 teaspoon vanilla extract
Ground ginger or ground black pepper, to taste (optional)

ICING:
1 tablespoon unsalted butter
3 tablespoons milk
1½ cups sifted confectioners' sugar
Pinch of salt
½ teaspoon vanilla extract
Ground ginger or ground black pepper, to taste (optional)

Instructions:

FOR THE CAKE: Preheat the oven to 375°F. Lightly grease an 8-inch square cake pan. Combine the chocolate and milk in a large heatproof bowl set over a pan of simmering water for 5 minutes. Blend with a mixer. Remove from the heat and cool. Sift the flour once into a bowl. Add the baking soda and salt to the flour, then sift the dry ingredients together three more times. With an electric mixer, cream the butter and sugar. Add the butter mixture, vanilla, and chocolate mixture to the flour; beat vigorously for 1 minute. If using ginger or black pepper, add it to the batter. Pour the batter into the prepared pan. Bake for 20–25 minutes until a toothpick inserted into the center comes out clean. Cool completely in the pan.

FOR THE ICING: Heat the butter and milk in a small saucepan until melted. In a bowl, mix together the sugar and salt. Add the hot milk, stirring to blend. Add the vanilla and beat with an electric mixer on low to medium speed for 1 minute. Add the ginger or black pepper to the icing, if using. Spread on the cooled cake.

Quantity: 10 servings

Bicerin

This very unusual, rich, layered drink of Turin, Italy, warms us with memories of the earlier days of women drinking chocolate at the time of Mass.

Ingredients:

¾ cup whole milk or cream
3 ounces dark chocolate, finely chopped or shaved
1 cup espresso or very strong coffee
Lightly sweetened whipped cream, flavored with vanilla or cinnamon or both, to taste

Instructions:

Heat the milk or cream slowly over low heat in a double boiler, stirring frequently, until steaming; be careful not to scorch it. Add the chopped chocolate to the steaming milk. Stir slowly over low heat, not allowing the mixture to boil. Remove from the heat.

Pour ¼ cup of the warm chocolate into each of four heatproof glasses. Using the bottom of a tablespoon held against the side of the glass to create a separate layer, pour ¼ cup of espresso into each glass. Again using a tablespoon, pour an equal layer of whipped cream over the top of each drink. The cream should be hand-whipped to a consistency just thick enough to float on top of the drink.

Quantity: 4 servings

Red Chile Bizcochitos (Little Cookies)

Thank you to Hannah Gross for this recipe for Christmas cookies customary in Mexico and known as the New Mexico state cookie. They can be shaped to celebrate other local customs, including the Day of the Dead.

Ingredients:

¼ cup unsweetened cocoa powder
3 cups flour
1½ teaspoons baking powder
½ teaspoon salt
¾ cup sugar
1 teaspoon ground cinnamon
1¼ cups butter
¼–½ teaspoon ground dried red chipotle chile, to taste
¼ teaspoon vanilla extract
1¼ teaspoons aniseed
1 large egg
6 ounces dark chocolate, broken into pieces

Instructions:

Preheat the oven to 400°F. Sift together the cocoa powder, flour, baking powder, and salt into a medium bowl and set aside. Combine ¼ cup of the sugar with the cinnamon in a small bowl and set aside. Put the butter, ground chile, and the remaining ½ cup sugar into the bowl of a standing mixer fitted with the paddle attachment, and beat on medium speed until fluffy, about 1 minute. Add the vanilla, aniseed, and egg and beat, stopping the mixer once or twice to scrape down the sides of the bowl with a rubber spatula, until well mixed, about 1 minute. Reduce the speed to low, then gradually add the flour mixture, scraping the sides of the bowl as needed, and beat until the dough begins to gather into a ball and comes cleanly away from the sides of the bowl, about 2 minutes. Transfer the dough to a lightly floured surface and divide in half. Shape each half into a smooth ball. Cover with a clean dish towel and set aside to rest for 15–20 minutes.

Roll out half of the dough on a lightly floured surface or between sheets of parchment paper to a thickness of about ⅛ inch. Form into desired shapes with a cookie cutter (Day of the Dead or other special occasion cookie cutter shapes may be found online), and arrange 1 inch apart on ungreased cookie sheets. Bake until golden, about 10 minutes. Transfer the cookies to a wire rack and sprinkle lightly with the reserved cinnamon-sugar mixture while still warm. Repeat the process with the remaining half of dough. Cool completely.

Line a baking sheet with parchment paper or waxed paper. Melt the chocolate in a large heatproof bowl set over a pan of simmering water, stirring until smooth. Dip the cookies halfway into the melted chocolate and place on the prepared baking sheet to cool, or place the cookies on the prepared baking sheet and drizzle the chocolate on top of the cookies with a fork. The chocolate will harden as it cools.

Quantity: 3–5 dozen, depending on the size of the cookie cutter

Chocolate Matzah Brickle

This easy-to-prepare concoction works for Passover or really any time. We enjoyed combining roasted almonds, candied orange peel, cocoa nibs, and candied ginger. Thank you to our friend Ruth Belkin for this recipe.

Ingredients:

2 pounds dark chocolate, chips or broken into pieces
¼ cup vegetable oil
½–1 teaspoon vanilla extract or almond extract
1 box matzah sheets, broken into quarters
1 cup nuts, chopped
1 cup dried fruits, chopped

Instructions:

Line a large baking sheet with parchment paper or waxed paper. Melt the chocolate in a large heatproof bowl set over a pan of simmering water. Once melted, thin the chocolate with the vegetable oil; stir in the vanilla or almond extract. Coat the matzah, nuts, and dried fruits with the chocolate and spread onto the prepared baking sheet. Place the sheet in the refrigerator for at least ½ hour to cool. Once cool and hardened, remove from the pan and break into bite-size bits. Store in a closed container.

Quantity: 10 servings

Chocolate Charoset Truffles

This is a great combination of chocolate and *charoset*, the Passover fruit concoction representing the building of granaries by the Hebrew slaves.

Ingredients:

3 pounds dark or bittersweet chocolate, broken into pieces
¼ cup pistachios
¼ cup pecans
⅛ cup almonds
⅛ cup pine nuts
½ tart apple
¼ navel orange, with rind
A few drops of sweet white wine
A few drops of honey
Pinch of fresh or ground ginger (or to taste)
Pinch of ground cinnamon (or to taste)

Instructions:

Line a large baking sheet with parchment paper or waxed paper. Grind the nuts, apples, and orange separately in a food processor. The nuts should be as close to a powder as possible without becoming "butter." Combine the nuts, apple, orange, wine, honey, ginger, and cinnamon in a bowl, mixing well. The *charoset* filling should have a smooth, thick texture. Roll the *charoset* into 1-inch balls. Melt the chocolate in a large heatproof bowl set over a pan of simmering water; remove from the heat. Using two forks, dip the balls into the melted chocolate and place on the prepared baking sheet; refrigerate until the chocolate has set.

Quantity: 24 truffles

Timeline of Chocolate and Religion

1275 Jacobus de Vorgine, archbishop of Genoa, writes the *Golden Legend* story of St. Nicholas's coins.

1492 Jews are expelled from Spain, which leads them to new lands and new business opportunities including trading cacao.

1496 Jews are expelled from Portugal.

1502 Europeans first encounter chocolate in the New World when Columbus and his crew sight cacao beans in a canoe in Honduras.

1528 Cortés brings chocolate-making equipment to Spain.

1544 Dominicans present drinking chocolate to the Spanish court through the presentation of the Kekchi Maya delegation.

1571 The Inquisition is formally established in New Spain, endangering Jews who fled from Spain to the New World.

1580 Spain annexes Portugal, causing many conversos living in Portugal to return to Spain.

c. 1600–1650   Some Jews in New Spain amass wealth as traders of cacao. Inquisition records document Jewish chocolate usage and trade.

1641   Chocolate first arrives in North America in St. Augustine, Florida, during a voyage (ending in a shipwreck) that had been bound for Spain.

1650   Jacob the Jew opens the first coffeehouse in England, in Oxford, which also serves chocolate.

1655   Don Esteban Gammarra is assured that the Jews of Amsterdam are expert chocolate makers.

1663   Emanuel Soares de Rinero is granted the first permit to fabricate chocolate in Brabant, Belgium.

1664   Louis XIV dictates that all of the property in the Caribbean belongs to the French crown. Cocoa farmer Benjamin d'Acosta de Andrade loses his factories and plantations.

1685   Jews are expelled from the French colonies, ending chocolate trade in Martinique.

1701   The first known business record of the import of chocolate in New York by a Jew.

1725   Abraham d'Andrade is arrested for making chocolate in the city of Bayonne, France.

1752   Obadiah Brown builds an early water mill for chocolate grinding in Providence, Rhode Island.

1761   Chocolate makers of Bayonne, France, found a guild to exclude Jews from making or selling chocolate.

1763   Caffè al Bicerin is founded and named for the specialty drink of Turin.

1772   Aaron Lopez buys chocolate from Joseph Pinto for Passover in Newport, Rhode Island.

1772   First recorded sale of Baker's chocolate.

1779–1781   Rebecca Gomez makes and advertises chocolate in New York City.

1824   John Cadbury opens his coffee, tea, and cocoa business.

1894   Wilbur Chocolate makes Wilbur Buds, preceding Hershey's Kisses by over ten years.

1940s   Stephen Klein, founder of Bartons Bonbonniere, provides immigration assistance and jobs to refugees of the Holocaust.

1934   Elite launches Para chocolate line.

1940s   Pietro Ferrero develops Nutella.

1948   Chocolate Pilot, Uncle Wiggly Wings, Gail S. Halvorsen drops chocolate over Berlin.

1950s   Chocolate spread becomes a popular, cost-effective accompaniment to meals in Israel, especially for soldiers in the army.

1978   The Klein family sells Bartons.

1990s   Rolf Bloch, CEO of the Swiss chocolate company Camille Bloch and president of the Swiss Federation of Jewish Communities, leads the effort to bring to light Swiss injustices to Jews during the Holocaust.

2001   "CBE [cocoa butter equivalent] wars" in European Union end.

A Consumer's Guide to Buying Ethically Produced Chocolate

What Is the Best Chocolate?

PEOPLE OFTEN ASK ME TO RECOMMEND MY FAVORITE chocolate or what I consider to be the best chocolate. As detailed in chapter 10, I would say that the best chocolate derives from companies that are guided by human and religious values that mesh with our own. There are many different value systems in the world, including Judaism. The company list below outlines how such values may be used to help you be a more socially conscious consumer when deciding which chocolate to buy. It looks at a sampling of chocolate companies and how they perform in the areas of charity, eco-practices, worker justice, and quality of ingredients. If you know of other companies to add to this list, please contact me at www.jews-onthechocolatetrail.org.

Al Nassma

Umm Nahad, Al Ain Road, Exit 26, PO Box 11-75-84, Dubai, UAE
971-4-223-9289 | www.al-nassma.com

QUALITY: Local food.

GENERAL NOTES: Uses camel milk and acacia honey. Not kosher: contains camel milk; not halal–certified.

Alter Eco
Chocolats Halba

2325 Third Street, Suite 324, San Francisco, CA 94107
415-701-1212 | www.alterecofoods.com

ECO-PRACTICES: Certified carbon neutral.

WORKER JUSTICE: Fair trade–certified.

QUALITY: Organic; 100 percent natural; contains no emulsifiers or artificial additives; organic cane sugar. Options include toasted quinoa, mint, or orange peel. Single origin from Peruvian Amazon or the Ecuador coast.

GENERAL NOTES: Also sells other fair trade products such as sugar, rice, and quinoa. Named France's #1 fair trade brand; awarded the best organic or fair trade product line at the International Chocolate Salon show; and received the Acterra Award for sustainability. Chocolate is processed in Switzerland. No kosher certification.

Askinosie Chocolate

514 E. Commercial, Springfield, MO 65803
417-862-9900 | www.askinosie.com

CHARITY: Chocolate University teaching local children about social entrepreneurship, direct trade, and sustainability; runs projects building wells in Africa; 100 percent of proceeds from chocolate tours support Chocolate University.

ECO-PRACTICES: Green packaging and construction of factory; cocoa shells for mulch; reuses cocoa bean bag in the strings for chocolate wrappings.

WORKER JUSTICE: Direct contact with farmers through approach known as "stake in outcome"; 10 percent of net profits go to the farmers.

QUALITY: Unofficially organic. Single origin chocolate from the Philippines, Mexico, Guatemala, Honduras, and Ecuador.

GENERAL NOTES: Financials are seen by farmers; Askinosie says this arrangement is better than fair trade since they have direct contact. Use the online "Choc-o-lot" system to trace the story of your bar.

Barry-Callebaut

Aalstersestraat 122, B-9280 Lebbeke-Wieze, Belgium
(011)+32-53-73-10211 | www.barry-callebaut.com

WORKER JUSTICE: Signed onto Harkin-Engel Cocoa Protocol, 2005, the Cocoa Industry Protocol, partner in the International Cocoa Initiative; "interested in fair trade, organic, and in making sure no child labor was used." Supports all certifications and an organic cocoa program in Tanzania called Biolands.

GENERAL NOTES: World's largest cocoa and chocolate manufacturer; produces couverture for manufacturers and consumers. Some kosher options. First multinational company to be granted a global kosher certificate in the 1970s.

Bartons Candy

1035 Mill Road, Allentown, PA 18106
610-366-1606 | www.bartonscandy.com/index.php

GENERAL NOTES: See Ms. Chocolate (www.misschocolate.com/passover.php) for Passover fundraising of Bartons' Kosher for Passover line. Some products are certified kosher dairy and some are identified as pareve.

Blommer

600 West Kinzie Street, Chicago, IL 60654
800-621-1606 | www.blommer.com

CHARITY: In the Ivory Coast, Blommer supports improvements to community infrastructure, including schools, labs, and maternity wards.

ECO-PRACTICES: A line of Rainforest Alliance certified products.

WORKER JUSTICE: Does not use any forced labor, meaning any work or service performed involuntarily under threat of physical or other penalty; does not employ child labor, specifically anyone under the age of sixteen. Supports and partners with Cocoa Livelihoods program. Member of the World Cocoa Foundation, Côte d'Ivoire Alliance of Farmers, Olam International, Blommer Chocolate (CIFOB), Sulawesi Alliance of Farmers (SAFOB), and Processors Alliance for Cocoa Traceability and Sustainability (PACTS).

QUALITY: Line of organic.

GENERAL NOTES: Four generation family owned; North America's largest cocoa bean processor and chocolate manufacturer.

Cadbury

Linden Road, Bournville B30 2LU, Birmingham, England
(011)+44-121-458-2000 | www.cadbury.co.uk

CHARITY: Donates books and bicycles to Ghana to further education among local children.

ECO-PRACTICES: Multiple sustainability goals for Kraft in 2015.

WORKER JUSTICE: Dairy Milk line is fair trade in some countries.

GENERAL NOTES: Owned by Kraft. In turn, Cadbury owns Green & Black's, which is fair trade and organic. See www.greenandblacks.com.

Camille Bloch

Grand-Rue, CH-2608, Courtelary, Switzerland
(011)+41-(0)32-945-1200 | www.camillebloch.ch/en

WORKER JUSTICE: Member of the World Cocoa Foundation.

GENERAL NOTES: Third-generation Jewish family ownership. Under the rabbinic supervision of Rabbi Westheim; kosher for Passover.

Chocolats Latour

Cincinnati, OH | 513-591-0085 | http://chocolatslatour.com

ECO-PRACTICES: Uses boxes made from recycled craft paper; cellophane bags are compostable.

WORKER JUSTICE: Selects fairly traded chocolate from Equal Exchange and El Rey from Venezuela. Uses as many local ingredients as possible. No formal certification.

GENERAL NOTES: Makes the chocolate in her Cincinnati home kitchen.

Dagoba

1192 Illinois Street, San Francisco, CA 94107; or
1105 Benson Way, Ashland, OR 97520
866-972-6879 (toll-free) or 415-401-0080 | www.dagobachocolate.com

ECO-PRACTICES: Recyclable packaging and Rainforest Alliance certified™.

WORKER JUSTICE: Cacao from farmer co-ops in Tanzania and Dominican Republic.

QUALITY: Organic.

GENERAL NOTES: Owned by Hershey. Certified kosher by Kosher Supervision of America (KSA).

Divine

4 Gainsford Street, London, England, SE1 2NE
(011)+44-(0)20-7378-6550 | www.divinechocolate.com

WORKER JUSTICE: Fair trade—45 percent owned by farmer co-op called Kuapa Kokoo in Ghana.

QUALITY: Not organic; dairy and butter in some products; sourced from Ghana.

GENERAL NOTES: Makes fair trade kosher coins that would be great for Chanukah gelt. Certified kosher by Triangle-K.

El Ciebo

Av. Juan Pablo II No. 2560, El Alto, La Paz, Bolivia
703-745-7945 (US) | www.elceibo.org

WORKER JUSTICE: Grown by the farmers of El Ceibo farmer cooperative in Alto Beni. Ninety percent of the whole production of the 1,200 families is fermented and dried by the producers.

QUALITY: Organic; all beans from Bolivia.

GENERAL NOTES: Developed in consultation with Chloé Doutre-Roussel.

Elite/Max Brenner

260 5th Avenue, 9th floor, New York, NY 10011
212-388-0030 | www.maxbrenner.com

WORKER JUSTICE: Not fair trade or organic.

QUALITY: Owned by Strauss-Elite. Chocolate sold in shops is certified kosher dairy by Bet–Shemesh Rabbinate.

Endangered Species

5846 W. 73rd Street, Indianapolis, IN 46278
800-293-0160 | http://chocolatebar.com

CHARITY:
- Donates 10 percent of net profits to support species and habitat conservation
- Donates to non-profits
- Endangered Species Chocolate Foundation

ECO-PRACTICES: Rainforest Alliance Certified™; implements green practices including packaging, shipping, and processing. Forest Stewardship Council, African Wildlife Foundation, and Project Ecuador.

Endangered Species (continued)

WORKER JUSTICE: Very high concern for worker's rights. "Ethically traded"; supports local farmers and forests. No slave labor. Purchases beans from co-ops with safe social and environmental practices.

QUALITY: Organic single origin from Sacha, Ecuador, and the Ivory Coast.

GENERAL NOTES: Certified kosher by Orthodox Union.

Equal Exchange

50 United Drive, West Bridgewater, MA 02379
774-776-7400 | www.equalexchange.coop/chocolate-bars

WORKER JUSTICE: Worker owned; fair trade–certified; from small-scale farmer co-ops in Dominican Republic (Conacado), Peru (Cacvra), and Panama.

QUALITY: Certified organic Swiss process in Switzerland.

GENERAL NOTES: Founded in 1986. Swiss standards; no additives such as emulsifiers or corn syrup. Other products included in the chocolate, such as sugar and vanilla, come from farmer co-ops. Kosher: drinking chocolates certified by Kashrut Council of Canada; bars are certified by Rabbi Abraham Hochwald, chief rabbi of the Northern Rhine, Germany.

Gnosis Chocolate

Brooklyn, NY | 646-688-5549 | www.gnosischocolate.com

CHARITY: Donates 10 percent of profits to replant trees.

ECO-PRACTICES: Certified Forest Stewardship Council (FSC) packaging.

QUALITY: Certified organic; beans from Bali, Ecuador, and Peru; certified raw.

GENERAL NOTES: Certified kosher by International Kosher Council.

Godiva

333 West 34th Street, New York, NY 10007
800-946-3482 | www.godiva.com

WORKER JUSTICE: Not fair trade. Belongs to the World Cocoa Foundation.

QUALITY: Not organic.

GENERAL NOTES: Recipes in Belgium and the U.S. differ. Certified kosher by Orthodox Union.

Green & Black's

25 Berkeley Square, London, England W1J 6HN
(011)+44-0207-633-5900 | www.greenandblacks.com/us

WORKER JUSTICE: Maya Gold line is 100 percent fair trade–certified.

QUALITY: Organically grown cacao, certified by the California Certified Organic Farmers (CCOF). Beans from Belize and Dominican Republic.

GENERAL NOTES: Owned by Cadbury and Kraft.

Hawaiian Vintage

1050 Bishop Street #162, Honolulu, HI 96813
808-735-8494 | www.hawaiianchocolate.com

QUALITY: Not organic; local beans.

GENERAL NOTES: First new variety of cocoa in eighty years.

Hershey's

100 Chrystal A Drive, Hershey, PA, 17033-0810
800-468-1714 | www.hersheys.com

WORKER JUSTICE: Not fair trade. Member of the World Cocoa Foundation.

QUALITY: Not organic.

GENERAL NOTES: Also owns Dagoba and Scharffen-Berger. Nearly all chocolate products certified kosher by Orthodox Union.

Kallari

c/o Harry Wils & Co.
Rommel Santos, 505 Jefferson Avenue, Secaucus, NJ 07094
908-834-1614 | www.kallarichocolate.com

ECO-PRACTICES: Rainforest Alliance–certified.

WORKER JUSTICE: Farmer co-op 100 percent profit.

QUALITY: Organic; local bean, Cacao Nacional, from small indigenous Kichwa farmers in Ecuador.

Lake Champlain Chocolates

750 Pine Street, Burlington, VT 05401
800-465-5909 | www.lakechamplainchocolates.com

WORKER JUSTICE: Member of the World Cocoa Foundation.

QUALITY: Has an organic/fair trade–certified line of chocolate, including cocoa, hot chocolate, and chocolate bars.

GENERAL NOTES: Belgian-style chocolate. Certified kosher by Star-D Kosher.

Malie Kai

PO Box 1146, Honolulu, HI 96807
808-599-8600 | www.maliekai.com

QUALITY: Single origin/small batch; lecithin. Local beans from Oahu.

Newman's Own Organics

7010 Soquel Drive, Suite 200, Aptos, CA 95001
831-685-2866 | www.newmansownorganics.com/index.php

ECO-PRACTICES: Rainforest Alliance–certified.

QUALITY: Certified organic by Oregon Tilth.

GENERAL NOTES: Family owned. Certified kosher by Orthodox Union.

Omanhene

5441 S. 9th Street, Milwaukee, WI 53221
414-744-8780 | www.omanhene.com

WORKER JUSTICE: Factory workers and farmers have a stake in the company.

QUALITY: Single sourced from and processed in Ghana.

GENERAL NOTES: The name Omanhene in the Twi language means the "Paramount Chief."

Original Beans

Keizersgracht 253 1015 EB Amsterdam, Netherlands
+1-503-692-3323 ext. 10 (US) | www.originalbeans.com

CHARITY: Plants trees.

ECO-PRACTICES: Restores forests and uses lot numbers to track trees. For each chocolate bar purchased a tree is planted in the rainforest.

Rescue Chocolate

39 Plaza Street West #M1 Brooklyn, NY 11217
347-875-0078 | www.rescuechocolate.com

CHARITY: 100 percent net profits donated to animal rescue organizations.

WORKER JUSTICE: Chocolate from Ghana/Callebaut.

QUALITY: Processed in small batches in Brooklyn.

GENERAL NOTES: Belgian tradition. Pareve, OK certification; some is kosher for Passover. "Don't Passover Me" matzah texture.

Seeds of Change

3209 Richards Lane, Santa Fe, NM 87507
888-762-4240 | http://seedsofchangechocolate.com

CHARITY: Donates 1 percent of its net sales to promote sustainable organic farming initiatives worldwide.

ECO-PRACTICES: Recycled packaging; sustainable forest initiative; promotes biodiversity.

WORKER JUSTICE: Beans from Bolivia and Brazil.

QUALITY: Certified organic by Oregon Tilth; no GMOs.

GENERAL NOTES: Owned by Mars. Certified kosher by Orthodox Union.

Shaman

Mount Laurel, NJ | www.shamanchocolates.com

CHARITY: Supports Huichol Indians.

WORKER JUSTICE: Fair trade–certified.

QUALITY: Organic certified.

GENERAL NOTES: Huichol practice pagan customs.

Sunspire

The Hain Celestial Group, Inc., 4600 Sleepytime Drive, Boulder, CO 80301
800-434-4246 | www.sunspire.com

WORKER JUSTICE: Fair trade–certified. Member of the World Cocoa Foundation.

QUALITY: Organic certified.

GENERAL NOTES: Kosher.

Taza

561 Windsor Street, Somerville, MA 02143-4192
617-623-0804 (office) 617-284-2232 (store) | www.tazachocolate.com

ECO-PRACTICES: Recycle and green—Pedal Paver deliveries; UPS carbon-neutral program.

WORKER JUSTICE: Direct trade.

QUALITY: Small batch; beans from Latin America and Caribbean.

GENERAL NOTES: Enter batch number to see how chocolate is made; Mesoamerican tradition of chocolate grinding; 100 percent stone ground. Certified kosher pareve by Orthodox Union.

Terra Nostra

PO Box 71054, Vancouver, BC V6N 4J9
888-439-4443 | www.terranostrachocolate.com

WORKER JUSTICE: Member of "equitable trade" or "equi-trade."

QUALITY: Organic certified.

Theo

3400 Phinney Avenue, N. Seattle, WA 98103
206-632-5100 | www.theochocolate.com

ECO-PRACTICES: Uses green energy to power factory; sustainable packaging and printing methods; education during tours about social and environmental accountability.

WORKER JUSTICE: Fair trade, living wage, and education for families of growers.

QUALITY: Small batch organic.

GENERAL NOTES: Claims to be the first fair trade, organic bean to bar factory in the United States. Certified kosher by Square-K.

Valrhona

14 Avenue du President Roosevelt, 26600 Tain L'Hermitage, France
(011)+33-(0)475-07-9062 | www.valrhona.com

WORKER JUSTICE: Works on reducing waste. Some lines are fair trade. Member of the World Cocoa Foundation.

QUALITY: Some organic lines; some single origin options from places such as Manjari, Guanaja, and Honduras.

GENERAL NOTES: Some lines are certified kosher by Triangle-K, although some packaging omits the marking.

Vintage Plantations

461 Frelinghuysen Avenue, Newark, NJ 07114
908-354-9304 | www.vintageplantations.com

ECO-PRACTICES: First rainforest certified chocolate company; sun-dried beans.

WORKER JUSTICE: Direct contact with farmers.

QUALITY: Single origin; small batch from Ecuador.

Zotter

8333 Riegersburg, Bergl 56A, Austria
(011)+43-(0)3152-5554 | www.zotter.at/en/

WORKER JUSTICE: Austrian fair trade–certified.

QUALITY: Organic.

GENERAL NOTES: White chocolate was labeled as chocolate. US regulations require labeling as "white chocolate."

Chocolate Museums and Tours around the World

CREATE YOUR OWN CHOCOLATE TRAIL OF MUSEUMS and factory tours using this list. I encourage you to visit each website listed or call for additional details on hours, availability, and fees. For further chocolate experiences as you travel, you may wish to search for chocolate shows and festivals which happen all over the world, including Ashland (Oregon), Bayonne (France), Bruges, New York, Paris, Tokyo, and Turin (Italy).

BRAZIL

Chocolate Caseiro Prawer
Avenida das Hortênsias, 4100
Gramado, Brazil
CEP: 95670-000
(54) 3286-1580
www.prawer.com.br

CANADA

The Chocolate Museum
73 Milltown Blvd.
St. Stephen, NB E3L 1G5
New Brunswick, Canada
(506) 466-7848
www.chocolatemuseum.ca

Le Choco-Musée Érico
634 rue Saint-Jean, G1R 1P8
Quebec, Canada
(418) 524-2122
www.chocomusee.com

Le Musée du Chocolat de la Confiserie Bromont

679 rue Shefford Bromont, J2L 1C2
Quebec, Canada
(450) 534-3893
www.museeduchocolatdebromont.ca

COSTA RICA

Cacao Trails—The Chocolate Tour

Limón, Hone Creek, Costa Rica
(506) 2756-8186
www.cacaotrails.com/tours_cacao/tour_chocolate.htm

CUBA

Museo del Chocolate

Mercaderes Street and Amargura
Havana, Cuba
(011)+53-866-4431
www.havana-guide.com/museo-del-chocolate.html

EUROPE

Chocolate Museum Heindl

Willendorfergasse 2-8
1230
Vienna, Austria
(011)+43 (0)1-667 21 10-0
www.heindl.co.at/en/about-heindl/
    chocolate-museum

Choco Story

Wijnzakstraat 2 (Sint-Jansplein)
8000
Bruges, Belgium
(011)+32-50-61-22-37
www.choco-story.be/ENG/
    museum.htm

Roose's Chocolate World

Havenstraat 1
8000
Bruges, Belgium
(011)+32-50-34-78-60
www.chocolate-world.be/index.
    asp?taal=en

Chocolaterie DUVAL Bruxelles

Rue des Chardons 19
1030
Brussels, Belgium
(011)+32-2-242-94-66
www.chocolaterieduval.com/
    english/visits_workshops/
    standard_visits_1.htm

Le Chocolatier Manon Factory Tour

Rue Tilmont 64
1090
Brussels, Belgium
(011)+32-2-425-26-32
www.chocolatiermanon.com/
    factory.htm

Museum of Cocoa and Chocolate

Rue de la Tete d'Or 9-11
1000
Brussels, Belgium
(011)+32-2-514-20-48
www.mucc.be/EN/index_en.htm

Planète Chocolat

Rue du Lombard 24
1000
Brussels, Belgium
(011)+32-2-425-26-32
www.planetechocolat.be/planete_
    demo_uk.html

Temple du Chocolat Côte d'Or

Brusselsesteenweg 450
B-1500 Halle
Brussels, Belgium
(011)+32-02-362-37-47
www.cotedor.be/cotedor/page?
    siteid=cotedor-prd&locale=
    befr1&PagecRef=555

Le Musée du Chocolat Jacques

Rue de l'industrie 16
B-4700
Eupen, Belgium
www.chocojacques.be/fr/musee

Choco Story Okolády

Celetná 10 (Staré msto)
110 00
Prague, Czech Republic
(011)+420 224-242-953
www.choco-story-praha.cz

Cadbury World

Linden Road, Bournville, B30 2LU
Birmingham, England
(011)+44-121-458-2000
www.cadburyworld.co.uk/
    CadburyWorld/Pages/
    CadburyWorld.aspx

Choco-Musée Puyodebat

Rue des Gouverneurs 9
64100
Bayonne, France
(011)0033-559-59-4842
www.chocolats-puyodebat-
    bayonne.fr/notre-musée-
    lieu-dinitiation-cacao-
    chocolat-i-10.html

L'Atelier du Chocolat de Bayonne

7 Alley Gibeleou
64100
Bayonne, France
(011)05-59-55-70-23
www.atelierduchocolat.fr/visitez_
    chocolaterie_bayonne.aspx

Chocolaterie de Beussent Lachelle

66 Route de Desvres
62170
Beussent, France
(011)03-21-86-17-62
www.choco-france.com

Planèt Musée du Chocolat

14 Avenue Beau Rivage
64200
Biarritz, France
(011)05-59-23-27-72
www.planetemuseeduchocolat.com

Michel Cluizel's Chocolatrium Musée

Route de Conches
27240
Damville, France
(011)+33-02-32-35-20-75
http://chocolatrium.com

Le Musée Du Chocolat Hautot

851 Route de Valmont
76400
Fécamp, France
(011)+33-02-35-27-62-02
http://chocolats-hautot.com/musee-
   chocolats-hautot.html

Musée Les Secrets du Chocolat

Rue du Pont du Péage
F-67118
Geispolsheim, France
(011)+33 (0)3-88-55-04-90
www.musee-du-chocolat.com

Le Paradis du Chocolat Musée

Château Louis XI, rue des Remparts
38260
La Côte Saint André, France
(011)+33-04-74-20-35-89
www.paradis-chocolat.com/
   musee-du-chocolat.htm

Le Musée du Chocolat Des Lis Chocolat

6 rue Louis Blériot
77140
Nemours, France
(011)+33-01-64-29-20-20
www.deslischocolat.com/
   page.php?lg=fr&rub=03

Chocolaterie du Drakkar et Musée du Chocolat

ZA Bayeux Intercom
14400 Nonant
Normandy, France
(011)+33 (0)2-31-10-00-05
www.musee-chocolat.com
   or
www.chocolateriedrakkar.com/
   index_010.htm

Musée du Bonbon Haribo

30 700 Uzés
Pont des Charrettes, France
(011)+33-04-66-22-74-39
www.haribo.com/planet/fr/
   info/main/use/popup/index.
   php?cat=1&nav=1&subnav=1

Le Musée du Chocolat

Z.A.E.S. du Moulin Rouge
24120
Terrasson Lavilledieu, France
33 (0)5-53-51-57-36
www.bovetti.com/FR/
   le-musee-du-chocolat/
   visite-du-musee-du-chocolat

Musée Art du Chocolat

13 place Paul Saissac
81310 Lisle Sur Tarn
Toulouse, France
(011)+33-05-63-33-6979
www.musee-art-chocolat.com

Rausch Plantagen Schokoland Museum

Wilhelm-Rausch-Strasse 4, 31228
   Peine
Berlin, Germany
(011)+49-517-1990120
   www.rausch-schokolade.com/
   index.html

Schokoladen Museum

Am Schokoladenmuseum 1a
50678
Cologne, North Rhine-Westphalia,
  Germany
(011)+49-221-931888-0
www.chocolatemuseum-cologne.com

Halloren Schokoladenmuseum

Delitzscher Strasse 70
06112
Halle, Germany
(011)+490345-5642-192
www.halloren.de/marke/
  schokoladenmuseum.php

Csokoládé Múzeum

1162 Budapest Bekecs Street 22
Budapest, Hungary
(011)+36-1-401-5000
www.csokolade-muzeum.hu

La Casa del Cioccolato Perugina

Stahilmento Nestl
Divisione Prodotti Dolciari
Strada Pieraiola 207/C
San Sisto
Perugia, Italy
(011)+39-527-6796
www.perugina.it/Templates/
  PaginaIntroduzione.
  aspx?pageid=361

Museo del Cioccolato Antica Norba

S.r.l. Sede Legale Via Caceres, 3
Sede Produttiva Via Capo dell'
  Acqua, 20
04010
Norma, Italy
(011)+39-0773354548
www.museodelcioccolato.com

Caffarel Chocolate Museum

Via Gianavello 41
10062
Luserna San Giovanni
Torino (Piemonte), Italy
www.curious-food-lover.com/
  culinary-activity/7333/
  caffarel-chocolate-museum

Chocoladefabriek

Prinseneiland 43
1013 LL
Amsterdam, Netherlands
(011)+31 (0)20-420-07-72
www.dechocoladefabriek.nl/
  www-choc-eng/ydc.html

Gemeentemuseum Weesp

Nieuwstraat 41
Weesp, Netherlands
(011)+311-029 4491245
www.weesp.nl/index.php?
  mediumid=15&pagid=1339

Museo del Chocolate

Calle José Maria Goy 5
24700
Astorga, León, Spain
(011)+34-98-7616220
www.museochocolateastorga.com

Museu de la Xocolata

Carrer Comerç 36
08003
Barcelona, Spain
(011)+34-932-68-7878
http://pastisseria.cat/ct/
  PortadaMuseu

Chocolate Comes Artesano

Calle Sant Josep, 29
46410
Sueca (Valencia), Spain
(011)+34-96-170-19-42
www.chocolatescomes.com/
  museo.htm

Chocolates Clavileño Museo del Chocolate

Calle de Colón N° 187
03570
Villajoyosa, Alicante, Spain
www.chocolatesclavileno.com/
museo.htm

Valor Chocolate Museum

Pianista Gonzalo Soriano, 13
03570
Villajoyosa, Alicante, Spain
(011)+34 965 89 09 50
www.valor.es/museo/
museodelchocolate.asp

Cailler Chocolate Factory

La Maison Cailler, rue Jules Bellet 7
1636
Broc, Switzerland
(011)+41 (0)26-921-59-60
www.cailler.ch/en/Home.aspx

Chocolat Frey Le Monde Du Cacao Exhibition

Bresteneggstrasse 4
5033
Buchs, Switzerland
(011)+41-062 836 26 26
www.chocolatfrey.ch

SchoggiLand Maestrani Factory Tour

Toggenburgerstrasse 41
9230
Flawil, Switzerland
(011)+41 071 228 38 11
www.maestrani.ch/lang-en/
fuehrungen-a-events/
fabrikbesichtigungen.html

Swiss Chocolate Train

Train travels to and from Montreaux
on the Swiss Riviera, to Gruyères
Cheese Factory, to Broc and the
Cailler-Nestlé Chocolate Factory.
www.raileurope.com/european-
trains/chocolate-train/index.html

ISRAEL

De Karina

Kibbutz Ein Zivan
Golan Heights
(011)972 04-699-3622
www.de-karina.co.il

Elite

5 Gilboa Street
Nazareth Illit
(011)972 04-650-8258
www.strauss-group.com

Galita Chocolate Farm

Kibbutz Deganya Bet
(011)972 04-675-5608
www.galita.com

Ornat

5008 Hasharon Industrial Park
Sharon 60920
(011)972 09-891-3389

JAPAN

Ishiya Chocolate Factory
2-2-11-63 Miyanosawa
Nishi-ku, Sapporo, 063-0052
Japan
(011)+81 (0)11-666-1481
www.shiroikoibito.ishiya.co.jp

KOREA

Chocolate Museum
Daejeong-eup Ilgwa-ri 511-18
Seogwipo-si Jeju Special Self-Governing Province, Korea
(011)+82-64-792-3121
www.chocolatemuseum.org

NEW ZEALAND

Silky Oak Chocolate Company Museum and Factory Tours
1131 Links Road, Hastings
Hawkes Bay, New Zealand
(011)+64 6 845 0908
www.silkyoakchocs.co.nz/museum.htm

UNITED STATES

Askinosie Chocolate
514 E. Commercial
Springfield, MO 65803
417-862-9900
www.askinosie.com

Candy Americana Museum
48 North Broad Street
Lititz, PA 17543
717-626-3249
www.wilburbuds.com/docs/
   museum.html

Ethel M. Chocolates Factory Tour
2 Cactus Garden Drive
Henderson, NV 89014
800-471-0352
www.ethelm.com/about_us/
   factory_tour.aspx

Hershey's Chocolate World
251 Park Boulevard
Hershey, PA 17033
717-534-4900
www.hersheys.com/chocolateworld

Hershey Story

63 West Chocolate Avenue
Hershey, PA 17033
717-534-3439
www.hersheystory.org

Lake Champlain Chocolates Factory Tour

750 Pine Street
Burlington, VT 05401
802-864-1807
www.lakechamplainchocolates.com/
    about-us/visit-our-factory

Mast Brothers Chocolate

111 N. 3rd Street
Brooklyn, NY 11249
718-388-2625
http://mastbrothers.com/about

New American Chocolate: TCHO Tour

Pier 17
San Francisco, CA 94111
415-981-0189
www.tcho.com/explore/tour

South Bend Chocolate Tours

3300 W. Sample Street
South Bend, IN 46619
574-233-2577
www.southbendchocolate.com

Taza

561 Windsor Street
Somerville, MA 02143-4192
617-632-0804
www.tazachocolate.com

Theo Chocolate

3400 Phinney Avenue
N. Seattle, WA 98103
206-632-5100
www.theochocolate.com/
    our-story/the-factory.php

Notes

INTRODUCTION

1. Abraham Cresques, known as the "map Jew" or the "compass Jew," drew the Catalan map, perhaps the most famous and comprehensive image of the then known world. See Meyer Kayserling, *Christopher Columbus and the Participation of Jews in Spanish and Portuguese Discoveries* (New York: Longman's Green, 1894), 5–6, 13, 48, 113.

2. Eli Rosenblatt, "Christopher Columbus: Jew?" *The Jewish Daily Forward*, February 8, 2008, accessed November 22, 2011, www.forward.com/articles/12638/#ixzz1eYODaj86.

3. Louis Evan Grivetti and Howard-Yana Shapiro, eds., *Chocolate: History, Culture and Heritage* (Hoboken, NJ: John Wiley & Sons, 2009), 927.

CHAPTER 1: DID JEWS INTRODUCE CHOCOLATE TO FRANCE?

1. Sophie D. and Michael D. Coe, *The True History of Chocolate* (London: Thames & Hudson, 1996), 155–56; Susan J. Terrio, *Crafting the Culture of French Chocolate* (Berkeley: University of California Press, 2000), 72ff.

2. Jonathan I. Israel, *European Jewry in the Age of Mercantilism 1550–1750* (Oxford: Clarendon Press, 1989), 66; Grivetti and Shapiro, eds. *Chocolate*, 923. More about coffeehouses may be found in the following sources: Norma Aubertin-Potter and Alyx Bennet, *Oxford Coffee Houses 1651–1800* (Oxford: Hampden Press, 1987), 13; Ellis Markman, *The Coffee House: A Cultural History* (London: Weidenfeld and Nicolson, 2004), 30. The excitement of coffeehouse culture and its cultural generativity may be seen in the work of Steve Johnson, *Where Good Ideas Come From: The Natural History of Innovation* (New York: Riverhead Books, 2010).

3. Jonathan Irvine Israel, *Diasporas within Diasporas: Jews, Crypto-Jews and the World Maritime Empires (1540–1740)* (Leiden, the Netherlands: Brill Publishers, 2002), 440.

4. Frédéric Duhart, *Le Chocolat au Pays Basque* (Donastia, Spain: Elkar Éditions, 2006), 22.

5. Ralph G. Bennett, "The Sephardic Path to North America," accessed 2006, www.sefarad.org/publication/lm/030/bennett.html.

6. Gérard Nahon, "The Portuguese Nation of Saint-Esprit-lès Bayonne: The American Dimension," in *The Jews and Expansion of Europe to the West 1450–1800*, ed. Paolo Bernardini and Norman Fiering (New York: Berghahn Books, 2001), 257; Mordechai Arbell, "Jewish Settlements in the French Colonies in the Caribbean (Martinique, Guadeloupe, Haiti, Cayenne) and the 'Black Code,'" in *The Jews and Expansion of Europe*, 292.

7. Elliott Horowitz, "Coffee, Coffeehouses and the Nocturnal Rituals of Early Modern Jewry," *Association for Jewish Studies Review* 14 (1989): 42.

8. Hanne Trautner Kromann, *The History of Jews in Denmark*, Jewish Gen Scandinavia—SIG (Scandinavia Special Interest Group), accessed 2007, www.jewishgen.org/scandinavia/history.htm.

9. Christian Teubner, *The Chocolate Bible* (New York: Penguin Books, 1997), 71.

10. "Cocoa in France," The Worldwide Gourmet, accessed 2006, www.theworldwidegourmet.com/products/articles/cocoa-in-france.

11. Israel, *Diasporas within Diasporas*, 22, 27, 132, 247, 253; William Gervase Clarence-Smith, *Cocoa and Chocolate 1765–1914* (New York: Routledge, 2000), 94.

12. Gerard Nahon, "The Sephardim of France," in *The Sephardi Heritage: Essays on the History and Cultural Contribution of the Jews of Spain and Portugal*, ed. R. D. Barnett and W. M. Schwab (New York: Ktav Publishing House, Inc., 1971), 51.

13. Esther Benbassa, *The Jews of France: A History from Antiquity to the Present*, trans. M. B. DeBevoise (Princeton, NJ: Princeton University Press, 1999), 52.

14. Jonathan Irvine Israel, *Dutch Primacy in World Trade 1585–1740* (Oxford, UK: Clarendon Press, 1989), 261; Israel, *Diasporas within Diasporas*, 268; Fernand Braudel, *Civilization and Capitalism, 15th–18th Century*, vol. 1, *The Structures of Everyday Life: The Limits of the Possible*, trans. Sian Reynolds (New York: Harper and Row, 1979), 249; Clarence-Smith, *Cocoa and Chocolate 1765–1914*, 107.

15. Eugenio Piñero, "The Cacao Economy of the Eighteenth Century Province of Caracas and the Spanish Cacao Market," in *The Atlantic Staple Trade: The Economics of Trade*, vol. 2 of *An Expanding World: The European Impact on World History 1450–1800*, ed. Susan Socolow

(London: Variorum, 1996), 501. A Jamaican Jew, Isaac Nunes, had contact with a brother living in Bayonne; Stephen Alexander Fortune, *Merchants and Jews: The Struggle for British West Indian Commerce 1650–1750*, Center for Latin American Studies Book (Gainesville: University of Florida Press, 1984), 133.

16. Duhart, *Le Chocolat au Pays Basque*, 20.

17. Clarence-Smith, *Cocoa and Chocolate*, 67.

18. The shop was run by Monsieur Lemoine, and the review was written by Grimod de la Reynère in *L'Almanach des Gourmands*, quoted in Nathalie Bailleux, et al., eds., *The Book of Chocolate* (Paris: Flammarion, 1995), 101.

19. Mort Rosenblum, *Chocolate: A Bittersweet Saga* (New York: North Point Press, 2005), 12. Terrio, *Crafting the Culture*, 73; and Antony Wild, *The East India Company Book of Chocolate* (London: Harper Collins, 1995), 13.

20. Zvi Avneri, "Bayonne," *Encyclopaedia Judaica*, 2nd ed. ed. Fred Skolnik (Detroit, MI: Macmillan Reference USA / Keter Publishing House, 2007), 3, 231.

21. Joan Nathan, *Quiches, Kugels and Couscous: My Search for Jewish Cooking in France* (New York: Alfred A. Knopf, 2010), 320.

22. Duhart, *Le Chocolat au Pays Basque*, 20.

23. Terrio, *Crafting the Culture*, 66ff., 77.

24. Ibid., 78.

25. Ibid., 78–79.

Complexities of Jewish Identity

a. Richard L. Kagan and Philip D. Morgan, eds., *Atlantic Diasporas: Jews, Conversos, and Crypto-Jews in the Age of Mercantilism 1500–1800* (Baltimore, MD: Johns Hopkins University Press, 2009), viii–ix, 4–5, 24.

b. Seymour B. Liebman, *The Jews in New Spain: Faith, Flame and Inquisition* (Florida: University of Miami Press, 1970), 152; Jorge Cañizares-Esguerra and Erik R. Seeman, *The Atlantic in Global History 1500–2000* (NJ: Prentice Hall, 2007), 40.

CHAPTER 2: THE INQUISITION: CHOCOLATE OUTED JEWS AND DIVIDED CHRISTIANS

1. Label at the Barcelona Museu de la Xocolata, www.pastisseria.com/en/PortadaMuseu.

2. Marcy Norton, *Sacred Gifts, Profane Pleasures: A History of Tobacco and Chocolate in the Atlantic World* (Ithaca, NY: Cornell University Press, 2010), 142.

3. Haim Beinart, "The Records of the Inquisition: A Source of Jewish and Converso History," *Proceedings of the Israel Academy of Sciences and Humanities* 2, no. 11 (1967): 213; Stanley M. Hordes, "The Inquisition as Economic and Political Agent," *The Americas* 39, no. 1 (July 1982): 29.

4. Francesca Trivellato, "Sephardic Merchants in the Early Modern Atlantic and Beyond: Toward a Comparative Historical Approach to Business Cooperation," in *Atlantic Diasporas*, 120.

5. Arnold Wiznitzer, "Crypto-Jews in Mexico in the 17th Century," *Proceedings of the American Jewish Historical Society* 51 (June 1962): 264–66. Hordes, "The Inquisition," 119.

6. Martha Few, *Women Who Live Evil Lives: Gender, Religion, and the Politics of Power in Colonial Guatemala: 1650-1750* (Austin: University of Texas Press, 2002), 28–29, 32, 53–55, 64; Marcy Norton, *Sacred Gifts, Profane Pleasures*, 138.

7. Robert J. Ferry, *The Colonial Elite of Early Caracas: Formation and Crisis 1567–1767* (Los Angeles: University of California Press, 1989), 48, 62; Robert J. Ferry, "Don't Drink the Chocolate: Domestic Slavery and the Exigencies of Fasting for Crypto-Jews in Seventeenth-Century Mexico," *Nuevo Mundo Mundos Neuvos*, 2005, accessed November 2011, http://nuevomundo.revues.org/934; Robert Ferry, "Trading Cacao: A View from Veracruz: 1629–1645," *Nuevo Mundo Mundos Neuvos*, 2006, accessed November, 2011, http://nuevomundo.revues.org/1430; Stanley M. Hordes, *The Crypto-Jewish Community of New Spain, 1620–1649: A Collective Biography* (Ann Arbor, MI: Dissertation Services, 1980 / Dissertation, Tulane University, May 1980), 68, 71, 81, 83.

8. Stanley M. Hordes, e-mail message to author, December 28, 2010.

9. Stanley M. Hordes, *To the End of the Earth: A History of the Crypto-Jews of New Mexico* (New York: Columbia University Press, 2005), 42, 53–54, 83–84, 92, 109; Ferry, *Trading Cacao*, 16–17; Hordes, *Crypto-Jewish Community*, 71; Liebman, *New Spain*, 317, 327.

10. Norton, *Sacred Gifts*, 179.

11. Ferry, *Trading Cacao*, 52; Hordes, *End of the Earth*, 81.

12. Ferry, *Trading Cacao*, 25ff., 41, 57, 63.

13. David M. Gitlitz and Linda Kay Davidson, *A Drizzle of Honey: The Lives and Recipes of Spain's Secret Jews* (New York: St Martin's Griffin: 1999), 106; David Gitlitz, *Secrecy and Deceit: The Religion of the Crypto-Jews* (Philadelphia, PA: Jewish Publication Society; Albuquerque: University of New Mexico Press, 1996), 57, 355; Liebman, *New Spain*, 47, 79, 258. Between Juan Méndez de Villaviciosa and Ana Suarez, arranged by another merchant, the bride's mother, and the bride's grandmother, from Inquisition testimony (October 24, 1642).

14. Ferry, *Trading Cacao*, 8–9.

15. "Process or Trial of Gabriel de Granada, Mexico 1642," *Publication of the American Jewish Historical Society* 7 (1899): 93, 95.
16. Liebman, *New Spain*, 47, 83, 84; Gitlitz, *Drizzle of Honey*, 44.
17. Gitlitz, *Secrecy and Deceit*, 356, 358.
18. Gitlitz, *Drizzle of Honey*, 103.
19. Ferry, *Trading Cacao*, 9.
20. Gitlitz, *Secrecy and Deceit*, 364, as reported by Isabel Rodriguez and Juan Pacheco de León from approximately 1650.
21. Ferry, *Trading Cacao*, 13.
22. Gitlitz, *Secrecy and Deceit*, 398–99.
23. Ferry, *Trading Cacao*, 14.
24. Ferry, "Don't Drink," 12.
25. Gitlitz, *Secrecy and Deceit*, 397.
26. Ibid., 398.
27. Ferry, "Don't Drink," 11.
28. Ferry, *Trading Cacao*, 12.
29. Ferry, *Trading Cacao*, 5, 14, 15.
30. Ibid; Liebman, *New Spain*, 2–4, 10, 15, 203.
31. Hordes, *End of the Earth*, 60.

The Inquisition

a. Liebman, *New Spain*, 16, 33.
b. Arnold Wiznitzer, "Crypto-Jews in Mexico in the 16th Century," *The American Jewish Historical Quarterly* 51 (1962): 175–76.
c. Richard Greenleaf, *Zumárraga and the Mexican Inquisition, 1536–1543*, Academy of American Franciscan History Monograph Series, vol. 4 (Washington, DC: Academy of American Franciscan History, 1961), 89.
d. Hordes, "The Inquisition," 26, 28, 36.
e. Liebman, *New Spain*, 24, 28, 168–69.
f. Coe, *True History*, 138–9.

Cacao in Central America

a. J. H. Elliott, *Empires of the Atlantic World: Britain and Spain in America 1492–1830* (New Haven, CT: Yale University Press, 2006); Ferry, "Trading Cacao", 21. Louisa Schell Hoberman, "Merchants in 17th Century Mexico City," *Hispanic American Historical Review* 57 (August 1977): 21, 25–29, 91, 111, 206–7.

CHAPTER 3: JEWS DIP INTO CHOCOLATE IN THE AMERICAN COLONIAL PERIOD

Chocolate Pudding

a. Esther Levy, *The Jewish Cookery Book, on Principles of Economy, adapted for Jewish Housekeepers with the addition of many useful medicinal recipes and other valuable information related to housekeeping and domestic management* (Philadelphia, PA: W. S. Turner, 1871), 94. This is the first known American Jewish cookbook.

Detailed charts of chocolate shipping and production information may be found at the website for *On the Chocolate Trail* at www.jews-onthechocolatetrail.org/booksupplement/.

1. Jacob R. Marcus, *The Colonial American Jew, 1492–1776* (Detroit, MI: Wayne State University Press, 1970), 673.

2. Anthony M. Sammarco, *The Baker Chocolate Factory: A Sweet History* (Charleston, SC: History Press, 2009).

3. Elvira N. Solis, "Note on Isaac Gomez and Lewis Moses Gomez from an Old Family Record," *Publications of the American Jewish Historical Society* (1893–1961): 1903; vol. 11, *American Jewish Historical Society Journal*, 140, 142.

4. Malcolm Stern, *First American Jewish Families: 600 Genealogies, 1654–1977* (Cincinnati, OH: American Jewish Archives; Waltham, MA: American Jewish Historical Society, 1978), 185.

5. James Gay, "Chocolate Production and Uses in 17th and 18th Century North America," in Grivetti and Shapiro, *Chocolate*, 283, 285, 289; "Franklin's Print Shop," accessed November, 2011, www.history.org/history/teaching/enewsletter/volume9/jan11/featurearticle.cfm.

6. James Gay, interview with the author, February 2008, Williamsburg, Virginia. However, the earliest records for chocolate in North America date to the middle of the seventeenth century and consist of the following:

   • First report: A manuscript dated September 29, 1641 reports the plight of a ship named the *Nuestra Señora del Rosario y el Carmen* traveling the Bahamas Channel to Spain. Caught in a hurricane, the captain tossed much of the cargo in order to save the ship. However, he elected not to throw the valuable chocolate/cocoa beans overboard. After the storm passed, the ship finally landed at St. Augustine, Florida. Conversos were among the settlers of St. Augustine, Florida, in 1565 and may have enjoyed these first tastes of the shipwrecked cocoa. See Saul S. Friedman, *Jews and the American Slave Trade* (New Brunswick, NJ: Transaction Publishers, 1998), 103. The drenched cargo included thirty-two crates of chocolate and nine chocolate grinding stones. Ultimately, the chocolate was auctioned off to locals and then distributed to a long list of men and boys. See

Beatriz Cabezon and Louis Evan, "Paleography and the St. Augustine Chocolate Saga," in Grivetti and Shapiro, *Chocolate*, 669–98.

- Second report: A lovely chocolate cup, Rochester Museum item 875/99, manufactured sometime between 1655 and 1675 in Delft, the Netherlands, used by Native Americans perhaps as decoration, was found in the Hudson Valley. Peter G. Rose, "Dutch Cacao Trade in New Netherland During the 17th and 18th Centuries," in Grivetti and Shapiro, *Chocolate*, 379. Also, e-mail correspondence with George R. Hamell, collections manager, Rock Foundation Collection, Rochester Museum, August 4, 2009: "The present cup on loan to the Museum of the City of New York and another similar cup from a contemporary archeological site were probably acquired at Fort Orange–Beverwijck [Albany], which the Seneca and Iroquois [Haudenosaunee] frequented for trade. There are also references to visits to trade and to attend councils at New Amsterdam. It is also possible the cups and other Euroamerican ceramics known from Seneca and the lower Iroquois [Haudenosaunee] archeological village sites were directly acquired from Euroamerican colonists on the lower Mohawk Valley or in the Hudson Valley, or indirectly from native or Euroamerican traders traveling through Seneca and Iroquois [Haudenosaunee] communities during the seventeenth century."

- Third report: The diary of Massachusetts Bay mint-master John Hull records that in the winter of 1667–68 "our ship *Providence* ... cast away on the French shore ... carrying ... cocoa." Gay, "Chocolate Production," in Grivetti and Shapiro, *Chocolate*, 281.

- Fourth report: In 1670 the city of Boston granted permission to Dorothy Jones and Jane Barnard to open a "Coffee and Chucaletto" house. Ibid.

- Fifth report: British customs records show cocoa arriving in America in 1682: "1682 ... Jamaica ... to ... Boston." Ibid.

7. Celia D. Shapiro, "Nation of Nowhere: Jewish Role in Colonial American Chocolate," in Grivetti and Shapiro, *Chocolate*, 59.

8. Marquez was endenizened in New York, October 16, 1695, and made a freeman on September 17, 1697. See Stern, *First American Jewish Families*, 185; Liber 30 of Conveyances Registers Office Borough of Manhattan, New York City, "An Account of his Majesty's Revenue of the Province of New York," P255/Box#19, American Jewish Historical Society (AJHS), New York.

9. Leo Hershkowitz, "Some Aspects of the New York Jewish Merchant and Community, 1654–1820," *American Jewish Historical Quarterly* 66, nos. 1–4 (September 1976–June 1977): 25.

10. Oppenheim Collection, 255/18/4, American Jewish Historical Society, New York.

11. Marcus, *The Colonial American Jew*, 2:1486n16; 2:1494n38; Celia
    D. Shapiro, "Nation of Nowhere," 58; Hershkowitz, "Aspects," 22;
    correspondence Daniel Gomez to Aaron Lopez, Microfilm 597, New
    York, June 19, 1753, American Jewish Archives (AJA), Cincinnati, OH;
    Daniel Gomez Ledger, Microfilm 597, AJA, Cincinnati, OH.

12. Virginia Barnett and Jan K. Gilliam, *Food in the Eighteenth Century
    Chesapeake* (Williamsburg, VA: Colonial Williamsburg Foundation
    Library, 1991), 71, 74.

13. The first coffeehouse in England was founded in Oxford by Jacob the
    Jew (see chap. 1); Mary R. M. Goodwin, *The Coffeehouses of the
    17th and 18th Centuries* (Williamsburg, VA: Colonial Williamsburg
    Foundation Library, Research Report Series, 1956).

14. Gay, "Chocolate Production," in Grivetti and Shapiro, *Chocolate*, 285.
    An entry in the daybook of Josiah DuBois 1807–1820 notes that the
    town of New Paltz paid for half a pound of chocolate "for relief of
    John A. Freer and family ... A family of color" on September 15, 1819,
    and again on October 19, 1819.

15. *The Providence Gazette and Country Journal*, March 25, 1775, 4.

16. Mary R. M. Goodwin, "Christmas in Colonial Virginia," in *Library
    Research Report Series* (Williamsburg, VA: Colonial Williamsburg
    Foundation, 1955), xxix.

17. Ibid., xxxii.

18. *Essex Gazette*, January 11, 1774, 94.

19. "Report of the Committee of Commerce and Manufactures on the
    Memorials of Sundry Manufacturers of Chocolate, February, 8, 1797,"
    Early American Imprints, Series I, Rockefeller Library, Williamsburg, VA.

20. To learn about chocolate preparation in the colonial period, see the
    website for *On the Chocolate Trail* at www.jews-onthechocolatetrail.org.

21. *The Boston News-Letter*, July 2, 1772, 2.

22. John Scharffenberger and Robert Steinberg, *The Essence of Chocolate*
    (New York: Hyperion, 2006), 55. In England in the latter part of the
    eighteenth century, chocolate drop confections modeled after a treat
    from Naples were known similarly as *diavolino* or *diablotin*. See Peter
    Brown, *Pleasures of the Table: Fairfax House—Ritual and Display in
    the European Dining Room 1600–1900* (York, UK: York Civic Trust,
    1997), 79.

23. *A New England Weekly Journal*, November 25, 1728.

24. *Boston Gazette*, May 18, 1761.

25. Gerald W. R. Ward, "Silver Chocolate Pots of Colonial Boston," in
    Grivetti and Shapiro, *Chocolate*, 144.

26. Grivetti and Shapiro, *Chocolate*, 893.

27. "[1702] Monday, October 26 From thence to Billericay. Visited languishing Mr. Sam Whiting, I gave him 2 Balls of Chockalett and a pound of Figgs, which very kindly accepted....

"[1707] March 31 Visited Mr. Gibbs, presented him with a pound of Chockalett and 3 of Cousin Moodey's sermons....

"[1707] I gave Mr. Stoddard for Madam Stoddard two half pounds of Chockolat, instead of Commencement Cake and a Thesis." Thomas M. Halsey, *The Diary of Samuel Sewall 1674–1729* (New York: Farrar, Straus and Giroux, 1973), 476, 563, 570.

28. "I go to Mr. Belcher's where I drink warm chockelat and no beer; find myself much refresh'd by it after great Sweating to day, and yesterday.... October 20, 1697 I wait on the Lieutenant Governour at Dorchester and there meet with Mr. Torry, breakfast together on venison and chockalatte." Ibid., 626, 380.

29. Rose, "Dutch Cacao Trade," in Grivetti and Shapiro, *Chocolate*, 379.

30. *Boston Evening-Post*, December 14, 1747, 2.

31. Edith B. Gelles, ed., *The Letters of Abigail Franks 1733–1748* (New Haven, CT: Yale University Press, 2004), 146–4.

32. Hershkowitz, "Aspects," 14.

33. Jonathan Sarna, "Jews in British America," in Bernardini and Fiering, *Jews and the Expansion of Europe to the West*, 524–25.

34. Gelles, *Letters of Abigail Franks*, 143.

35. David de Sola Pool, "The Mill Street Synagogue (1730–1817) of the Congregation Shearith Israel," pamphlet 930, AJHS, New York, 34, 36, 40.

36. David de Sola Pool and Tamar de Sola Pool, *An Old Faith in the New World: Portrait of Shearith Israel 1654–1954* (New York: Columbia University Press, 1955), 525.

37. Pool, "*Mill Street Synagogue*," 23, 40.

38. Willem Klooster, "Jews in Suriname and Curaçao," in Bernardini and Fiering, *Jews and the Expansion of Europe to the West*, 354.

39. Daniel Gomez Account Book, Microfilm 597, AJA, Cincinnati, OH; Oppenheim Collection of Daniel Gomez Shipping Notes, 255/18/2 AJHS, New York.

40. Daniel Gomez Account Book, Microfilm 597, AJA, Cincinnati, OH.

41. *New York Gazette,* or *The Weekly Post Boy* (February 5 and 12, 1759), in Oppenheim Collection, Daniel Gomez File/Box 4, AJHS, New York.

42. Lee M. Friedman, *Early American Jews* (Cambridge, MA: Harvard University Press, 1934), 75ff.

43. *New Jersey Journal*, September 3, 17, 19, and 24, 1788, 4.

44. *Mercantile Advertiser*, July 20, 1799, and August 1, 1799.

45. *The National Advocate*, March 15, 1815–June 26, 1815.

46. Gelles, *Letters of Abigail Franks*, 128 n8.

47. A couple of decades later, in 1790, Levy Solomons of Albany opened a chocolate factory to serve his Dutch customers. "Items Relating to the Solomons Family, New York," *Publication of the American Historical Society* 27 (1920): 376.

48. *New York Gazette and Weekly Mercury*, January 25, 1779, 2.

49. *Royal Gazette*, December 2, 1780, 3.

50. *New York Gazette and Weekly Mercury*, February 12, 1781, 4.

51. *New York Gazette and Weekly Mercury*, March 12, 1781, 4.

52. Friedman, *Early American Jews*, 75–76.

53. Bruce Macmillan Bigelow, *The Commerce of Rhode Island with the West Indies Before the American Revolution*, parts 1 and 2 (PhD diss., Brown University, 1930), 2:4.

54. Marcus, *The Colonial American Jew*, 2:649; 2:628.

55. Stanley F. Chyet, *A Merchant of Eminence: The Story of Aaron Lopez* (PhD diss., Hebrew Union College–Jewish Institute of Religion, 1960), 191.

56. Marcus, *The Colonial American Jew*, 2:642.

57. Sarna, "The Jews in British America," in Bernadini and Fiering, *Jews and the Expansion of Europe to the West*, 527.

58. Bruce Macmillian Bigelow, "Colonial Merchant of Newport," *New England Quarterly* 4, no. 4 (October, 1931): 776.

59. Marcus, *The Colonial American Jew*, 2:673.

60. Stanley F. Chyet, *Lopez of Newport* (Detroit, MI: Wayne State University Press, 1970), 28.

61. MS 231 Folder 1/9, AJA, Cincinnati, OH; Lopez Letterbook 640, February 21, 1781, 66, NHS, Newport, Rhode Island.

62. Aaron Lopez Account Book, 720/322, NHS, Newport, RI.

63. Aaron Lopez Store Blotter, 667, Newport Historical Society (NHS), Newport, RI.

64. Lopez Account Book, 118, NHS, Newport, RI.

65. Chyet, Lopez of Newport, 160. On a voyage from London that began in May of 1750, George Fisher described that because of the small allotment of food allowed by the captain, "myself and most of my family subsisted almost entirely on Coffee, Tea and chocolate, wherewith we were well provided." See *William & Mary Quarterly Historical Magazine*, series 1, vol. 17, no. 1 (July 1908): 133.

66. James B. Hedges, *The Browns of Providence Plantations: Colonial Years* (Cambridge, MA: Harvard University Press, 1952), 8–9.

67. MSS Book 650 Lopez Collection 1780–8, NHS, Newport, RI.

68. From the *Memorandum Book O* 554, Lopez Collection, 119, NHS, Newport, RI.

69. On June 16, 1773, John Baker of Boston charged James Baker 1 pound, 2 shillings, 6 pence for "one days work at your Chocolate Mill." Miller "Calendar," 5.

70. For nearly a century, 1725–1807, the American slave trade was quite connected with Rhode Island. Rhode Island merchants controlled between 60 and 80 percent of the American slave traffic. However, according to Bert Lippincott, librarian and genealogist at Newport Historical Society, only 1 percent of Lopez's trade dealt in slaves (interview with the author, September 10, 2009). See Saul S. Freidman, *Jews and the American Slave Trade* (New Brunswick, NJ: Transaction Publishers, 1998), 121. In Newport, the census of 1730 showed a population of 4,640 people plus 649 slaves, according to Weeden, *Rhode Island*, 192.

Prince Updike is not listed as a member of free Negro households in the 1774 town census, which suggests that he may not have been free during the time of his chocolate manufacturing activities.

According to Keith Stokes of the Newport Chamber of Commerce, in an e-mail message to author, September 2009: "Enslaved Africans and Mulattos (African and Indian mix) comprised nearly 20 percent of the entire Newport population by 1770. For the most part, slaves were trained to work within urban seaport economies, i.e., sail lofts, rope works, fish processing, rum making and spermaceti candles, etc. Many of these slaves were apprenticed and trained as artisans. Slaves in the households of Lopez, Rivera, and other Newport Jews were given Jewish names including Sara, Moses, Rebecca, etc. These close work, home, and religious relationships would create unique bonds between master and slave. When a five-year-old enslaved African boy drowned in Newport Harbor, Aaron Lopez funded the proper burial and marker. By 1780, the Free African Union Society was formed at Newport, a first of its kind in the Americas where former slaves organized and chartered a self-help organization with the Rhode Island General Assembly."

71. Eli Faber, *A Time for Planting: The First Migration 1654–1820*, vol. 1, *The Jewish People in America* (Baltimore, MD: Johns Hopkins University Press, 1992), 136.

72. For further information about Prince Updike, see *Spinner's Book* 715/36, NHS, Newport, RI.

73. Regarding Abraham or Abram Casey, see *Spinner's Book* 715/37, 40, NHS, Newport, RI. The *Rhode Island Newspaper* reports Abraham Casey's death in the September 25, 1844 issue. Regarding Cornelius Casey, see *Memorandum Book O*, Lopez Collection, 142, NHS, Newport, RI.

In an 1805 list of occupations, the *Book of Occupations* by George H. Richardson, NHS, Newport, RI, Casey is recorded as a chimney sweep. These later references suggest that Abraham must have been rather young when he was grinding chocolate for Lopez. We do not know whether Cornelius was his father, his brother, or even related.

Jews Retailed Chocolate before Baker's

a. Bruce Miller, "A Calendar of Walter Baker & Company, Inc., and Its Times," General Foods Corporation, 1940, Rockefeller Library, Williamsburg, VA.

b. *Boston Gazette and Country Journal*, July 14, 1760, 4.

c. *New York Gazette*, May 11, 1761, supplement 2.

d. *New York Gazette and Country Journal*, December 2, 1760, 2; *New York Mercury*, January 26, 1761, 4.

e. Special Collections 4477, AJA, Cincinnati, OH. In 1763 Nathan Hart did the same in an advertisement in *The Newport Mercury*, June 27, 1763, 4.

f. September 24, 1760, AJA, Cincinnati, OH; and Jacob Rader Marcus, *The Jew in the American World: A Source Book* (Detroit, MI: Wayne State University Press, 1996), 54.

g. Jacob Rader Marcus, *American Jewry: Documents Eighteenth Century* (Cincinnati, OH: Hebrew Union College Press, 1959), 350. Also, Special Collection 11496, AJA, Cincinnati, OH. Others in the retail business included:

[1773] Benjamin Levy, the first Jew to settle permanently in Baltimore, who ran the largest ad in the *Maryland Journal and Advertiser* for his chocolate and snuff business. *Paving Our Way: Early Maryland Jewish Life 1632–1845: A Living History Resource Kit*, presented by the Jewish Museum of Maryland, accessed 2006, www.jhsm.org/html/documents/PavingOurWay1.3.07.pdf.

[1770s] Abraham Wagg, who married Rachel Gomez, daughter of Mordecai and Rebecca on July 4, 1770, engaged in the business of wholesale grocer and chocolate manufacturer. Abraham G. Duker, "Emerging Culture Patterns in American Jewish Life: The Psycho Social Approach to the Study of Jewish Life in America," *Publications of the American Jewish Historical Society* 39 (September 1949–June 1950): 1–4.

[1770s] Benjamin Lyon and Isaac Werden in Canada competed for business, including chocolate sales. Jacob Rader Marcus, *Early American Jewry: The Jews of New York, England and Canada 1649–1794* (Philadelphia, PA: Jewish Publication Society, 1951), 236.

[1808] Jacob Philipson advertised chocolate and sugar in the *Missouri Gazette* when he announced the opening of his new store opposite the post office.

Business Advertisements from the *Missouri Gazette* 1808, AJA, Cincinnati, OH.

Colonial Chocolate Recipes

a. Hannah Glasse, *The Art of Cookery Made Plain and Easy, 1796 Edition* (New York: United States Historical Research Service, 1994), 341.

Jews Traded Cacao from Philadelphia

a. Maxwell Whiteman and Edwin Wolf, *The History of the Jews of Philadelphia from Colonial Times to the Age of Jackson*, 2nd ed. (Philadelphia, PA: Jewish Publication Society of America, 1957), 339, citing *Poulson's American Daily Advertiser* record of December 8, 1801.

Jewish Estate Inventories: Personal Chocolate Usage

a. Leo Hershkowitz, "Original Inventories of Early American Jews (1682–1763)," *American Jewish History*, 90n3 (September 2002): 283, 300–301, 307–8, 318–19, 409, 419, 425, 440–42. Aaron Lopez Estate Inventory, Death Notices, 1783, MS 231/1/4, AJA, Cincinnati, OH.

Jewish Chocolate Grinders Working for Aaron Lopez

a. Lopez Memorandum Book 459/491, NHS, Newport, RI; Lopez Memorandum Book R/118/318, NHS, Newport, RI; Lopez Memorandum Book 463/ 215, NHS, Newport, RI; Lopez Memorandum Book 716/327, NHS, Newport, RI.

CHAPTER 4: CHANUKAH AND CHRISTMAS CHOCOLATE MELT INTO GELT

1. Marvin Tameanko, "The Original Chanukah Gelt," American Numismatic Association, accessed March 2, 2009, http://theshekel.org/articles_chanukah_gelt_4.html.

2. Tina Wasserman, "Who Invented Chanukah Gelt?" *Reform Judaism*, Winter 2005, accessed March 2, 2009, http://reformjudaismmag.org/Articles/index.cfm?id=1081.

3. Amy Klein, "In Search of Chanukah Gelt," *Jewish Journal*, November 29, 2007; Mark Mietkiewicz, "Gelt Is Good: Net Clarifies Old Traditions, New Customs," *Jewish News Weekly of Northern California*, November 15, 2002; Yisrael Rice, "Why the Gelt?" Chabad Lubavitch, accessed March 2, 2009, www.chabad.org/holidays/chanukah/article_cdo/aid/103084/jewish/Why-the-Gelt.html; Eliezer Segal, *Holidays, History and Halakah* (New York: Jason Aronson, 2000), 87; "From Gelt to Gifts," an online column about the holidays, accessed March 2, 2009, acs.ucalgary.ca/~elsegal/Shokel/961121_Geltl.html.

4. "History of Chocolate," Chocoladefabriken Lindt & Sprüngli AG, Lindt Chocomania, accessed December 2006, www.lindt.com/1222/1228/1254/1255.asp; Sophie D. Coe, *America's First Cuisines* (Austin: University of Texas, 1994), 102–3.

5. Wasserman, "Who Invented Chanukah Gelt?"; Jenna Joselit, *The Wonders of America: Reinventing Jewish Culture 1880–1950* (New York: Hill and Wang, 1996), 233ff; Yehuda Shiff and Dani Dor, eds., *Israel 50* (Israel: Elite, 1997), issued in celebration of the sixty-fifth anniversary of Elite.

6. "Chocolate Coins," accessed December 2010, www.youtube.com/watch?v=g8HvhJ5Os6w&feature=related.

7. "Feast of St. Nicholas," Fish Eaters, accessed March 2, 2009, www.fisheaters.com/customsadvent3.html.

CHAPTER 5: CHOCOLATE REVIVES REFUGEES, SURVIVORS, AND IMMIGRANTS

1. Lisa Hoffman and Charles Atkins, "Elsa Hoffman's Gift—a Thanksgiving Story," November 24, 2005, accessed July 2011, www.charlesatkins.com/chocolate_thanksgiving.htm.

2. Gil Marks, *Encyclopedia of Jewish Food* (Hoboken, NJ: John Wiley & Sons, 2010), 171–72.

3. See information about some business controversies and questions related to Tootsie Rolls at the "Candy Professor," accessed April 2010, http://candyprofessor.com.

4. Steve Almond, *Candyfreak: A Journey through the Chocolate Underbelly of America* (Chapel Hill, NC: Algonquin Books, 2004), 140.

5. "World's Finest Chocolate," accessed July 2011, www.worldsfinest-chocolate.com.

6. Devan Sipher, "A Family Tree Just Covered in Chocolate," *New York Times*, December 25, 2011, MB3, accessed December 25, 2011, www.nytimes.com/2011/12/25/nyregion/jomart-chocolates-in-brooklyn-stays-in-the-family.html.

7. "Koppers Chocolate," accessed July 2011, www.kopperschocolate.com/main.html.

8. James Stevenson, "Talk of the Town: Chocolates," *New Yorker*, February 1966, 29. http://archives.newyorker.com/?i=1966-02-19#, 30.

9. Ellen Miller, *The Window Shop: Safe Harbor for Refugees* (Bloomington, IN: iUniverse, 2007); Joan Nathan, *The Jewish Holiday Kitchen* (New York: Schocken Books, 1988); "The Window Shop," accessed 2009, www.harvardsquare.com/History/Glimpses/The-Window-Shop.aspx.

10. Ernest Weil, interview with the author, September 9, 2007. Ernest Weil, *Love to Bake: Pastry Cookbook 40 Years of Fantasia Confections' Best 1948–1988* (San Francisco: Ernest Weil, 2006).

11. "Business and the Holocaust," accessed July 2011, www.stockmaven.com/medrepcN.htm.

12. Nick Bryant, "The Secret History of the Nazi Mascot," BBC News, August 21, 2007, accessed July 2011, http://news.bbc.co.uk/2/hi/europe/6945847.stm.

13. WW2 Talk, May 9, 2005, accessed July 2011, www.ww2talk.com/forum/news-articles/5343-death-chocolate.html; Paul Reynolds, "Nazis' Exploding Chocolate Plans," BBC News, September 4, 2005, http://news.bbc.co.uk/2/hi/uk_news/politics/4204980.stm.

14. Maureen Dowd, "Hitler's Talking Dogs," *New York Times*, July 13, 2011, A27.

15. Haim Gouri, *The Chocolate Deal*, trans. Seymour Simckes (New York: Holt, Rinehart and Winston, 1968), 132.

16. "Liberators' Testimonies," accessed July 2011, www.remember.org/liberators.html. Deprivation back home led to creative versions of cakes such as the "World War II (Vegan) Chocolate Cake," accessed July 2011, http://yummyplants.com/vegan-recipe/wwii-vegan-chocolate-cake. See the recipe on page 192.

17. "Chocolate in the 20th and 21st Centuries," Cadbury, accessed December 29, 2011, www.cadbury.co.uk/cadburyandchocolate/historyofchocolate/Pages/chocolate20th21st.aspx.

18. "Ration D Bars," Hershey Community Archives, accessed July 2011, www.hersheyarchives.org/essay/details.aspx?EssayId=26.

19. Hoffman and Atkins, "Elsa Hoffman's Gift."

20. Harry Herder, "Liberation of Buchenwald," Holocaust Cybrary: Remembering the Stories of the Survivors, accessed July 2012, www.remember.org/witness/herder.html.

21. Theo Richmond, *Konin: One Man's Quest for a Vanished Jewish Community* (London: Vintage Books, 1996), quoted in "The Liberation of Mauthausen, May 5, 1945," Scrapbookpages Blog, accessed June 2011, http://furtherglory.wordpress.com/2010/05/07/the-liberation-of-mauthausen-may-5-1945.

22. "Berlin Airlift," accessed November 2011, www.spiritoffreedom.org/airlift.html.

23. Gail S. Halvorsen, *The Berlin Candy Bomber* (Bountiful, UT: Horizon Publishers, 1990), 101, 104–5, 109, 113–23.

24. Michael O. Tunnell, *Candy Bomber: The Story of the Berlin Airlift's Chocolate Uncle* (Watertown, MA: Charlesbridge Publishing, 2010), 62, 67.

25. Margot Theis Raven, *Mercedes and the Chocolate Pilot: A True Story of the Berlin Airlift and the Candy That Dropped from the Sky* (MI: Sleeping Bear Press, 2002), 22, 137.

26. Gregg J. Rickman, *Swiss Banks and Jewish Souls* (New York: Transaction Publishers, 1999), 141.

27. Tom Bower, *Nazi Gold: The Full Story of the Fifty-Year Swiss-Nazi Conspiracy to Steal Billions from Europe's Jews and Holocaust Survivors* (New York: HarperCollins Publishers, 1997), 41ff., 303–4; Brigitte Sion, *Anti-Semitism: Knowing It Better, Fighting It Better* (Geneva: CICAD, 2002), 59–60.

28. Bower, *Nazi Gold*, 295.

29. Dr. Brigitte Sion, interview with the author, March 4, 2011.

30. Brigitte Sion, e-mail message to author, March 6, 2011.

31. Ibid.; Lawrence Grossman and David Singer, "Switzerland," *American Jewish Year Book* (New York: American Jewish Committee, 2002), 303.

32. Morris Freedman, "Orthodox Sweets for Heterodox New York: The Story of Bartons," *Commentary Magazine* (May 1952): 474.

33. A. Leib Scheinbaum, *The Klein Family Edition, the World That was America 1900–1945: Transmitting the Torah Legacy to America*, (The Living Memorial: A Project of the Hebrew Academy of Cleveland and Shaar Press, 2004), 417.

34. Freedman, "Orthodox Sweets," 473.

35. Ibid.

36. Ibid.

37. Freedman, "Orthodox Sweets," 473, 476–7, 478, 480.

38. Jeffrey Ariel Yoskowitz, "Creating a Kosher America: The Orthodox Union's Program to Reclaim Kashrut, 1945–65" (honors thesis, Department of History, Brown University, 2007); Yoskowitz, "A Seder Different from All Other Seders," *The Atlantic*, April 8, 2009, accessed April 2009, www.theatlantic.com/life/archive/2009/04/a-seder-different-from-all-other-seders/7340/; Yoskowitz, "The Kosher Chocolate Wars," *The Atlantic*, April 15, 2009, accessed April 2009, www.theatlantic.com/life/archive/2009/04/the-kosher-chocolate-wars/13045.

Complex Kosher for Passover Chocolate

a. David Golinkin, "A Responsum (*Tshuvah*) Regarding the Custom of Abstaining from Eating *Qitniyot* on Passover," personal website of Benjamin Mordechai Ben Baruch, http://home.earthlink.net/~bbenbaruch/qitniyot-kitniyot.htm; Nathan Jeffay, "Pesach Kitniyot Rebels Roil Rabbis as Some Ashkenazim Follow New, Permissive Ruling," *The Jewish Daily Forward*, April 1, 2009, www.forward.com/articles/104483; Eli J. Mansour, "Passover-Eating Rice on Pesach," *Daily Halacha*, www.dailyhalacha.com/displayRead.asp?readID=537; "The Year's Reformer: Efrat Rabbi Tilts Against Passover Food Restriction for Ashkenazi Jews," April 15, 2011, http://matzav.com/this-years-reformer-efrat-rabbi-tilts-against-passover-food-restrictions-for-ashkenazi-jews.

CHAPTER 6: ISRAELIS:
MESHUGA FOR CHOCOLATE

1. Shoshana Brickman, "Land of Milk, Honey ... and Chocolate," *Inbal Magazine*, 2008; "100 Tons of Chocolate Swiped from Israeli Factory," *Columbus Dispatch*, February 28, 2008.

2. Brinkers, a Dutch company that originally manufactured margarine, claims to have created the first chocolate spread in 1948; accessed April 2011, www.brinkers.com/thecompany/history/index.html.

3. "The Chocolate Soldier," accessed April 2011, http://en.wikipedia.org/wiki/Chocolate_Soldier_%28disambiguation%29; Jay Hurvitz, e-mail to author, April 23, 2011.

> Come, chocolate soldier
> Come to me to the outpost
> Sit and rest, have no fear
> And you'll return to your dust (ashes)
> The chef serves meat to the master chef
> The master chef serves meat to the cannons
> All people are brothers under the flowers
> The cannons roar, the children cry
> Come, chocolate soldier ...
> My brother was brave, he fell on his watch
> The rooms of his heart are now open to the grass and the dew
> My brother had blood, but that blood has been used up
> Even the general's orders won't bring him back
> Left, right, right and left, the battalion marches and sings
> Life is clumsy, death is short
> The entire battalion marches behind the rear of the master sergeant
> The master sergeant also goes the way of all flesh
> (TRANSLATED BY JAY HURVITZ)

4. The Vered Hagalil chocolate company, now owned by Unilever, could not compete with Elite, though it is still available (Janna Gur, interview with the author, February 27, 2011).

5. Shiff and Dor, *Israel 50*.

6. Amihai Zippor, "Full of Beans," *Jerusalem Post*, March 2, 2010, accessed December 21, 2011, www.holycacaochocolate.com/Press.html.

7. "Elite," accessed July 22, 2012, www.strauss-group.com/en/MenultemAboutUs/history/1930; Bernhard Press, *The Murder of the Jews in Latvia: 1941–1945* (Evanston, IL: Northwestern University Press, 2000), 20.

8. "The Smell of Chocolate," accessed June 2009, www.shiron.net/artist?type=lyrics&lang=1&prfid=342&wrkid=7401.

The Smell of Chocolate

Besof Ramat-Gan yesh makom meyuchad,
Sham efshar la'amod ulehariach shokolad.
Yesh sham bayit gavoha gavoha
Bli chalonot, im shalosh arubot
Ushloshim mechonot yom valayla ovdot
Veshiv'im poalim im sinar ukfafot
Mechinim shokolad bechol hatzurot.

Chorus:
Shokolad katan veshokolad gadol (sho-ko-ko-)
Shokolad yakar veshokolad bezol
Shokolad egozim veshokolad stam
La'ashirim, ulechulam
Vehareyach bechinam ...
vechol ha'ezrachim (tu-tu-tu-tu ...)
Otzrim umerichim (mmm ...)
Otzrim hayeladim sheratzim bashchuna
Otzer ha'otobus me'ever lapina
Hachatulim mafsikim livroach mehaklavim
Vehashotrim omdim leyad haganavim
Kulam mabitim el ha'arubot
Ule'at le'at, ha'af shelahem
Mitmaleh bereyach shel shokolad.

Chorus:
Shokolad katan veshokolad gadol....
Besof Ramat-Gan yesh makom meyuchad,
Sham efshar la'amod ulehariach shokolad.

At the edge of Ramat Gan there's a special place
Where you can stand and smell chocolate in the air
There's a big tall house
With three chimneys and no windows
And thirty machines inside working all day and night
Seventy workers in aprons and mitts
Making chocolate of every kind.

Chorus:
Small chocolate, big chocolate (*sho-ko-ko-*)
Expensive chocolate, cheap chocolate
Chocolate with nuts and plain
For the rich people, and for us all
And the smell is free
so all the citizens
Stop to sniff the air (mmm ...)
The kids stop running in the streets
The bus stops at the corner

The dogs stop chasing the cats
Even the policemen stand near the thieves
Everyone gazes up at the chimneys
And their noses slowly fill
With the sweet smell of chocolate

Chorus:
Small chocolate, big chocolate ...
There is a special place at Ramat Gan where it is possible to stand
and smell chocolate.

9. Shiff and Dor, *Israel 50.*

CHAPTER 7: PRE-COLUMBIAN PEOPLES IDOLIZED CHOCOLATE IN MESOAMERICA

1. View this at *Jews on the Chocolate Trail,* www.jews-onthechocolatetrail. org/2009/01/chocolate-in-mexico.

2. Liebman, *New Spain,* 19–20.

3. Wiznitzer, "Crypto Jews in Mexico in the 16th Century," 168–9; Wiznitzer, "Crypto-Jews in Mexico in the 17th Century," 262. See chapter 2.

4. Liebman, *New Spain,* 151; Hoberman, "Merchants," 27.

5. Lisa J. LeCount, "Like Water for Chocolate: Feasting and Political Ritual among the Late Classic Maya at Xunantunich, Belize," *American Anthropologist* 103, no. 4 (2001): 947–48.

6. Patricia A. McAnany and Satoru Murata, "America's First Connoisseurs of Chocolate," *Food & Foodways* 15 (2007): 5, 14, 20.

7. Meredith L. Dreiss and Sharon Edgar Greenhill, *Chocolate: Pathways to the Gods* (Tucson: University of Arizona Press, 2008), 4, 9.

8. LeCount, "Like Water," 948; McAnany and Murata, "America's First Connoisseurs," 20, 24–25, 27, 49. This concept of "world trees," a motif in Mesoamerican myth and art, recalls the four directions and connects the earth with the heavens.

9. Ana M. de Benítez, *Cocina Prehispanica* (Evanston, IL: Adler's Foreign Books, 1977), 113–20, based on the Codex Borgia, a Mesoamerican ritual and divinatory manuscript, written before the Spanish conquest of Mexico, in southern or western Puebla.

10. Fray Diego Durán, *Book of the Gods and Rites and the Ancient Calendar,* trans. and ed. Fernando Horcasitas and Doris Heyden (Norman, OK: University of Oklahoma Press, 1971), 130–32, 156–200.

11. Coe and Coe, *True History,* 44; Durán, *Book of the Gods,* 155–58, 215; Dreiss and Greenhill, *Chocolate,* 35, 44, 58; Dennis Tedlock, *2000 Years of Mayan Literature* (Los Angeles: University of California Press, 2010), 34–35.

12. Michael Coe and Rex Koontz, *The Maya* (London: Thames and Hudson, 2005), 42, 57, 218; Dreiss and Greenhill, *Chocolate*, 21, 27; Norton, *Sacred Gifts*, 24, 27, 29–30.

13. Meredith L. Dreiss and Sharon Edgar Greenhill, *Chocolate: Pathways to the Gods* (Tucson: University of Arizona Press, 2008), 66.

14. Sophie D. Coe, *America's First Cuisines* (Austin: University of Texas, 1994), 77–80; Coe and Koontz, *Maya*, 49, 173; Dreiss and Greenhill, *Chocolate*, 66–67, 69; Norton, *Sacred Gifts*, 35.

15. Tedlock, *2000 Years*, 35, 64, 66.

16. Cameron L. McNeil, "Traditional Cacao Use in Modern Mesoamerica," in *Chocolate in Mesoamerica: A Cultural History of Cacao*, ed. Cameron L. McNeil (Gainesville: University Press of Florida, 2009), 361, 363.

17. Seth Kugel, "Frugal Summer: Highs and Lows," *The New York Times Frugal Traveler Blog*, September 19, 2010, accessed, July 2011, http://frugaltraveler.blogs.nytimes.com/2010/09/14/frugal-summer-highs-and-lows; Dreiss and Greenhill, *Chocolate*, 76; McNeil, "Traditional Cacao Use," in McNeil, *Chocolate in Mesoamerica*, 363.

18. Dreiss and Greenhill, *Chocolate*, 42, 59.

19. McNeil, "Traditional Cacao Use," in McNeil, *Chocolate in Mesoamerica*, 357; Dreiss and Greenhill, *Chocolate*, 52.

20. Grivetti and Shapiro, *Chocolate*, 105.

History of Cacao

a. Coe and Coe, *True History*, 39; Coe and Koontz, *Maya*, 99, 174–75; Dreiss and Greenhill, *Chocolate*, 44; McAnany and Murata, "America's First Connoisseurs," 8; McNeil, "Introduction: The Biology, Antiquity, and Modern Uses of the Chocolate Tree," in McNeil, *Chocolate in Mesoamerica*, 9; Terry G. Powis et al., "Spouted Vessels and Cacao Use among the Preclassic Maya," *Latin American Antiquity* 13, no. 1 (March 2002): 91–94, 100.

CHAPTER 8: FAITH DIFFUSED CHOCOLATE AROUND THE WORLD

1. Cynthia Elyce Rubin, ed., *Bread and Chocolate: Culinary Traditions of Switzerland* (New York: New York Writer's House, 1993), 20, 57.

2. Ann Ball, "When the Church Said No to Chocolate," 3–4, accessed July 7, 2010, www.mexconnect.com/articles/1469-when-the-church-said-no-to-chocolate; Elisabeth Lambert Ortiz, "Mole Poblano and Turkey," in *The Wilder Shores of Gastronomy: Twenty Years of the Best Food Writing from the Journal Petits Propos Culinaires*, ed. Alan Davidson (Berkeley, CA: Ten Speed Press, 2002), 440–44. Rosenblum, *Chocolate*, 67ff.

3. A. J. R. Russell-Wood, *A World on the Move: The Portuguese in Africa, Asia, and America 1415–1808* (Manchester, UK: Carcanet Press, 1992), 92.

4. Liebman, *New Spain*, 124.

5. Forrest and Naijaj, "Sipping Sin," 42.

6. Norton, *Sacred Gifts*, 54.

7. Marcia Zoladz, "Cacao in Brazil or the History of a Crime," in *Food and Morality: Proceedings of the Oxford Symposium on Food and Cookery 2007*, ed. Susan Friedland (Devon, England: Prospect Books, 2008), 314.

8. Norton, *Sacred Gifts*, 55.

9. Maguelonne Toussaint-Samat, *History of Food*, trans. Anthea Bell (Oxford, UK: Blackwell Press, 1996), 576.

10. He compiled the *Historia general de las cosas de Nueva España* (*General History of the Things of New Spain, or the Florentine Codex*) in 1569.

11. Dreiss and Greenhill, *Chocolate*, 67.

12. *The History of the Indies of New Spain*, also known as the *Durán Codex* (c. 1581), *Book of the Gods and Rites* (1574–76), and *Ancient Calendar* (c. 1579). Fray Diego Durán, *Book of the Gods and Rites and the Ancient Calendar*, trans. and ed. Fernanco Horcasitas and Doris Heyden (Norman, OK: Oklahoma University Press, 1970).

13. Nathalie Bailleux et al., *The Book of Chocolate* (Paris: Flammarion, 1995), 71ff.

14. Forrest and Naijaj, "Sipping Sin," 44.

15. Norton, *Sacred Gifts*, 132.

16. Forrest and Naijaj, "Sipping Sin," 34.

17. Jean McClure Mudge, *Chinese Export Porcelain in North America* (New York: Clarkson N. Potter, Inc., 1986), 44.

18. McNeil, "Introduction," in McNeil, *Chocolate in Mesoamerica*, 22.

19. Brandon Head, *Food of the Gods: A Popular Account of Cocoa* (New York: Dutton, 1903), e-book from Project Gutenberg, 83.

20. Norton, *Sacred Gifts*, 77–78.

21. Ibid.

22. William G. Clarence-Smith, *Cocoa and Chocolate, 1765–1914* (London: Routledge, 2000), 17.

23. Norton, *Sacred Gifts*, 80–82. Valadés, the son of an Indian noblewoman and a Spanish conquistador who passed as pure Spanish, wrote *Rhetorica Christiana*.

24. Manuel Aguilar-Moreno, "The Good and Evil of Chocolate in Colonial Mexico," in McNeil, *Chocolate in Mesoamerica*, 278.

25. Norton, *Sacred Gifts*, 250.

26. Ibid., 251.

27. Ibid., 197.

28. Bailleux et al., *Book of Chocolate*, 75; Robert Ferry, "Trading Cacao," See Simon Martin, "Cacao in Ancient Maya Religion," in McNeil,

Chocolate in Mesoamerica, 274–5; Norton, *Sacred Gifts*, 140, 196–97, 251; Toussaint-Samat, *History of Food*, 576.

29. Martin, "Cacao," in McNeil, *Chocolate in Mesoamerica*, 164.

30. McNeil, "Introduction," in McNeil, *Chocolate in Mesoamerica*, 22; Aguilar-Moreno, "Good and Evil," in McNeil, *Chocolate in Mesoamerica*, 278; Norton, *Sacred Gifts*, 65–66.

31. Norton, *Sacred Gifts*, 249.

32. Ibid., 69–75.

33. Ibid.

34. Ibid., 74–76.

35. Ibid., 67.

36. Ibid., 68.

37. Ibid., 68–69.

38. Ibid., 231, 234.

39. Forrest, "Sipping Sin," 33, 41.

40. Norton, *Sacred Gifts*, 131, 242, 244; Toussaint-Samat, *History of Food*, 576; Forrest, "Sipping Sin," 34.

41. Norton, *Sacred Gifts*, 243, 245.

42. Aguilar-Moreno, "Good and Evil" in McNeil, *Chocolate in Mesoamerica*, 283. Hurtado supported this opinion by quoting popes such as Gregory XIII, Paulus V, and Pius V, who shared his view. See also Forest, "Sipping Sin," 42.

43. Aguilar-Moreno, "Good and Evil," in McNeil, *Chocolate in Mesoamerica*, 283; Bailleux et al., *Book of Chocolate*, 83.

44. Bailleux et al., *Book of Chocolate*, 80; J. Piero Camporesi, *Exotic Brew: The Art of Living in the Age of Enlightenment*, trans. Christopher Woodall (Cambridge, MA: Polity Press, 1994), 55; Janine Gasco, "The Social and Economic History of Cacao Cultivation in Colonial Soconusco, New Spain," in *Chocolate: Food of the Gods*, ed. A. Szogyi (Westport, CT: Greenwood Press, 1997), 200; Norton, *Sacred Gifts*, 169, 173–74, 259.

45. Camporesi, *Exotic Brew*, 42.

46. Ibid., 72.

47. Ibid., 111.

48. Ibid., 110.

49. Jean Anthelme Brillat Savarin, *A Handbook of Gastronomy*, trans. Adolphe Lalauze (London: J. C. Nimmo and Bain), 161.

50. Camporesi, *Exotic Brew*, 117, 140.

51. Ibid.

52. Ibid., 141–42.

53. Ibid., 145–47, 163–64.

54. Ibid., 64; Zoladz, "Cacao in Brazil," in Friedland, *Food and Morality*, 310–12.

55. Timothy Walker, "Slave Labor and Chocolate in Brazil: The Culture of Cacao Plantations in Amazonia and Bahia (17th–19th Centuries)," *Food and Foodways* 15 (January 2007): 75, 85, 155, 164.

56. Willem Klooster and Alfred Padula, *The Atlantic World: Essays on Slavery, Migration and Imagination* (Upper Saddle River, NJ: Pearson/Prentice Hall, 2005), 21.

57. Zoladz, "Cacao in Brazil," in Friedland, *Food and Morality*, 312.

58. Klooster and Padula, *Atlantic World*, 20; Zoladz, "Cacao in Brazil," in Friedland, *Food and Morality*, 311; Forrest, "Sipping Sin," 7.

59. Beatriz Cabezon, "Cacao, Haciendas and the Jesuits: Letters from New Spain 1693–1751," in Grivetti and Shapiro, *Chocolate*, 607–9.

60. Patricia Barriga and Beatriz Cabezon, "Sailors, Soldiers and Padres: California Chocolate 1542?–1840," in Grivetti and Shapiro, *Chocolate*, 440.

61. Ibid., 443.

62. Ibid.

63. Ibid., 445.

64. Ibid., 446.

65. Ibid.

66. Ibid., 441–42, 444, 447–48, 450–51.

CHAPTER 9: UTOPIAN CHOCOLATE SAVED SOULS: FROM CADBURY TO HERSHEY

1. See Bailleux et al., *Book of Chocolate*, 102.

2. Fry built upon the company of chocolate maker Churchman, who had advertised, "Mr Churchman's Chocolate Mills and works there which being a secret cannot be exposed to view." James Walvin, *Fruits of Empire: Exotic Produce and British Taste 1660–1800* (New York: New York University Press, 1997), 98–99; Bailleux, *Book of Chocolate*, 102.

3. Carol Off, *Bitter Chocolate: Investigating the Dark Side of the World's Most Seductive Sweet* (New York: Random House, 2006), 50.

4. Bertram Gordon, "Chocolate in England from Introduction to Industrialization," in Grivetti and Shapiro, *Chocolate*, 588.

5. Ibid., 589.

6. Emma Robertson, Marek Korczynski, and Michael Pickering, "Harmonious Relations? Music at Work in the Rowntree and Cadbury Factories," *Business History* 49, no. 2 (March 2007): 211–34.

7. Mark K. Smith, "Adult Schools and the Making of Adult Education," Encyclopedia of Information Education, 2004, accessed August 2010, www.infed.org/lifelonglearning/adult_schools.htm.

8. J. B. Priestley, *English Journey: Being a Rambling but Truthful Account of What One Man Saw and Heard and Felt and Thought During a Journey through England during the Autumn of the Year 1933* (London: William Heinemann, 1934), 95.

9. A. G. Gardiner, *Life of George Cadbury* (New York: Cassell and Company, 1923), 133, 281.

10. Deborah Cadbury, *The Chocolate Wars: The 150-Year Rivalry Between the World's Greatest Chocolate Makers* (New York: Public Affairs, 2010), 164.

11. Anne Vernon, *A Quaker Business Man: The Life of Joseph Rowntree 1836–1925* (Sydney, Australia: Allen and Unwin, 1958), 23, 27, 31, 60.

12. Ibid., 147.

13. Tammy L. Hamilton, archivist, Hershey Community Archives, e-mail message to author, July 14, 2010.

14. Joël Glenn Brenner, *The Emperors of Chocolate: Inside the Secret World of Hershey and Mars* (New York: Random House, 1999), 85.

15. Michael D'Antonio, *Hershey* (New York: Simon and Schuster, 2006), 86, 89, 91, 95, 102; Nicholas Westbrook, "Chocolate at the World's Fairs," in Grivetti and Shapiro, *Chocolate*, 185–205.

16. D'Antonio, *Hershey*, 114–5.

17. Brenner, *Emperors*, 114–16.

18. D'Antonio, *Hershey*, 130.

19. Brenner, *Emperors*, 133; D'Antonio, *Hershey*, 203; "Hershey Trust Company," Hershey Community Archives, accessed July 14, 2010, www.hersheyarchives.org/essay/details.aspx?EssayId=23&Rurl=%2fresources%2fsearch-results.aspx%3fType%3dBrowseEssay.

20. "Britain Wins EU Chocolate Battle," CNN World, accessed November 2011, www.cnn.com/2003/WORLD/europe/01/16/chocolate.war.

21. D'Antonio, *Hershey*, 91–92, 95, 119.

22. See more about this at: "Kissing Cousins: The Hershey's Kiss and the Wilbur Bud," accessed May 1, 2010, http://candyprofessor.com; on the naming of the Kiss, see "Hershey's: Why a Kiss Is Just a Kiss," accessed May 1, 2010, http://candyprofessor.com. See Zoe's Online Hershey Kisses Collection of more than fifty-five Kisses flavors, accessed June 2010, www.lauracarey.com/kisses.

23. Off, *Bitter Chocolate*, 61.

24. Lowell J. Satre, *Chocolate on Trial: Slavery, Politics and the Ethics of Business* (Athens, OH: Ohio State University Press, 2005), 8.

25. August Chevalier, "The Island of São Thomé," *Bulletin of the American Geographical Society* 42, no. 9 (1910): 665.

26. The Portuguese first populated São Tomé with Jewish children kidnapped from their parents in 1493. Also, Jews and New Christians were deported as undesirables to São Tomé, Cape Verde, and Angola with the expectation

that they would not survive there. Russell Wood, *A World on the Move: The Portuguese in Africa, Asia, and America 1415–1808* (Manchester, UK: Carcanet Press, 1992), 107–8; Dagmar Schaffer, *Portuguese Exploration to the West and the Formation of Brazil 1450–1800: Catalogue of an Exhibition* (Providence, RI: John Carter Brown Library, 1988), 17.

27. Satre, *Chocolate on Trial*, 10.

28. Gillian Wagner, *The Chocolate Conscience* (London: Chatto and Windus, 1987), 93.

CHAPTER 10: SHOPPING FOR THE BEST CHOCOLATE: VALUES AND ETHICS

1. Brian Woods and Kate Blewett, *Slavery: A Global Investigation* (London: True Vision, BBC, 2001), http://freedocumentaries.org/film.php?id=192.

2. Ross W. Jamieson, "The Essence of Commodification: Caffeine Dependencies in the Early Modern World," *Journal of Social History* 35, no. 2 (Winter 2001): 269–94.

3. Bill Guyton, World Cocoa Foundation, interview with the author and e-mail message to the author, September 27, 2010: "The vast majority of cocoa in Africa is grown on nearly two million small, independent family farms that are less than 5 acres in size (many of which have been farmed in the same way for generations by the same families). African cocoa farmers and families face a number of challenges: low yields due to aging trees, pests and diseases that attack their cocoa trees, difficulty obtaining farming supplies, and limited access to credit." See World Cocoa Foundation, accessed September 2010, www.worldcocoafoundation.org/index.html.

4. Walker, "Slave Labor and Chocolate in Brazil," 79.

5. Satre, *Chocolate on Trial*; Off, *Bitter Chocolate*, 96; Sudarsan Raghavan, "Two Boys Tell of Descent into Slavery," *JSOnline: Milwaukee Journal Sentinel*, June 25, 2001, accessed September, 2010, http://jsonline.com; Christian Parenti, "Chocolate's Bittersweet Economy," CNN Money, February 15, 2008, accessed September 2010, http://money.CNN.com.

6. Jorge Amado, *The Violent Land*, trans. Samuel Putnam (New York: Alfred Knopf, 1965), 273.

7. Sarah Moss and Alexander Badenoch, *Chocolate: A Global History* (Chicago: University of Chicago Press, 2009), 80ff.

8. Put the issue of the abuses and scandals of child slave trafficking right into the Passover seder by using *A Haggadah for a Chocolate Seder*, which may be found at the website for *On the Chocolate Trail* at www.jews-onthechocolatetrail.org/booksupplement/. See recent coverage for updates on the Harkin Engel Protocol. Deadlines were delayed until 2008 and then still not fully implemented. Thousands of children have been assisted; however, the total estimated number of children in cacao

agricultural work is 1.8 million. See http://harkin.senate.gov/press/
release.cfm?i=332330.

9. Leslie Josephs, "Selling Candy with a Conscience," *Wall Street Journal*, accessed December 24, 2010, http://online.wsj.com/article SB10001424052748704278404576037921787419978.html.

10. "Sweetening the Supply of Cocoa," Kraft Foods, accessed November 2011, www.kraftfoodscompany.com/deliciousworld/sustainability/sweetening_cocoa.aspx.

11. Shawn Askinosie, interview with the author, July 15, 2008.

12. "Chocolate University," Askinosie Chocolate. When he travels he sends reports back to the students. The factory shuts down when they visit. Curriculum components relate to the chocolate business. They develop service projects for local Africans, such as a deep water wells in Tenende, Tanzania. They underwrote a computer lab for the Springfield homeless children and families, and more.

13. Judy Logback, lecture, April 8, 2010, at Food Emporium Chocolate Room, New York; Jill Santopietro, "When Chocolate Is a Way of Life," *New York Times*, November 5, 2008.

14. Judy Logback, e-mail message to author, May 22, 2010.

15. Rainforest Alliance, accessed April 2010, www.rainforest-alliance.org.

16. David Wolfe, *Superfoods: The Food and Medicine of the Future* (Berkeley, CA: North Atlantic Books, 2009), 36.

17. For FDA guidelines and definition of white chocolate, see "Guidance for Industry: Standard of Identity for White Chocolate," U.S. Food and Drug Administration, July 17, 2008, accessed July 2011, www.fda.gov/Food/GuidanceComplianceRegulatoryInformation/GuidanceDocuments/FoodLabelingNutrition/ucm059076.htm.

18. Andrew Osborn, "Chocolate War Over after 30 Years," *The Guardian*, January 16, 2003, accessed April 2010, www.guardian.co.uk/uk/2003/jan/17/foodanddrink; Colin Blane, "EuroChocolate War Ends," BBC News, May 25, 2000, accessed April 2010, http://news.bbc.co.uk/2/hi/europe/764305.stm.

19. Judy Logback, e-mail message to author, May 22, 2010.

20. Bachya ben Asher ben Hlava, *Shulchan Shel Arba*, 497, cited in Jonathan Brumberg-Kraus, "'Torah on the Table': A Sensual Morality," in *Food and Morality: Proceedings of the Oxford Symposium on Food and Cookery 2007*, ed. Susan R. Friedland (Totnes, UK: Prospect Books, 2008), 47.

AFTERWORD

1. Dr. Howard Marcus, snail mail communication, February 16, 2010.

Glossary

Ashkenazi (plural, Ashkenazim): A Jewish person of Eastern European descent.

bain-marie: A cooking technique used for melting chocolate, by which one melts the chocolate in a bowl laid atop a pot of hot water.

bean to bar: Processing of the cocoa bean into chocolate, rather than using melted chocolate from slabs or from disks.

bicerin: An Italian layered drink of espresso, hot chocolate, and milk or cream, named for the glass in which it is served.

bloom on the chocolate: A whitish tinge that suggests improper temperatures in storage, perhaps too cold or too warm. It is still edible, however.

cacao: May refer to the bean, the pod, or the tree. Cacao and cocoa may be used interchangeably.

chocolate: Processed cacao beans in a liquid or solid form; before the end of the eighteenth century this often referred to the beverage.

cocoa butter: The yellowish fat derived from the cacao bean.

cocoa liquor: Liquid form of chocolate that contains equal parts of cocoa butter and cocoa solids.

cocoa powder: A low-fat component of chocolate made from the roasted beans. May be mixed with milk solids for preparing hot cocoa.

cocoa solids: These give chocolate color, flavor, and a low melting point; cocoa butter aids its smoothness. Cocoa solids also contain the greatest concentration of the psychoactive chemicals caffeine and theobromine, which are mostly absent in the other part of chocolate, the cocoa butter or fat.

conversos: Jews from the Iberian Peninsula who converted to Christianity to avoid persecution during the Spanish Inquisition, many of whom maintained secret Jewish practices at home.

dreidel: The children's game of Chanukah using a spinning top; the winner is sometimes paid in coins.

emulsifier: An additive such as soy lecithin that creates a smoother chocolate. Additives are used in place of longer conching.

gelt: The Yiddish word for money.

hechsher: A mark of rabbinic certification that a food or an item is kosher.

Inquisition: Established in 1478 by Catholic monarchs Ferdinand II of Aragon and Isabella of Castille to ensure orthodoxy of Catholic religion and elimination of heresies.

jicara **(Spanish),** *xicara* **(Portuguese):** A term for a gourd used as a vessel for drinking chocolate.

kashrut: Jewish dietary laws. When a food is permissible according to the laws of kashrut, it is kosher.

metate, *piedre, pierre,* **chocolate stone, or quern:** A stone for warming and crushing cacao beans to make chocolate.

molinollo, **mill, stirrer, or stick:** Used for mixing the chocolate beverage in a pot.

pareve: Containing neither dairy nor meat. According to Jewish dietary law, meat and dairy cannot be mixed, so a pareve food may be eaten at either a dairy or meat meal.

Seder: Ritual meal for Passover.

Sephardi (plural, Sephardim): A Jewish person of Iberian descent.

tecomate: A deep clay cup used for drinking chocolate in Mesoamerica.

torta di nocciole con cioccolata calda: Hot chocolate soup poured over a fresh hazelnut cake.

white chocolate: A confection comprised of cocoa butter, milk solids, and sugar without cocoa mass or cocoa liquor; some do not consider it chocolate.

Resources for Further Learning

ON THE CHOCOLATE TRAIL WEBSITE

For further learning and engagement around chocolate, additional resources may be found at the *On the Chocolate Trail* website, www.jews-onthechocolatetrail.org/booksupplement/, including the following:

- Lesson plans for teaching about Jews and chocolate
- *A Haggadah for a Chocolate Seder* for Passover
- Selected responsa and Jewish texts related to chocolate, cocoa, or cacao
- Detailed charts of citations and data for "Jews Dip into Chocolate in the American Colonial Period"

BIBLIOGRAPHY

Bailleux, Nathalie, et al. *The Book of Chocolate*. Paris: Flammarion, 1995.

Brenner, Joël Glenn. *The Emperors of Chocolate: Inside the Secret World of Hershey and Mars*. New York: Random House, 1999.

Coe, Sophie D., and Michael D. Coe. *The True History of Chocolate*. London: Thames and Hudson, 1996.

Dreiss, Meredith L., and Sharon Edgar Greenhill. *Chocolate: Pathway to the Gods*. Tucson: University of Arizona Press, 2008.

Grivetti, Louis Evan, and Howard-Yana Shapiro, eds. *Chocolate: History, Culture and Heritage*. Hoboken, NJ: John Wiley & Sons, 2009.

Lebovitz, David. *The Great Book of Chocolate*. Berkeley, CA: Ten Speed Press, 2004.

Lopez, Ruth. *Chocolate: The Nature of Indulgence*. New York: Harry N. Abrams, in association with the Field Museum, 2002.

McNeil, Cameron L., ed. *Chocolate in Mesoamerica: A Cultural History of Cacao*. Gainesville: University of Florida Press, 2009.

Norton, Marcy. *Sacred Gifts, Profane Pleasures: A History of Tobacco and Chocolate in the Atlantic World*. Ithaca, NY: Cornell University Press, 2008.

Presilla, Maricel E. *The New Taste of Chocolate: A Cultural and Natural History of Cacao with Recipes*. Berkeley, CA: Ten Speed Press, 2000.

Rosenblum, Mort. *Chocolate: A Bittersweet Saga of Dark and Light*. New York: North Point Press, 2005.

Terrio, Susan J. *Crafting the Culture of French Chocolate*. Berkeley: University of California Press, 2000.

DVDs

Chocolate: The Bitter Truth of Child Trafficking, five-part documentary report, www.youtube.com/watch?v=LD85fPzLUjo, 2010.

Chocolate Country, a film about farmers in Dominican Republic's Loma Guaconejo and their approach to cooperative chocolate production and shipping directly to the United States, accompanied by the music of local folk musicians, www.chocolatecountryfilm.com, 2010.

Cocoa Slave Tastes Sweet Freedom, a film about the rescue of a twelve-year-old slave on a cocoa farm and his reunion with his mother; http://news.bbc.co.uk/panorama/hi/front_page/newsid_8584000/8584847.stm, 2010.

The Dark Side of Chocolate, an investigation into trafficking of children in cacao plantations of West Africa, www.thedarksideofchocolate.org, 2010; also available inexpensively from www.greenamerica.org.

Credits

A version of "Christmas and Chanukah Chocolate Melt Together" was first published in *Petits Propos Culinaires* 89, January 2010. Used by permission.

A small section of the chapter "Israelis: *Meshuga* for Chocolate" originally appeared on, "The Jew and the Carrot," a *Jewish Daily Forward* and Hazon partnership blog. Used by permission.

A version of "Camel's Milk in My Chocolate?" was posted at parkmemoirs.com, a blog created by Jeff Yoskowitz, and also at www.jews-onthechocolatetrail.org. Used by permission.

"Our Dark Addictions: Chocolate, Coffee and Tea" by Deborah Prinz in the *Sacred Table: Creating a Jewish Food Ethic*, edited by Mary L. Zamore, © 2011 by Central Conference of American Rabbis. All rights reserved. Used by permission. A version of this piece originally appeared on, "The Jew and the Carrot," a *Jewish Daily Forward* and Hazon partnership blog.

Reproduction of Negro Cornelius Casey entry from the *Lopez Memorandum Book* 142c, Newport Historical Society. Used by permission.

Photo of the Chocolate Candy Bar Bomb, The National Archives of the U.K., Ref KV4/284. Used by permission.

Photo of cocoa tree and pods from Wikimedia Commons. Used by permission.

Photo of *A Man Scraping Chocolate*, anonymous artist, Spanish School, 1680–1780, oil on canvas, North Carolina Museum of Art, Raleigh, North Carolina, gift of Mr. and Mrs. Benjamin Cone, G69.20.1. Used by permission.

Photo of *mendiants* taken by Paola Paska. Used by permission.

Photo of the Santa Catalina Bakery in Valencia taken by Juan Costa, Sinagoga Conservador la Javurá. Used by permission.

Photo of St. Nicholas coins from the St. Nicholas Center. Used by permission.

Index

Page numbers in italics refer to illustrations. See the "Index for Recipes" for recipes.

Index of Recipes

Bible Study/Midrash

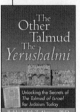

The Book of Job: Annotated & Explained
Translation and Annotation by Donald Kraus; Foreword by Dr. Marc Brettler
Clarifies for today's readers what Job is, how to overcome difficulties in the text, and what it may mean for us. Features fresh translation and probing commentary.
5½ x 8½, 256 pp, Quality PB, 978-1-59473-389-5 **$16.99**

Masking and Unmasking Ourselves: Interpreting Biblical Texts on Clothing & Identity *By Dr. Norman J. Cohen*
Presents ten Bible stories that involve clothing in an essential way, as a means of learning about the text, its characters and their interactions.
6 x 9, 240 pp, HC, 978-1-58023-461-0 **$24.99**

The Other Talmud—*The Yerushalmi*: Unlocking the Secrets of The Talmud of Israel for Judaism Today *By Rabbi Judith Z. Abrams, PhD*
A fascinating—and stimulating—look at "the other Talmud" and the possibilities for Jewish life reflected there.   6 x 9, 256 pp, HC, 978-1-58023-463-4 **$24.99**

The Torah Revolution: Fourteen Truths That Changed the World
By Rabbi Reuven Hammer, PhD   A unique look at the Torah and the revolutionary teachings of Moses embedded within it that gave birth to Judaism and influenced the world.   6 x 9, 240 pp, HC, 978-1-58023-457-3 **$24.99**

Ecclesiastes: Annotated & Explained
Translation and Annotation by Rabbi Rami Shapiro; Foreword by Rev. Barbara Cawthorne Crafton
5½ x 8½, 160 pp, Quality PB, 978-1-59473-287-4 **$16.99**

Ethics of the Sages: *Pirke Avot*—Annotated & Explained   *Translation and Annotation by Rabbi Rami Shapiro*   5½ x 8½, 192 pp, Quality PB, 978-1-59473-207-2 **$16.99**

The Genesis of Leadership: What the Bible Teaches Us about Vision, Values and Leading Change *By Rabbi Nathan Laufer; Foreword by Senator Joseph I. Lieberman*
6 x 9, 288 pp, Quality PB, 978-1-58023-352-1 **$18.99**

Hineini in Our Lives: Learning How to Respond to Others through 14 Biblical Texts and Personal Stories *By Rabbi Norman J. Cohen, PhD*   6 x 9, 240 pp, Quality PB, 978-1-58023-274-6 **$16.99**

A Man's Responsibility: A Jewish Guide to Being a Son, a Partner in Marriage, a Father and a Community Leader *By Rabbi Joseph B. Meszler*   6 x 9, 192 pp, Quality PB, 978-1-58023-435-1 **$16.99**

The Modern Men's Torah Commentary: New Insights from Jewish Men on the 54 Weekly Torah Portions *Edited by Rabbi Jeffrey K. Salkin*
6 x 9, 368 pp, HC, 978-1-58023-395-8 **$24.99**

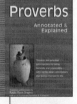

Moses and the Journey to Leadership: Timeless Lessons of Effective Management from the Bible and Today's Leaders *By Rabbi Norman J. Cohen, PhD*
6 x 9, 240 pp, Quality PB, 978-1-58023-351-4 **$18.99**; HC, 978-1-58023-227-2 **$21.99**

Proverbs: Annotated & Explained
Translation and Annotation by Rabbi Rami Shapiro
5½ x 8½, 288 pp, Quality PB, 978-1-59473-310-9 **$16.99**

Righteous Gentiles in the Hebrew Bible: Ancient Role Models for Sacred Relationships
By Rabbi Jeffrey K. Salkin; Foreword by Rabbi Harold M. Schulweis;
Preface by Phyllis Tickle 6 x 9, 192 pp, Quality PB, 978-1-58023-364-4 **$18.99**

Sage Tales: Wisdom and Wonder from the Rabbis of the Talmud
By Rabbi Burton L. Visotzky 6 x 9, 256 pp, HC, 978-1-58023-456-6 **$24.99**

The Wisdom of Judaism: An Introduction to the Values of the Talmud
By Rabbi Dov Peretz Elkins 6 x 9, 192 pp, Quality PB, 978-1-58023-327-9 **$16.99**

Or phone, fax, mail or e-mail to: **JEWISH LIGHTS** Publishing
Sunset Farm Offices, Route 4 • P.O. Box 237 • Woodstock, Vermont 05091
Tel: (802) 457-4000 • Fax: (802) 457-4004 • www.jewishlights.com
Credit card orders: (800) 962-4544 (8:30AM–5:30PM EST Monday–Friday)
Generous discounts on quantity orders. SATISFACTION GUARANTEED. Prices subject to change.

Bar/Bat Mitzvah

The Mitzvah Project Book
Making Mitzvah Part of Your Bar/Bat Mitzvah ... and Your Life
By Liz Suneby and Diane Heiman; Foreword by Rabbi Jeffrey K. Salkin; Preface by Rabbi Sharon Brous
The go-to source for Jewish young adults and their families looking to make the world a better place through good deeds—big or small.
6 x 9, 224 pp, Quality PB Original, 978-1-58023-458-0 **$16.99** For ages 11–13

The Bar/Bat Mitzvah Memory Book, 2nd Edition: An Album for Treasuring the Spiritual Celebration
By Rabbi Jeffrey K. Salkin and Nina Salkin
8 x 10, 48 pp, 2-color text, Deluxe HC, ribbon marker, 978-1-58023-263-0 **$19.99**

For Kids—Putting God on Your Guest List, 2nd Edition: How to Claim the Spiritual Meaning of Your Bar or Bat Mitzvah *By Rabbi Jeffrey K. Salkin*
6 x 9, 144 pp, Quality PB, 978-1-58023-308-8 **$15.99** For ages 11–13

The Jewish Prophet: Visionary Words from Moses and Miriam to Henrietta Szold and A. J. Heschel *By Rabbi Dr. Michael J. Shire*
6½ x 8½, 128 pp, 123 full-color illus., HC, 978-1-58023-168-8 **$14.95**

Putting God on the Guest List, 3rd Edition: How to Reclaim the Spiritual Meaning of Your Child's Bar or Bat Mitzvah *By Rabbi Jeffrey K. Salkin*
6 x 9, 224 pp, Quality PB, 978-1-58023-222-7 **$16.99**; HC, 978-1-58023-260-9 **$24.99**

Putting God on the Guest List Teacher's Guide
8½ x 11, 48 pp, PB, 978-1-58023-226-5 **$8.99**

Teens / Young Adults

Text Messages: A Torah Commentary for Teens
Edited by Rabbi Jeffrey K. Salkin
Shows today's teens how each Torah portion contains worlds of meaning for them, for what they are going through in their lives, and how they can shape their Jewish identity as they enter adulthood.
6 x 9, 304 pp (est), HC, 978-1-58023-507-5 **$24.99**

Hannah Senesh: Her Life and Diary, the First Complete Edition
By Hannah Senesh; Foreword by Marge Piercy; Preface by Eitan Senesh; Afterword by Roberta Grossman
6 x 9, 368 pp, b/w photos, Quality PB, 978-1-58023-342-2 **$19.99**

I Am Jewish: Personal Reflections Inspired by the Last Words of Daniel Pearl
Edited by Judea and Ruth Pearl 6 x 9, 304 pp, Deluxe PB w/ flaps, 978-1-58023-259-3 $18.99
Download a free copy of the *I Am Jewish Teacher's Guide* at www.jewishlights.com.

The JGirl's Guide: The Young Jewish Woman's Handbook for Coming of Age
By Penina Adelman, Ali Feldman and Shulamit Reinharz
6 x 9, 240 pp, Quality PB, 978-1-58023-215-9 **$14.99** For ages 11 & up

The JGirl's Teacher's and Parent's Guide
8½ x 11, 56 pp, PB, 978-1-58023-225-8 **$8.99**

Tough Questions Jews Ask, 2nd Edition: A Young Adult's Guide to Building a Jewish Life *By Rabbi Edward Feinstein*
6 x 9, 160 pp, Quality PB, 978-1-58023-454-2 **$16.99** For ages 11 & up

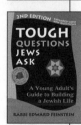

Tough Questions Jews Ask Teacher's Guide
8½ x 11, 72 pp, PB, 978-1-58023-187-9 **$8.95**

Pre-Teens

Be Like God: God's To-Do List for Kids
By Dr. Ron Wolfson
Encourages kids ages eight through twelve to use their God-given superpowers to find the many ways they can make a difference in the lives of others and find meaning and purpose for their own.
7 x 9, 144 pp, Quality PB, 978-1-58023-510-5 **$15.99** For ages 8–12

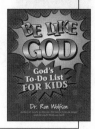

The Book of Miracles: A Young Person's Guide to Jewish Spiritual Awareness
By Lawrence Kushner, with all-new illustrations by the author.
6 x 9, 96 pp, 2-color illus., HC, 978-1-879045-78-1 **$16.95** For ages 9–13

Children's Books

Around the World in One Shabbat
Jewish People Celebrate the Sabbath Together
By Durga Yael Bernhard
Takes your child on a colorful adventure to share the many ways Jewish people celebrate Shabbat around the world.
11 x 8½, 32 pp, Full-color illus., HC, 978-1-58023-433-7 **$18.99** *For ages 3–6*

It's a ... It's a ... It's a Mitzvah
By Liz Suneby and Diane Heiman; Full-color Illus. by Laurel Molk
Join Mitzvah Meerkat and friends as they introduce children to the everyday kindnesses that mark the beginning of a Jewish journey and a lifetime commitment to *tikkun olam* (repairing the world). 9 x 12, 32 pp, Full-color illus., HC, 978-1-58023-509-9 **$18.99** *For ages 3–6*

What You Will See Inside a Synagogue
By Rabbi Lawrence A. Hoffman, PhD, and Dr. Ron Wolfson; Full-color photos by Bill Aron
A colorful, fun-to-read introduction that explains the ways and whys of Jewish worship and religious life. 8½ x 10½, 32 pp, Full-color photos, Quality PB, 978-1-59473-256-0 **$8.99** *For ages 6 & up*
(A book from SkyLight Paths, Jewish Lights' sister imprint)

Because Nothing Looks Like God
By Lawrence Kushner and Karen Kushner
Real-life examples of happiness and sadness—from goodnight stories, to the hope and fear felt the first time at bat, to the closing moments of someone's life—invite parents and children to explore, together, the questions we all have about God, no matter what our age. 11 x 8¾, 32 pp, Full-color illus., HC, 978-1-58023-092-6 **$18.99** *For ages 4 & up*

The Book of Miracles: A Young Person's Guide to Jewish Spiritual Awareness
Written and illus. by Lawrence Kushner
Easy-to-read, imaginatively illustrated book encourages kids' awareness of their own spirituality. Revealing the essence of Judaism in a language they can understand and enjoy. 6 x 9, 96 pp, 2-color illus., HC, 978-1-879045-78-1 **$16.95** *For ages 9–13*

In God's Hands   *By Lawrence Kushner and Gary Schmidt*
Brings new life to a traditional Jewish folktale, reminding parents and kids of all faiths and all backgrounds that each of us has the power to make the world a better place—working ordinary miracles with our everyday deeds.
9 x 12, 32 pp, Full-color illus., HC, 978-1-58023-224-1 **$16.99** *For ages 5 & up*

In Our Image: God's First Creatures
By Nancy Sohn Swartz
A playful new twist to the Genesis story, God asks all of nature to offer gifts to humankind—with a promise that the humans would care for creation in return. 9 x 12, 32 pp, Full-color illus., HC, 978-1-879045-99-6 **$16.95** *For ages 4 & up*

The Jewish Family Fun Book, 2nd Ed.
Holiday Projects, Everyday Activities, and Travel Ideas with Jewish Themes
By Danielle Dardashti and Roni Sarig
The complete sourcebook for families wanting to put a new spin on activities for Jewish holidays, holy days and the everyday. It offers dozens of easy-to-do activities that bring Jewish tradition to life for kids of all ages.
6 x 9, 304 pp, w/ 70+ b/w illus., Quality PB, 978-1-58023-333-0 **$18.99**

The Kids' Fun Book of Jewish Time   *By Emily Sper*
A unique way to introduce children to the Jewish calendar—night and day, the seven-day week, Shabbat, the Hebrew months, seasons and dates.
9 x 7½, 24 pp, Full-color illus., HC, 978-1-58023-311-8 **$16.99** *For ages 3–6*

What Makes Someone a Jew?   *By Lauren Seidman*
Reflects the changing face of American Judaism. Helps preschoolers and young readers (ages 3–6) understand that you don't have to look a certain way to be Jewish. 10 x 8½, 32 pp, Full-color photos, Quality PB, 978-1-58023-321-7 **$8.99** *For ages 3–6*

When a Grandparent Dies: A Kid's Own Remembering Workbook for
Dealing with Shiva and the Year Beyond   *By Nechama Liss-Levinson*
8 x 10, 48 pp, 2-color text, HC, 978-1-879045-44-6 **$15.95** *For ages 7–13*

Life Cycle
Marriage/Parenting/Family/Aging

The New Jewish Baby Album: Creating and Celebrating the Beginning of a Spiritual Life—A Jewish Lights Companion
By the Editors at Jewish Lights; Foreword by Anita Diamant; Preface by Rabbi Sandy Eisenberg Sasso
A spiritual keepsake that will be treasured for generations. More than just a memory book, *shows you how—and why it's important*—to create a Jewish home and a Jewish life. 8 x 10, 64 pp, Deluxe Padded HC, Full-color illus., 978-1-58023-138-1 **$19.95**

The Jewish Pregnancy Book: A Resource for the Soul, Body & Mind during Pregnancy, Birth & the First Three Months *By Sandy Falk, MD, and Rabbi Daniel Judson, with Steven A. Rapp* Medical information, prayers and rituals for each stage of pregnancy. 7 x 10, 208 pp, b/w photos, Quality PB, 978-1-58023-178-7 **$16.95**

Celebrating Your New Jewish Daughter: Creating Jewish Ways to Welcome Baby Girls into the Covenant—New and Traditional Ceremonies *By Debra Nussbaum Cohen; Foreword by Rabbi Sandy Eisenberg Sasso* 6 x 9, 272 pp, Quality PB, 978-1-58023-090-2 **$18.95**

The New Jewish Baby Book, 2nd Edition: Names, Ceremonies & Customs—A Guide for Today's Families *By Anita Diamant* 6 x 9, 320 pp, Quality PB, 978-1-58023-251-7 **$19.99**

Parenting as a Spiritual Journey: Deepening Ordinary and Extraordinary Events into Sacred Occasions *By Rabbi Nancy Fuchs-Kreimer, PhD*
6 x 9, 224 pp, Quality PB, 978-1-58023-016-2 **$17.99**

Parenting Jewish Teens: A Guide for the Perplexed
By Joanne Doades Explores the questions and issues that shape the world in which today's Jewish teenagers live and offers constructive advice to parents.
6 x 9, 176 pp, Quality PB, 978-1-58023-305-7 **$16.99**

Judaism for Two: A Spiritual Guide for Strengthening and Celebrating Your Loving Relationship *By Rabbi Nancy Fuchs-Kreimer, PhD, and Rabbi Nancy H. Wiener, DMin; Foreword by Rabbi Elliot N. Dorff, PhD*
Addresses the ways Jewish teachings can enhance and strengthen committed relationships. 6 x 9, 224 pp, Quality PB, 978-1-58023-254-8 **$16.99**

The Creative Jewish Wedding Book, 2nd Edition: A Hands-On Guide to New & Old Traditions, Ceremonies & Celebrations *By Gabrielle Kaplan-Mayer*
9 x 9, 288 pp, b/w photos, Quality PB, 978-1-58023-398-9 **$19.99**

Divorce Is a Mitzvah: A Practical Guide to Finding Wholeness and Holiness When Your Marriage Dies *By Rabbi Perry Netter; Afterword by Rabbi Laura Geller*
6 x 9, 224 pp, Quality PB, 978-1-58023-172-5 **$16.95**

Embracing the Covenant: Converts to Judaism Talk About Why & How
By Rabbi Allan Berkowitz and Patti Moskovitz 6 x 9, 192 pp, Quality PB, 978-1-879045-50-7 **$16.95**

The Guide to Jewish Interfaith Family Life: An InterfaithFamily.com Handbook
Edited by Ronnie Friedland and Edmund Case
6 x 9, 384 pp, Quality PB, 978-1-58023-153-4 **$18.95**

A Heart of Wisdom: Making the Jewish Journey from Midlife through the Elder Years
Edited by Susan Berrin; Foreword by Rabbi Harold Kushner
6 x 9, 384 pp, Quality PB, 978-1-58023-051-3 **$18.95**

Introducing My Faith and My Community: The Jewish Outreach Institute Guide for the Christian in a Jewish Interfaith Relationship
By Rabbi Kerry M. Olitzky 6 x 9, 176 pp, Quality PB, 978-1-58023-192-3 **$16.99**

Making a Successful Jewish Interfaith Marriage: The Jewish Outreach Institute Guide to Opportunities, Challenges and Resources *By Rabbi Kerry M. Olitzky with Joan Peterson Littman*
6 x 9, 176 pp, Quality PB, 978-1-58023-170-1 **$16.95**

A Man's Responsibility: A Jewish Guide to Being a Son, a Partner in Marriage, a Father and a Community Leader *By Rabbi Joseph B. Meszler*
6 x 9, 192 pp, Quality PB, 978-1-58023-435-1 **$16.99**; HC, 978-1-58023-362-0 **$21.99**

So That Your Values Live On: Ethical Wills and How to Prepare Them
Edited by Rabbi Jack Riemer and Rabbi Nathaniel Stampfer
6 x 9, 272 pp, Quality PB, 978-1-879045-34-7 **$18.99**

Inspiration

God of Me: Imagining God throughout Your Lifetime
By Rabbi David Lyon Helps you cut through preconceived ideas of God and dogmas that stifle your creativity when thinking about your personal relationship with God. 6 x 9, 176 pp, Quality PB, 978-1-58023-452-8 **$16.99**

The God Upgrade: Finding Your 21st-Century Spirituality in Judaism's 5,000-Year-Old Tradition *By Rabbi Jamie Korngold; Foreword by Rabbi Harold M. Schulweis* A provocative look at how our changing God concepts have shaped every aspect of Judaism. 6 x 9, 176 pp, Quality PB, 978-1-58023-443-6 **$15.99**

The Seven Questions You're Asked in Heaven: Reviewing and Renewing Your Life on Earth *By Dr. Ron Wolfson* An intriguing and entertaining resource for living a life that matters. 6 x 9, 176 pp, Quality PB, 978-1-58023-407-8 **$16.99**

Happiness and the Human Spirit: The Spirituality of Becoming the Best You Can Be *By Rabbi Abraham J. Twerski, MD* Shows you that true happiness is attainable once you stop looking outside yourself for the source. 6 x 9, 176 pp, Quality PB, 978-1-58023-404-7 **$16.99**; HC, 978-1-58023-343-9 **$19.99**

A Formula for Proper Living: Practical Lessons from Life and Torah *By Rabbi Abraham J. Twerski, MD* 6 x 9, 144 pp, HC, 978-1-58023-402-3 **$19.99**

The Bridge to Forgiveness: Stories and Prayers for Finding God and Restoring Wholeness *By Rabbi Karyn D. Kedar* 6 x 9, 176 pp, Quality PB, 978-1-58023-451-1 **$16.99**

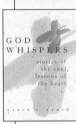

The Empty Chair: Finding Hope and Joy—Timeless Wisdom from a Hasidic Master, Rebbe Nachman of Breslov *Adapted by Moshe Mykoff and the Breslov Research Institute* 4 x 6, 128 pp, Deluxe PB w/ flaps, 978-1-879045-67-5 **$9.99**

The Gentle Weapon: Prayers for Everyday and Not-So-Everyday Moments— Timeless Wisdom from the Teachings of the Hasidic Master, Rebbe Nachman of Breslov *Adapted by Moshe Mykoff and S. C. Mizrahi, together with the Breslov Research Institute* 4 x 6, 144 pp, Deluxe PB w/ flaps, 978-1-58023-022-3 **$9.99**

God Whispers: Stories of the Soul, Lessons of the Heart *By Rabbi Karyn D. Kedar* 6 x 9, 176 pp, Quality PB, 978-1-58023-088-9 **$15.95**

God's To-Do List: 103 Ways to Be an Angel and Do God's Work on Earth *By Dr. Ron Wolfson* 6 x 9, 144 pp, Quality PB, 978-1-58023-301-9 **$16.99**

Jewish Stories from Heaven and Earth: Inspiring Tales to Nourish the Heart and Soul *Edited by Rabbi Dov Peretz Elkins* 6 x 9, 304 pp, Quality PB, 978-1-58023-363-7 **$16.99**

Life's Daily Blessings: Inspiring Reflections on Gratitude and Joy for Every Day, Based on Jewish Wisdom *By Rabbi Kerry M. Olitzky* 4½ x 6½, 368 pp, Quality PB, 978-1-58023-396-5 **$16.99**

Restful Reflections: Nighttime Inspiration to Calm the Soul, Based on Jewish Wisdom *By Rabbi Kerry M. Olitzky and Rabbi Lori Forman-Jacobi* 5 x 8, 352 pp, Quality PB, 978-1-58023-091-9 **$16.99**

Sacred Intentions: Morning Inspiration to Strengthen the Spirit, Based on Jewish Wisdom *By Rabbi Kerry M. Olitzky and Rabbi Lori Forman-Jacobi* 4½ x 6½, 448 pp, Quality PB, 978-1-58023-061-2 **$16.99**

Kabbalah/Mysticism

Jewish Mysticism and the Spiritual Life: Classical Texts, Contemporary Reflections *Edited by Dr. Lawrence Fine, Dr. Eitan Fishbane and Rabbi Or N. Rose* Inspirational and thought-provoking materials for contemplation, discussion and action. 6 x 9, 256 pp, HC, 978-1-58023-434-4 **$24.99**

Ehyeh: A Kabbalah for Tomorrow *By Rabbi Arthur Green, PhD* 6 x 9, 224 pp, Quality PB, 978-1-58023-213-5 **$18.99**

The Gift of Kabbalah: Discovering the Secrets of Heaven, Renewing Your Life on Earth *By Tamar Frankiel, PhD* 6 x 9, 256 pp, Quality PB, 978-1-58023-141-1 **$16.95**

Seek My Face: A Jewish Mystical Theology *By Rabbi Arthur Green, PhD* 6 x 9, 304 pp, Quality PB, 978-1-58023-130-5 **$19.95**

Zohar: Annotated & Explained *Translation & Annotation by Dr. Daniel C. Matt; Foreword by Andrew Harvey* 5½ x 8½, 176 pp, Quality PB, 978-1-893361-51-5 **$16.99**
(A book from SkyLight Paths, Jewish Lights' sister imprint)

Spirituality

The Jewish Lights Spirituality Handbook: A Guide to Understanding, Exploring & Living a Spiritual Life *Edited by Stuart M. Matlins*
What exactly is "Jewish" about spirituality? How do I make it a part of my life? Fifty of today's foremost spiritual leaders share their ideas and experience with us.
6 x 9, 456 pp, Quality PB, 978-1-58023-093-3 **$19.99**

The Sabbath Soul: Mystical Reflections on the Transformative Power of Holy Time *Selection, Translation and Commentary by Eitan Fishbane, PhD*
Explores the writings of mystical masters of Hasidism. Provides translations and interpretations of a wide range of Hasidic sources previously unavailable in English that reflect the spiritual transformation that takes place on the seventh day.
6 x 9, 208 pp, Quality PB, 978-1-58023-459-7 **$18.99**

Repentance: The Meaning and Practice of *Teshuvah*
By Dr. Louis E. Newman; Foreword by Rabbi Harold M. Schulweis; Preface by Rabbi Karyn D. Kedar
Examines both the practical and philosophical dimensions of *teshuvah*, Judaism's core religious-moral teaching on repentance, and its value for us—Jews and non-Jews alike—today. 6 x 9, 256 pp, HC, 978-1-58023-426-9 **$24.99**

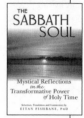

Aleph-Bet Yoga: Embodying the Hebrew Letters for Physical and Spiritual Well-Being
By Steven A. Rapp; Foreword by Tamar Frankiel, PhD, and Judy Greenfeld; Preface by Hart Lazer
7 x 10, 128 pp, b/w photos, Quality PB, Lay-flat binding, 978-1-58023-162-6 **$16.95**

A Book of Life: Embracing Judaism as a Spiritual Practice
By Rabbi Michael Strassfeld 6 x 9, 544 pp, Quality PB, 978-1-58023-247-0 **$19.99**

Bringing the Psalms to Life: How to Understand and Use the Book of Psalms
By Rabbi Daniel F. Polish, PhD 6 x 9, 208 pp, Quality PB, 978-1-58023-157-2 **$16.95**

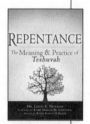

Does the Soul Survive? A Jewish Journey to Belief in Afterlife, Past Lives & Living with Purpose *By Rabbi Elie Kaplan Spitz; Foreword by Brian L. Weiss, MD*
6 x 9, 288 pp, Quality PB, 978-1-58023-165-7 **$16.99**

Entering the Temple of Dreams: Jewish Prayers, Movements and Meditations for the End of the Day *By Tamar Frankiel, PhD, and Judy Greenfeld*
7 x 10, 192 pp, illus., Quality PB, 978-1-58023-079-7 **$16.95**

First Steps to a New Jewish Spirit: Reb Zalman's Guide to Recapturing the Intimacy & Ecstasy in Your Relationship with God *By Rabbi Zalman M. Schachter-Shalomi with Donald Gropman* 6 x 9, 144 pp, Quality PB, 978-1-58023-182-4 **$16.95**

Foundations of Sephardic Spirituality: The Inner Life of Jews of the Ottoman Empire
By Rabbi Marc D. Angel, PhD 6 x 9, 224 pp, Quality PB, 978-1-58023-341-5 **$18.99**

God & the Big Bang: Discovering Harmony between Science & Spirituality
By Dr. Daniel C. Matt 6 x 9, 216 pp, Quality PB, 978-1-879045-89-7 **$18.99**

God in Our Relationships: Spirituality between People from the Teachings of Martin Buber *By Rabbi Dennis S. Ross* 5½ x 8½, 160 pp, Quality PB, 978-1-58023-147-3 **$16.95**

Judaism, Physics and God: Searching for Sacred Metaphors in a Post-Einstein World
By Rabbi David W. Nelson 6 x 9, 352 pp, Quality PB, inc. reader's discussion guide,
978-1-58023-306-4 **$18.99**; HC, 352 pp, 978-1-58023-252-4 **$24.99**

Meaning & Mitzvah: Daily Practices for Reclaiming Judaism through Prayer, God, Torah, Hebrew, Mitzvot and Peoplehood *By Rabbi Goldie Milgram*
7 x 9, 336 pp, Quality PB, 978-1-58023-256-2 **$19.99**

Minding the Temple of the Soul: Balancing Body, Mind, and Spirit through Traditional Jewish Prayer, Movement, and Meditation *By Tamar Frankiel, PhD, and Judy Greenfeld*
7 x 10, 184 pp, Illus., Quality PB, 978-1-879045-64-4 **$18.99**

One God Clapping: The Spiritual Path of a Zen Rabbi *By Rabbi Alan Lew with Sherril Jaffe*
5½ x 8½, 336 pp, Quality PB, 978-1-58023-115-2 **$16.95**

The Soul of the Story: Meetings with Remarkable People
By Rabbi David Zeller 6 x 9, 288 pp, HC, 978-1-58023-272-2 **$21.99**

Tanya, the Masterpiece of Hasidic Wisdom: Selections Annotated & Explained
Translation & Annotation by Rabbi Rami Shapiro; Foreword by Rabbi Zalman M. Schachter-Shalomi
5½ x 8½, 240 pp, Quality PB, 978-1-59473-275-1 **$16.99**

These Are the Words, 2nd Edition: A Vocabulary of Jewish Spiritual Life
By Rabbi Arthur Green, PhD 6 x 9, 320 pp, Quality PB, 978-1-58023-494-8 **$19.99**

Social Justice

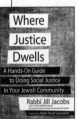

Where Justice Dwells
A Hands-On Guide to Doing Social Justice in Your Jewish Community
By Rabbi Jill Jacobs; Foreword by Rabbi David Saperstein
Provides ways to envision and act on your own ideals of social justice.
7 x 9, 288 pp, Quality PB Original, 978-1-58023-453-5 **$24.99**

There Shall Be No Needy
Pursuing Social Justice through Jewish Law and Tradition
By Rabbi Jill Jacobs; Foreword by Rabbi Elliot N. Dorff, PhD; Preface by Simon Greer
Confronts the most pressing issues of twenty-first-century America from a deeply Jewish perspective. 6 x 9, 288 pp, Quality PB, 978-1-58023-425-2 **$16.99**
There Shall Be No Needy Teacher's Guide 8½ x 11, 56 pp, PB, 978-1-58023-429-0 **$8.99**

Conscience
The Duty to Obey and the Duty to Disobey
By Rabbi Harold M. Schulweis
Examines the idea of conscience and the role conscience plays in our relationships to government, law, ethics, religion, human nature, God—and to each other.
6 x 9, 160 pp, Quality PB, 978-1-58023-419-1 **$16.99**; HC, 978-1-58023-375-0 **$19.99**

Judaism and Justice
The Jewish Passion to Repair the World
By Rabbi Sidney Schwarz; Foreword by Ruth Messinger
Explores the relationship between Judaism, social justice and the Jewish identity of American Jews. 6 x 9, 352 pp, Quality PB, 978-1-58023-353-8 **$19.99**

Spirituality/Women's Interest

New Jewish Feminism
Probing the Past, Forging the Future
Edited by Rabbi Elyse Goldstein; Foreword by Anita Diamant
Looks at the growth and accomplishments of Jewish feminism and what they mean for Jewish women today and tomorrow.
6 x 9, 480 pp, HC, 978-1-58023-359-0 **$24.99**

The Divine Feminine in Biblical Wisdom Literature
Selections Annotated & Explained
Translation & Annotation by Rabbi Rami Shapiro
5½ x 8½, 240 pp, Quality PB, 978-1-59473-109-9 **$16.99**
(A book from SkyLight Paths, Jewish Lights' sister imprint)

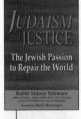

The Quotable Jewish Woman
Wisdom, Inspiration & Humor from the Mind & Heart
Edited by Elaine Bernstein Partnow
6 x 9, 496 pp, Quality PB, 978-1-58023-236-4 **$19.99**

The Women's Haftarah Commentary
New Insights from Women Rabbis on the 54 Weekly Haftarah Portions, the 5 Megillot & Special Shabbatot
Edited by Rabbi Elyse Goldstein
Illuminates the historical significance of female portrayals in the Haftarah and the Five Megillot. 6 x 9, 560 pp, Quality PB, 978-1-58023-371-2 **$19.99**

The Women's Torah Commentary
New Insights from Women Rabbis on the 54 Weekly Torah Portions
Edited by Rabbi Elyse Goldstein
Over fifty women rabbis offer inspiring insights on the Torah, in a week-by-week format.
6 x 9, 496 pp, Quality PB, 978-1-58023-370-5 **$19.99**; HC, 978-1-58023-076-6 **$34.95**

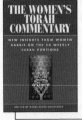

Spirituality/Crafts

Jewish Threads: A Hands-On Guide to Stitching Spiritual Intention into Jewish Fabric Crafts *By Diana Drew with Robert Grayson*
Learn how to make your own Jewish fabric crafts with spiritual intention—a journey of creativity, imagination and inspiration. Thirty projects.
7 x 9, 288 pp, 8-page color insert, b/w illus., Quality PB Original, 978-1-58023-442-9 **$19.99**

(from SkyLight Paths, Jewish Lights' sister imprint)

Beading—The Creative Spirit: Finding Your Sacred Center through the Art of Beadwork *By Wendy Ellsworth*
Invites you on a spiritual pilgrimage into the kaleidoscope world of glass and color.
7 x 9, 240 pp, 8-page full-color insert, b/w photos and diagrams, Quality PB, 978-1-59473-267-6 **$18.99**

Contemplative Crochet: A Hands-On Guide for Interlocking Faith and Craft *By Cindy Crandall-Frazier; Foreword by Linda Skolnik*
Will take you on a path deeper into your crocheting and your spiritual awareness.
7 x 9, 208 pp, b/w photos, Quality PB, 978-1-59473-238-6 **$16.99**

The Knitting Way: A Guide to Spiritual Self-Discovery
By Linda Skolnik and Janice MacDaniels
Shows how to use knitting to strengthen your spiritual self.
7 x 9, 240 pp, b/w photos, Quality PB, 978-1-59473-079-5 **$16.99**

The Painting Path: Embodying Spiritual Discovery through Yoga, Brush and Color *By Linda Novick; Foreword by Richard Segalman*
Explores the divine connection you can experience through art.
7 x 9, 208 pp, 8-page full-color insert, b/w photos, Quality PB, 978-1-59473-226-3 **$18.99**

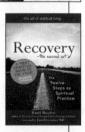

The Quilting Path: A Guide to Spiritual Self-Discovery through Fabric, Thread and Kabbalah *By Louise Silk* Explores how to cultivate personal growth through quilt making. 7 x 9, 192 pp, b/w photos, Quality PB, 978-1-59473-206-5 **$16.99**

The Scrapbooking Journey: A Hands-On Guide to Spiritual Discovery
By Cory Richardson-Lauve; Foreword by Stacy Julian
Reveals how this craft can become a practice used to deepen and shape your life.
7 x 9, 176 pp, 8-page full-color insert, b/w photos, Quality PB, 978-1-59473-216-4 **$18.99**

Travel

Israel—A Spiritual Travel Guide, 2nd Edition: A Companion for the Modern Jewish Pilgrim *By Rabbi Lawrence A. Hoffman, PhD*
Helps today's pilgrim tap into the deep spiritual meaning of the ancient—and modern—sites of the Holy Land.
4¾ x 10, 256 pp, Illus., Quality PB, 978-1-58023-261-6 **$18.99**
Also Available: **The Israel Mission Leader's Guide** 5½ x 8½, 16 pp, PB, 978-1-58023-085-8 **$4.95**

Twelve Steps

Recovery—The Sacred Art: The Twelve Steps as Spiritual Practice
By Rami Shapiro; Foreword by Joan Borysenko, PhD
Draws on insights and practices of different religious traditions to help you move more deeply into the universal spirituality of the Twelve Step system.
5½ x 8½, 240 pp, Quality PB Original, 978-1-59473-259-1 **$16.99**
(A book from SkyLight Paths, Jewish Lights' sister imprint)

100 Blessings Every Day: Daily Twelve Step Recovery Affirmations, Exercises for Personal Growth & Renewal Reflecting Seasons of the Jewish Year *By Rabbi Kerry M. Olitzky; Foreword by Rabbi Neil Gillman, PhD* 4½ x 6½, 432 pp, Quality PB, 978-1-879045-30-9 **$16.99**

Recovery from Codependence: A Jewish Twelve Steps Guide to Healing Your Soul
By Rabbi Kerry M. Olitzky 6 x 9, 160 pp, Quality PB, 978-1-879045-32-3 **$13.95**

Twelve Jewish Steps to Recovery, 2nd Edition: A Personal Guide to Turning from Alcoholism & Other Addictions—Drugs, Food, Gambling, Sex...
By Rabbi Kerry M. Olitzky and Stuart A. Copans, MD; Preface by Abraham J. Twerski, MD
6 x 9, 160 pp, Quality PB, 978-1-58023-409-2 **$16.99**

About Jewish Lights

People of all faiths and backgrounds yearn for books that attract, engage, educate, and spiritually inspire.

Our principal goal is to stimulate thought and help all people learn about who the Jewish People are, where they come from, and what the future can be made to hold. While people of our diverse Jewish heritage are the primary audience, our books speak to people in the Christian world as well and will broaden their understanding of Judaism and the roots of their own faith.

We bring to you authors who are at the forefront of spiritual thought and experience. While each has something different to say, they all say it in a voice that you can hear.

Our books are designed to welcome you and then to engage, stimulate, and inspire. We judge our success not only by whether or not our books are beautiful and commercially successful, but by whether or not they make a difference in your life.

For your information and convenience, at the back of this book we have provided a list of other Jewish Lights books you might find interesting and useful. They cover all the categories of your life:

Bar/Bat Mitzvah	Life Cycle
Bible Study / Midrash	Meditation
Children's Books	Men's Interest
Congregation Resources	Parenting
Current Events / History	Prayer / Ritual / Sacred Practice
Ecology / Environment	Social Justice
Fiction: Mystery, Science Fiction	Spirituality
Grief / Healing	Theology / Philosophy
Holidays / Holy Days	Travel
Inspiration	Twelve Steps
Kabbalah / Mysticism / Enneagram	Women's Interest

Stuart M. Matlins, Publisher

Or phone, fax, mail or e-mail to: **JEWISH LIGHTS Publishing**
Sunset Farm Offices, Route 4 • P.O. Box 237 • Woodstock, Vermont 05091
Tel: (802) 457-4000 • Fax: (802) 457-4004 • www.jewishlights.com
Credit card orders: (800) 962-4544 (8:30AM–5:30PM EST Monday–Friday)
Generous discounts on quantity orders. SATISFACTION GUARANTEED. Prices subject to change.